THE RED WINE HEADACHE COOK BOOK

OVER 300
SIMPLE
&
DELI-
CIOUS
RECIPE
IDEAS USING SCIENTIFICALLY
TESTED LOW-HISTAMINE INGREDIENTS

Ella Elizabeth

Nucleus Books

Published in Great Britain in 2010 by
Nucleus Books Ltd.

Produced in collaboration with
One Life Clinic Ltd. London

The Red Wine Headache Cookbook is a general recipe book. While the recipes are intended to be beneficial to health, this book in no way replaces medical advice. You must consult a doctor about any specific medical complaints. While all reasonable care has been taken during the preparation of this book, the publisher, author, or their consultants cannot accept responsibility for any consequences arising from its use or the information it contains.

A catalogue record for this book is available from the British Library

ISBN: 978-0-9567513-0-0

Printed at Progressive Printers Limited
Nottingham
NG5 1EJ
www.progressiveprinters.co.uk

For Daniel x

Contents

Foreword by Dirk Budka

You've probably heard of histamine. It's the chemical our bodies produce when we have an allergic reaction. But there's much more to histamine than itchy eyes and a runny nose. We all need a bit of it for our immune systems to work. But too much will make us ill: If our bodies can't safely break all our histamine down, we can become very ill indeed. This condition is called Histaminosis, (sometimes known as Histamine Intolerance or HIT.)

Histaminosis is a spectrum disorder: At the mild end are those sufferers who get a headache after drinking a glass of red wine, while at the severe end are those at risk of scrombroid poisoning, anaphylaxis and death. Most are somewhere in-between, but they may not realise it because the symptoms are so common. Impairment and misfunction of histamines leads to joint/muscle pain (rheumatoid arthritis), anxiety & depression, and low defence towards certain viruses and bacteria.

About 2% of the population suffer from severe Histaminosis, experiencing chronic symptoms that limit their capacity to enjoy life. More than 10% of the population have some sensitivity to Histamine, becoming occasionally unwell and missing out on time at work, at leisure, or with their families. Compare those figures to the estimated 4% who suffer from the 'common' food allergies (like peanuts or shellfish) and you can see that sensitivity to histamine affects far more people. Histaminosis is clearly a serious public health issue.

Our bodies' histamine is not only liberated by environmental factors such as pollen, pollution, stings or bites. We can also have histamine reactions to food and drink. Much of the food we regard as safe – healthy even – is actually slightly toxic. We only cope with it thanks to our hardworking immune systems.

To make matters worse, histamine naturally occurs in most foods. In fact, there are very few zero-histamine foods. Normally, this histamine would be made safe by special enzymes in our gut: diamine oxidase (DAO), monoamine oxidase-b (MAO-b) and histamine-N.methyltransferase (HNMT). Histaminosis sufferers often can't make enough of these enzymes, which is why they get ill. The histamine-rich foods common to our western diet don't give those poor enzymes much of a chance, either. Human evolution has yet to catch up with the convenience food industry.

Clearly, adopting a lower-histamine diet is a significant step towards easing Histaminosis. This is why I'm so happy that Ella has written this wonderful book. Using only scientifically tested low-histamine ingredients, she's created a remarkable collection of mouth-watering recipes. Here, Ella has shown that it's easy to adopt a lower-histamine lifestyle without having to feel 'deprived' by dietary restrictions.

Dirk Budka - One Life Clinic, London

Who Needs A Low-Histamine Diet?

Some people imagine a leaky bucket being filled with water faster than it can drain away. Our bodies' tolerance to histamine is like that bucket: each new challenge - a meal, a drink, a high pollen count - fills the bucket up a little more, until it finally overflows. And that's when we feel ill.

By easing off our histamine exposure, the water level drops a little, and then we don't feel so bad. But remember, that bucket is still nearly full. It won't be so long before it overflows again!

So how much histamine is too much? Well, that's the trouble: Everybody's tolerance is different. Some people are extremely susceptible and have to carefully manage their exposure to histamine, while others may go through life without ever realising they've been affected.

I lived my first twenty-five years blissfully unaware that histamine was a problem for me, until it suddenly became a problem in a very big way! (See 'My Story') I didn't know the warning-signs. Take a look at some of the symptoms below:

- Stomach pain
- Bloating
- Heartburn & acid reflux
- Joint & muscle pain
- Asthma
- Hay fever
- Frequent common colds
- Tension or cluster headaches
- Migraine
- "Red Wine" (or chocolate) headaches
- Panic attacks
- Mood changes & depression
- Dizziness
- Palpitations
- Low blood pressure
- Racing pulse (*tachycardia*)
- Irregular heartbeat (*arrhythmia*)
- Menstrual pain
- Pre-menstrual tension
- Premature ejaculation
- Dry nose
- Eczema
- Hives (*urticaria*)
- Prickly Heat
- Itchy or red skin

With such a wide range of symptoms, Histaminosis is difficult to diagnose and far too often overlooked. I know people whose lives were blighted by miserable, chronic symptoms for years: symptoms that just wouldn't go away, no matter what pills or potions they took.

Not appreciating histamine's significance, their doctors grew impatient and unsympathetic; "You're sensitive," they'd be dismissively told, "You need to learn to live with it." I've sometimes wondered if many healthcare professionals would be willing to 'live with' feeling awful all of the time? Of course not! They'd do something about it.

Who Needs A Low-Histamine Diet?

Yet with Histamine Intolerance *you* can do something about it! Empower yourself to manage how histamine makes you feel. Take charge over that aspect of your life: The food and drink that you consume.

The "*No*" List

Sometimes it feels as though a complete list of foods for Histaminosis sufferers to avoid could fill a book on its own. And here's the bad news: the foods that our society most likes to eat are often the very same foods that are most likely to make us ill. Some are even promoted for their healthful properties! Some popular foods that are very high in histamine, or that trigger histamine-release in our bodies, include:

Red meats e.g. beef & pork

Game meats like rabbit or grouse

Poultry e.g. chicken, duck & goose

Charcuterie like sausages or ham

Fish, including Shellfish and other seafood

Vegetarian meat alternatives derived from soybeans, such as tofu; or from the mycoprotein, Quorn™

Mushrooms and truffles

Fermented cheeses, e.g. Brie, Camembert, Gruyere, Cheddar, Roquefort & Parmesan

Yogurt, especially the pro-biotic kind

Potatoes & Tomatoes
Spinach

Soft fruits, like strawberries, raspberries & blackcurrants

Citrus fruits, like oranges, limes and grapefruit

Dried fruits, such as raisins and sultanas

Pineapple

Chocolate & Vanilla

All nuts except almonds

Anything made with vinegar, such as ketchup, pickles, vinaigrette and mayonnaise

Fermented products, like soy sauce or sauerkraut

Anything made with bakers' yeast such as bread, or brewers' yeast like Marmite, Vegemite or Cenovis

Most alcoholic beverages, especially red wine & beer

Coffee and tea

Cola and other soda drinks

Who Needs A Low-Histamine Diet?

"So What *Can* I Eat?"

This is the Histaminosis sufferer's dilemma. Imagine walking into any big supermarket with a different kind of shopping list: A list of foods you *mustn't* buy. Frustratingly, the aisles seem full of products made with high-histamine ingredients, or manufactured by histamine-liberating processes. The modern food industry just isn't geared up to cater for histamine-sensitive diners. Little wonder then, that some extreme sufferers become afraid of food. They cocoon themselves with a meagre handful of bland, 'safe' foodstuffs. That breaks my heart. Food should be about love and joy, not fear. Not to mention the inevitable malnutrition that comes with such fanatically limiting regimes.

If you're particularly histamine intolerant, then your symptoms may be a constant roar rather than an occasional murmur. You might start noticing the benefits of 'Going Low-Histamine' very quickly or it may take a little longer. Perhaps you're one of the fortunate ones; troubled only by the occasional headache after red wine or strong cheese, or maybe you experience bloating and gas after eating a pizza. If so, try eating the lower-histamine meals from this book just two or three times each week.

I refuse to be ruled by the "No" lists, telling us what we can't eat. The Red Wine Headache Cookbook is my "Yes" list!

Please note -

Everybody is different. Identify the specific ingredients that trouble *you* the most, and work out the level of histamine you can safely consume without getting ill. You're the expert at this. Your body will tell you if you learn to listen.

This book describes an effective dietary way to reduce or prevent symptoms of Histaminosis and HIT, but it is not a manual for self-diagnosis or self-treatment. If you suffer from any chronic symptoms you must see a doctor, even if only to rule out any other conditions. You should always seek consultation and supervision from an appropriate medical professional about any matters regarding your health and diet.

Ella Elizabeth, Autumn 2010

Soups & Starters

'Spring Rolls'

Ingredients -
For 2 or 4 people -

2 or 4	Spring onions
30ml or 60ml	Sesame oil
1 or 2 medium	Carrots
1 or 2 cloves	Fresh garlic
3 or 6 cms	Fresh ginger
1 or 2 small	Fresh chilli
25g or 50g	Green peas
50g or 100g	Bean sprouts
40g or 80g	Sesame seeds
¼ or ½ whole	Cucumber
2 or 4 sheets	Filo pastry - de frosted (approx. 24cm by 50cm)
45 ml or 90ml	Agave nectar - light

Method

Finely slice spring onions and gently fry in ½ oil for 1 min to soften. Cut carrots into matchsticks, add to the pan. Continue to cook for 2-3 mins.

Prepare garlic and ginger by finely dicing, sprinkle with sea salt, crush with the back of a knife. Finely chop chilli, removing seeds. Stir *only* ½ of the garlic, ginger and chilli into the pan. Cover the other ½, set aside.

Then add the green peas, bean sprouts and seeds to the pan. Stir to coat in oil. Remove from heat. Cut the cucumber into matchsticks. Add to the pan, season to taste, cover.

Preheat the oven to 220°c. Cut each sheet of filo into 6 equal size pieces. Brush half of the pieces with oil and lay the remaining pieces on top. With a corner of each piece facing you, put a large tsp of filling on top.

Fold the side corners into the centre, making sure they overlap. Brush the top corner with oil, roll the bottom corner up and over the filling tightly. Grease a baking tray and place each roll on it's seam. Bake for 10 mins until light brown and crispy.

For the 'Sweet Chilli Dipping Sauce' - While rolls bake, heat the already crushed garlic, ginger and chopped chilli in the seasoned pan for 1 min. Remove from heat and stir in agave.

Hints & tips

Serve with 'Sauteed Pak Choi' (aka 'Bok Choi'.) Chop 1 (or 2) shallots or small onions, fry in 15ml (or 30ml) sesame oil in a pan or wok. Stir the shallots and halved pak choi stems into the pan. After 3-4 minutes -

Add 30ml (or 60ml) apple juice. Add 40g (or 80g) sesame seeds to the pan. Stir in the pak choi leaves. Once they wilt, remove from heat, serve.

If using fresh poultry (organic if possible and not stored even for one day) cut it into thin strips and start to cook in the pan at the same time as the spring onions. **Make sure the meat is fully cooked before using as filling.**

'Soda Bread'

Ingredients

For 2 or 4 people - (1 or 2 loaves)

250g or 500g	Wholegrain Self Raising flour
1 or 2g	Sea salt - ground
50g or 100g	Fortified dairy-free spread*
150ml or 300ml	Almond milk

Sweet bread ideas - Try apple, pear, ginger, almond or rhubarb.

Savoury bread ideas - Try garlic, sage & onion, rosemary, basil, parsley, coriander or thyme. Beetroot, parsnip or sweet potato, smashed pea and mint, sunflower or sesame seeds.

Method

Sieve the flour and salt together.

Chop the butter or fortified dairy-free spread* into small chunks, add to the flour and mix with a fork making small fine 'breadcrumbs'.

Make a well in the 'crumbs' and pour in the milk slowly while stirring. Mix until you have a rough dough.

Preheat the oven to 220°c. Lightly flour your workspace, mould the dough with your fingers into a ball and place on the flour. Knead the dough until it is smooth and round.

When making sweet or savoury bread, grate fruits and vegetables, crush nuts, seed, garlic and herbs. Add 125 or 250ml of your chosen ingredient to the dough as you knead it. Mix well. Add a little flour or milk if the dough becomes a little too dry or wet.

Press the dough into a circle until it is approx. 1 ½ cm thick. Use a sharp knife to make a deep cross on top.

Grease a baking tray and place the dough on top. Brush with milk.

Bake in the oven for 15 minutes. The bread is ready when the top is firm and the base sounds hollow when tapped. If not, return to the oven for a few extra minutes.

Hints & tips

Large quantities of bicarb are not suitable for HIT. This soda bread uses self raising flour for minimal bicarb. Enjoy soda bread sparingly.

Soda bread can be used for croutons and also to serve soup in (make half portions.) Also blitz breadcrumbs together with herbs or seeds and olive oil to make savoury crumbs.

'Roast Parsnip Soup'

Ingredients

For 2 or 4 people -

125g or 250g	Red lentils
2 or 4	Parsnips
15ml or 30ml	Rapeseed oil
1 or 2	Red onion
20g or 40g	Butter
1 or 2	Carrots
3 or 6 cms	Fresh ginger
1 or 2 cloves	Fresh garlic
1 or 2	Apple
½ or 1 litre	Root vegetable 'stock'

Method

Boil a kettle of water. Cover red lentils with the water, bring to the boil again then simmer for 20 mins.

Preheat the oven to 200°c. Dice the parsnips and toss in rapeseed oil and season. Add to an oven proof tin and roast in the oven for 20 mins.

Meanwhile, roughly chop the onion and fry gently in butter for 2 mins. Chop the carrot and stir into the onion pan to coat in oil. Reduce the heat, cover and cook for 5 mins.

Prepare ginger and garlic by finely dicing. Then sprinkle with sea salt, and crush with the back of a knife. Stir into the pan for a minute.

Slice but do not peel the apple then stir into the hot pan. Pour over the vegetable 'stock', cover and bring to the boil, simmer for 10 minutes.

Stir the lentils well into the soup pan. Then carefully pour the contents of the pan into a blender (you may need to do so in two batches.)

Once the parsnips are ready, add to the blender and blitz soup to a smooth consistency. Return to the pan and gently heat but do not boil. Season to taste and serve warm.

Hints & tips

Serve topped with parsnip (or other root vegetable) crisps - see recipe.

This is a real 'whistles and bells' parsnip soup - feel free to leave out some of the extra ingredients for a simpler dish. For example, you may not add the lentils if the soup is to be served as a starter to a meal.

When blending hot soup, try removing the middle part of the lid and covering instead with a clean tea towel to avoid burning.

'Minestrone Verde'

Ingredients

For 2 or 4 people -

½ or 1	Swede
125g or 250g	Green beans
1 or 2	Onion
1 or 2	Leek
1 or 2 sticks	Celery
2 or 4 cloves	Fresh garlic
45ml or 90ml	Rapeseed oil
25g or 50g	Butter
1 or 2 litres	Root vegetable 'stock' (see recipe)
100g or 200g	Fusilli pasta - brown
½ or 1whole	Cabbage
2 or 4 handfuls	Fresh basil
50g or 100g	Green peas
200g or 400g	Cannelini beans

Method

Working quickly so the vegetables remain crisp, finely chop the swede, green beans, onion, leek and celery. Place in a bowl of cold water.

Prepare garlic by finely dicing. Sprinkle with sea salt, and crush with the back of a knife. Heat the oil and butter and add the garlic once the butter has melted. Fry gently for 2 mins.

Drain and add the chopped vegetables, plus the peas, and fry for 5 mins until the vegetables begin to soften.

Stir in the stock, plus the pasta, bring to the boil then reduce the heat to simmer, covered, for 15 minutes.

Meanwhile, finely slice the cabbage and tear the basil. After the 15 minutes cooking time - add the cabbage, basil and beans. Season to taste with sea salt and ground black pepper.

Continue to simmer for another 5 minutes until the pasta has cooked.

Remember this method calls for fusilli pasta. If using broken spaghetti or tiny pasta pieces you'll need to add pasta to the vegetables a little later. Maybe even use rice next time!

Try serving this spring-time dish with a dollop of fresh homemade basil pesto (see recipe), garlic buttered soda bread and a drizzle of olive oil.

Hints & tips

Ever heard the saying that Minestrone should contain 10 vegetables?

Alternatives include - courgettes, broccoli, cauliflower, collards, sprouts, green peppers, parsnip, watercress, or chilli for a spicy kick!

Non-Verde versions add carrot, babycorn, red, yellow or orange pepper with a splash of beetroot juice.

'Aloo Tikka & Raita'

Ingredients -

For 2 or 4 people -

<u>For the Aloo Tikka -</u>

2 or 4 small	Sweet potato
1 or 2	Red onion
15ml or 30ml	Rapeseed oil
50g or 100g	Green peas
1 or 2 small	Fresh chilli
1 or 2 cloves	Fresh garlic
70g or 140g	Gram flour
½ or 1 litre	Rapeseed oil

<u>For the Raita -</u>

125ml or 250ml	Homemade mayo (see recipe)
¼ or ½ whole	Cucumber
2 or 4 sprigs	Fresh mint

Method

Boil kettle. Peel and dice the sweet potato, add to a pan and cover with water. Bring to the boil for 10 mins until soft. Retain and freeze any cooking liquor for future stocks. Put the potato back in the pan for 2 mins on a low heat to 'dry out' the water.

Dice the red onion and fry gently in 1 (or 2 tbsp) oil for 2-3 mins until soft. Stir in the peas for a further 2 mins.

Finely chop the fresh chilli and remove the seeds. Prepare garlic by finely dicing, sprinkle with sea salt and crush with the back of a knife. Add both to the pan for another min.

Put the vegetables together in a large bowl. Add a pinch of unrefined sea salt and ground black pepper. Roughly mash to combine. Allow to cool as you prepare the mayonnaise. Put mayo in fridge to keep fresh.

In a second bowl, stir the gram flour with a little water to make a paste (120 or 240ml). Mould the 'Aloo Tikka' mix into 4 patties per person.

Heat the remaining oil in a small frying pan. Dip 2 or 3 patties into the paste then carefully add into the pan. Cook until light brown. Repeat.

Finely chop the cucumber and the mint and stir into the mayo. Season.

Hints & tips

'Aloo Tikka' and 'Raita' taste delicious when served with 'Chappati' or 'Poppadom' (see recipes.)

To turn the 'Raita' into 'Tzatiki' simply add 1 (or 2) cloves of crushed fresh garlic. For added bite, add ¼ or ½ finely chopped de-seeded chilli.

Also try serving with Mango Chutney.

'Mock-a-Leekie'

Ingredients

For 2 or 4 people -

2 or 4 small	Swede
½ or 1 litre	Root vegetable 'stock'
1 or 2	White onion
30ml or 60ml	Rapeseed oil
25g or 50g	Butter
2 or 4	Leeks
2 or 4 stalks	Celery
1 or 2 cloves	Fresh garlic
200g or 400g	Haricot beans
½ or 1 whole	Sweetheart cabbage
100ml or 200ml	Almond milk (or filtered water)

Method

Cut the swedes into chunks - if serving the soup inside the empty swedes - see the 'Hints & tips' below.

Cover the swede pieces with the root vegetable 'stock', bring to the boil then simmer for 15 mins until soft.

While the swede cooks, cut the onion into small pieces. Heat the oil and butter - add the onion once the butter has melted. Fry gently for 2 mins.

Chop the leeks and celery into 1cm pieces. Stir into the onion and butter. Continue to cook until tender but before they start to brown.

Prepare garlic by finely dicing. Sprinkle with sea salt, crush with the back of a knife. Add to the pan for a min.

Drain and rinse the haricot beans and cut the cabbage into thin strips.

Stir into the swede pan, heat through for 2-3 minutes. Add the gently fried onion, garlic, leek and celery.

If using, heat milk in a small pan but do not boil. If not, use filtered water instead. Pour into the soup pan. Stir well and remove from the heat.

Blitz the soup mix with a hand blender until smooth. Season with sea salt and ground black pepper. Reheat (don't boil) before serving.

Hints & tips

To serve soup in the swedes - wash and level the top and bottoms with a sharp knife. Cut a cross in the top and wrap in foil. Put in oven for 30 mins at 200°c. Allow to cool slightly and hollow out the filling in a similar way to a pumpkin or squash at Halloween (without the scary face!)

Cover swede flesh in root vegetable 'stock' - cook for 10 mins until soft. Continue with the method as before.

If using fresh poultry (organic if possible and not stored even for one day) boil small pieces with the swede, keep some back when blending the soup to stir through at the end. **Make sure the meat is fully cooked before serving.**

'Bruschetta'

Ingredients

For 2 or 4 people -

4 or 8 slices	Homemade soda bread - see recipe
1 or 2 cloves	Garlic
15ml or 30ml	Olive oil
2 or 4 large	*Carrots*
1 or 2	*Celery stick*
125 or 250ml	*Beetroot juice*
125 or 250ml	*Light 'stock'*

A handful of fresh basil.

Or -

300g or 600g	Green peas
25g or 50g	Butter

A handful of fresh mint.

Method

Make the bread as the 'Faux Mato' cooks or before making the smashed peas. Follow the recipe in this book.

To make the 'Faux Mato', dice the carrots and celery, cover with the beetroot juice and 'stock'. Bring to the boil and then simmer for 30 mins.

After the 30 minutes is up, remove the 'Faux Mato' from the heat. Mash the mix carefully so not to splash until you get a chunky texture, similar to that of chopped tomatoes.

Tear basil leaves and stir into the chunky mixture. Season generously.

To make the smashed peas, pour a couple of inches of water in the bottom of a pan. Place the peas in a colander over the top of the pan. Bring the water to boil and then simmer for 2-3 minutes until cooked.

Pour the water away and melt the butter in the hot pan. Tear mint into the butter and stir the peas through. Smash roughly with a fork. Season with sea salt and black pepper.

To assemble, toast the bread under a hot grill until lightly golden on each side. Rub one side of the bread with a clove of garlic and drizzle with oil.

Divide the topping between slices.

Hints & tips

Tear the soda bread into four, along the cross. Slice the wedges in half horizontally to make each slice.

Ideal as a starter served with a salad and parsnip wedges or crisps. For a more substantial meal, stir in gently caramelised red onion and 50g or 100g of seeds or white beans.

'Thai Delish Cakes'

Ingredients -

For 2 or 4 people -

125g or 250g	Red lentils
1 or 2 stalks	Lemongrass
2 or 4	Spring onions
30ml or 60ml	Rapeseed oil
1 or 2 cloves	Fresh garlic
3 or 6 cms	Fresh ginger
1 or 2 small	Fresh chilli
1 or 2 handfuls	Fresh coriander
60ml or 120ml	Oats - ground
1 or 2	Shallots
30ml or 60ml	Light tahini or almond nut butter
15ml or 30ml	Apple juice
15ml or 30ml	Agave nectar

Method

Boil a kettle of water. Cover red lentils with the water, bring to the boil again then simmer for 20 mins.

Remove the outer layers of the lemongrass and hit several times with a rolling pin to bruise it. Add to the pan for the last 10 mins simmering time. Remove once cooked.

Cut spring onion into thin rings and fry gently in ½ oil for 2 mins until soft. Prepare garlic and ginger by finely dicing, sprinkle with sea salt, crush with the back of a knife. Finely chop chilli, removing seeds. Stir *only* the ginger and ½ chilli into the pan.

Preheat the oven to 220°c. Remove the pan from the heat and tear in the coriander. Drain the red lentils and retain liquor. Stir in the spring onion - plus oats. Season with unrefined sea salt. Use your hands to mould mix into 2 patties per person.

Grease an oven tray and cook patties for 15 mins, turning once to brown.

For the 'Satay Sauce' - finely chop the shallots and gently fry in ½ oil in the seasoned pan for 2 mins. Add the already crushed garlic and chopped chilli for a min. Remove from heat.

Stir in the tahini or almond butter, juice and agave until well combined. Add a little red lentil 'stock' to thin the sauce to your preferred texture.

Hints & tips

Serve the 'Satay Sauce' and 'Thai Delish Cakes' with 'Gado Gado'. Cut a choice of carrots, celery, spring onion or cucumber into matchsticks, cauliflower or broccoli into florets and bean sprouts or green beans.

Lightly steam (if preferred) for 2-3 mins in a colander over a pan of boiling water. Or serve raw as crudities. Arrange together on a serving plate.

'Pinwheels'

Ingredients -

Makes 12 or 24 -

200g or 400g	Puff pastry - store bought or (see recipe.)
2 or 4	Leeks
20g or 40g	Butter
1 or 2 cloves	Fresh garlic
75 or 150ml	Double cream

Savoury options - replace the leek with finely chopped broccoli, courgette - even watercress or rocket!
Sweet options - Crushed almonds or finely chopped apple, pear, fig or mango with fresh ginger and agave nectar mixed together and spread.

Method

A real crowd pleaser that looks and tastes so delicious - even though it is quick and easy to prepare. Enjoy the sweet versions as a simple dessert or perhaps on a weekend morning?

Firstly, prepare the puff pastry following the recipe in this book. Wrap in cling film and leave to rest in the fridge. Allow 25 minutes. Alternatively, use frozen pastry and defrost at room temperature instead.

Meanwhile, wash and finely chop the leeks and put in a pan on the hob. Add ½ the butter and gently heat, stirring until all the butter has melted and coats the leeks. Cover pan with a lid and heat for 2-3 mins.

Prepare garlic by finely dicing then sprinkle with sea salt, crush with the back of a knife. Add to the pan, stir for a min. Season to taste.

Gently heat the cream in a separate pan, but do not allow to boil. Stir into the leeks, simmer uncovered for 5 mins as the sauce thickens. Cool.

On a film surface, roll out the pastry to ¼ cm thick. Evenly spread the leek mix on top. Roll tightly and wrap in the film. Refrigerate for 30 mins.

Preheat oven to 220°c. Cut pastry into 1 cm rings. Grease 1 (or 2) baking trays with ½ butter and place each pinwheel on it's side. Bake for 15-17 mins until lightly golden.

Hints & tips

Alternatively, try filo 'Spanakopita': Defrost 2 (or 4) sheets of filo. Combine finely chopped onion and garlic, 50g (or 100g) crumbled feta and a handful of watercress in a bowl.

Season to taste then assemble and bake as you would a 'Samosa' - see recipe in this book for method.

If using fresh poultry (organic if possible and not stored even for one day) finely dice and start to cook in the pan at the same time as the leeks. **Make sure the meat is fully cooked before serving.**

'French Onion Soup'

Ingredients

For 2 or 4 people -

500g or 1kg	Red, white and/or shallot onions
30ml or 60ml	Rapeseed oil
25g or 50g	Butter
1 or 2	Leeks
1 or 2 sprigs	Fresh rosemary
½ or 1 litre	Medium stock
¼ or ½	Homemade soda bread (see recipe)
Plus -	
1 or 2 cloves	Fresh garlic
10g or 20g	Olive oil
Or -	
2 or 4 slices	Fresh goats cheese

Method

Slice onions thinly using a mandolin or very sharp knife. Be very careful!

Heat the oil and butter - stir in the onion once the butter has melted. Cover pan with a lid as you cut the leek into thin rings. Add to the pan.

If you have greaseproof paper, cut a circle as wide as the pan. Splash with cold water and scrunch into a ball. Open up and shake and place directly on top of the onions and leek. If not, continue to cover pan with the lid.

Fry gently for 15 mins before removing the paper. Stir the onions and simmer until the onions turn a light golden brown (don't rush this part!)

Once browned, pour in the stock and bring to the boil. Finely chop and add rosemary. Reduce the heat to a simmer and cook for a further 15 mins.

As the soups simmers, cut the wedges of soda bread in half. Toast the slices of bread under a hot grill until lightly golden on each side.

Either - Rub one side of the toast with a clove of garlic and drizzle with oil. **Or** - Place slices of goats cheese onto each piece of bread and continue to toast until it melts.

Season to taste. Serve soup topped with the toasted bread croutons.

Hints & tips

Experiment with fresh herbs - try thyme, sage, marjoram or bay leaf.

Try a 'French Leek Soup' - or purists may leave out the leek altogether!

If making fresh bread, do so as the soup simmers. However for speed, next time you make soda bread, simply slice and freeze a portion. It toasts just as well from frozen!

'Kebabs'

Ingredients -

Makes 4 or 8 kebabs -

2 or 4 small	Red onion
15ml or 30ml	Rapeseed oil
1 or 2	Yellow pepper
¼ or ½ whole	Broccoli
30ml or 60ml	Olive oil
2 or 4 sprigs	Fresh mint
125g or 250g	Halloumi (fresh not aged.)

Options - Try replacing some of the vegetables above with; beetroot, courgette, cauliflower, celery, parsnip, sweet potato, carrots, sprouts!

Method

If using wooden skewers, always soak them in water for at least half an hour before using. This should avoid them burning whether you're BBQ-ing, grilling or cooking in the oven.

Preheat the oven to 220 °c. Don't peel the onions, cut a deep cross in the top of each and drizzle with oil. Wrap well in foil - cook for 10 mins. Cool then peel away the outer layer.

Once cool, cut the onions into quarters and add to a large bowl. Chop the pepper and broccoli to roughly the same size as the onions. Strip the herbs from the stem whole. Cut the halloumi into similar sized chunks.

Add to the bowl and toss thoroughly in the olive oil. Season with a pinch of unrefined sea salt and ground black pepper. Mix well to combine.

Thread the ingredients firmly onto the skewers, in an alternating pattern. Cover grill pan with foil and lightly brush with oil. Place skewers in a layer. Put in the oven for 15 mins, turning after 5 and 10 mins until crispy and slightly browned.

Carefully remove from the oven and drizzle with the remaining seasoned oil. For light meals, serve with cous cous, a fresh salad or part of a BBQ.

Hints & tips

Also try making 'Fruit Kebabs' - low histamine fruits include: apple, under-ripe pear, mango, star fruit, fig.

Drizzle with a little fruit coulis or melted homemade jam (see recipes.)

In place of the wooden skewers, try replacing with rosemary stems - they add an extra flavour to your kebabs!

If using fresh poultry (organic if possible and not stored even for one day) grill small pieces first, toss with the vegetables in the seasoned oil before adding to the skewers. **Make sure the meat is fully cooked before serving.**

'Carrot & Coriander Soup'

Ingredients

For 2 or 4 people -

4 or 8 large	Carrots
1 or 2	Apple
1 or 2	Red onion
30ml or 60ml	Rapeseed oil
3 or 6 cms	Fresh ginger
1 or 2 litres	Root vegetable 'stock' (see recipe)
2 or 4 handfuls	Fresh coriander
65g or 130g	Sunflower seeds

Drizzle of olive oil to serve.

Method

Do not take vegetables out of the fridge too early. Work quickly so the vegetables remain crisp.

Slice the carrots and the apple into small pieces and place into a bowl of cold water to keep fresh.

Slice the onion and fry gently in ½ oil for two minutes. Prepare ginger by finely dicing. Then sprinkle with sea salt, and crush with the back of a knife. Add to the oil for a minute.

Drain and carefully add the carrot and apple. Stir to coat well in the oil. Heat through on the hob for 5 mins.

Pour the stock into the pan and bring to the boil. Then cover and simmer for 20 minutes until the carrots and apple are soft.

Preheat the oven to 175°c.

Toss the seeds to coat in the remaining oil and season with sea salt and a little ground black pepper. Put in the oven, shaking at 10 and then at 15 mins until they are golden brown.

Add torn coriander to the soup mix. Using a food processor or hand-held blender, blitz the soup until smooth. Season to taste and reheat on the hob. Serve topped with the seeds and a drizzle of olive oil.

Hints & tips

Serve with homemade soda bread and butter. However, the soda bread needs a hotter oven to cook for 15 minutes (220°c) - so, prepare the seeds first and put in a sealed jar. Bake the bread as the soup simmers.

Carrot and apple also work as a nice combination in a salad. As the fruit is quite sharp - try serving with grilled halloumi or cubes of feta.

'Falafel'

Ingredients -

For 2 or 4 people -

1 or 2	Red onion
1 or 2 sticks	Celery
30ml or 60ml	Rapeseed oil
1 or 2	Red pepper
1 or 2 cloves	Fresh garlic
1 or 2 small	Fresh chilli
1 or 2 sprigs	Fresh herbs - coriander or mint
200g or 400g	Chickpeas
1 or 2	Organic egg yolk

Method

Finely chop the onion and celery. Gently fry in oil for 2-3 mins until they begin to soften.

Cut the pepper into small pieces and add to the pan. Stir to coat in oil and continue to fry gently for a minute.

Prepare garlic by finely dicing, sprinkle with sea salt and crush with the back of a knife. Cut the chilli into very small chunks, remove the seeds.

Add garlic and chilli to the pan while you finely chop the herbs. Remove the pan from the heat and also add the herbs, stir well to coat in oil.

Drain the chickpeas and add to a mixing bowl. Mash with a fork to break down the chickpeas without them becoming too smooth. Add the ingredients from the pan to the bowl and mix well to combine. Season.

Preheat the oven to 200°c. Beat the egg yolk in a small ramekin. Add to the bowl and stir well. Wet hands. Mould the mixture together with your hands to make 2 balls per person.

Lightly grease an oven tin and place the balls in around an inch apart. Cook in the oven for 25 minutes, turning after 15 mins, until golden on each side. Serve with pitta bread, cous-cous, lettuce and/or hummus.

Hints & tips

Easily convert this falafel recipe into a burger by moulding only 1 ball per person and serving in a homemade soda bread bun with salad and salsa.

If making cous-cous, try a simpler version of the 'Morrocan-style Salad' using oil, onion, herbs and seasoning.

Vary the white beans, fresh herbs and yellow, green or orange peppers.

'Creamed Broccoli Soup'

Ingredients

For 2 or 4 people -

50g or 100g	Fusilli pasta - brown
20g or 40g	Butter
3 or 6	Spring onions
2 or 4 sticks	Celery
1 or 2 sprigs	Fresh sage
½ or 1 whole	Broccoli
200g or 400g	Butter beans
1 or 2 cloves	Fresh garlic
½ or 1 litre	Light 'stock'
30ml or 60ml	Rapeseed oil

Serve with chunks of homemade soda bread and butter (see recipe.)

Method

Boil a kettle. Cover pasta with the water, bring to the boil then simmer for 15 minutes (drain really well.)

Meanwhile, cut the spring onions and celery into ½ cm pieces. Finely chop the sage. Gently melt the butter in a pan, add the onion, celery and sage.

Cut the broccoli into small pieces - plus stalk. Add to the pan and stir to coat in butter. Drain, add the beans.

Prepare garlic by finely dicing. Then sprinkle with sea salt, and crush with the back of a knife. Stir into the butter for a further minute.

Once the broccoli has softened a little, pour in the stock. Bring to the boil then simmer for 10 minutes.

As the soup simmers, heat the oil in a small pan. Carefully add the pasta. Keep the pasta sizzling and stir often to make sure it doesn't stick to the pan. After 7-8 mins, reduce the heat to medium for 10 mins. Season.

Remove the soup from the heat and blitz with a hand blender until smooth. Season to taste with unrefined sea salt and black pepper.

Reheat the soup to a simmer for 1-2 mins. Serve topped with the pasta.

Hints & tips

To make the soup extra creamy, stir through a little double cream once removed from the heat - but before blitzing. Alternatively, try feta or fresh goats cheese for a tangy taste.

Replace the broccoli with cabbage, cauliflower - maybe even sprouts!

In place of the pasta, add homemade soda bread croutons (see recipe.)

'Noodle Soup'

Ingredients -

For 2 or 4 people -

2 or 4	Spring onions
15 or 30ml	Sesame oil
1 or 2 cloves	Fresh garlic
3 or 6 cms	Fresh ginger
40g or 80g	Sesame seeds
1 or 2 stalks	Lemongrass
400 or 800ml	Medium 'stock'
150g or 300g	Egg free noodles
1 or 2 heads	Pak choi
100g or 200g	Sweetcorn
50g or 100g	Beansprouts
1 or 2 handfuls	Coriander

Optional -

1 or 2 finely chopped fresh chilli.

Method

Finely slice spring onions and gently fry in sesame oil for 1 min to soften.

Prepare garlic and ginger by finely dicing, sprinkle with sea salt, crush with the back of a knife. Stir with the seeds into the pan for 1-2 mins .

Remove the outer layers of the lemongrass and hit several times with a rolling pin to bruise it. Add to the pan to coat in oil. Pour stock over and bring to the boil.

Once boiling, add the noodles to the pan. Cover and reduce the heat to a simmer for 10 mins in total. Cut the pak choi stems from the leaves then cut stems and leaves into strips. After 2-3 mins, add stems to the pan.

For the last 2-3 mins cooking time, add the pak choi leaves, sweetcorn and bean sprouts to the pan.

Once the noodles are ready, take the pan off of the heat. Remove the lemongrass stalk from the soup.

Tear the coriander leaves into the pan and season to taste with unrefined sea salt and ground black pepper. Serve as a starter or side order, with homemade 'Spring Rolls' and 'Special Fried Rice' (see recipes.)

Hints & tips

Alternatively, make this soup with root vegetable or light 'stock.' Allow to cool then stir in a little double cream or almond milk and reheat to a simmer - but do not boil.

To make an Asian-style sauce, simply use less 'stock.' Another soup that can be made from the basis of a sauce recipe is a creamy 'Faux Mato'. Using either the 'Simple Pasta Sauce' or 'Ketchup' recipes - simply add more root vegetable 'stock' and stir in a little double cream.

If using fresh poultry (organic if possible and not stored even for one day) cut it into very thin strips and start to cook in the pan at the same time as the spring onions. **Make sure the meat is fully cooked before serving.**

Take a Month to Change Your Life

Low histamine isn't a diet in the typical sense: it's neither a weight-loss nor a 'detox' plan. It's a 'recharge' diet that becomes part of your life.

First make sure that your doctor has ruled out any other medical condition. Then using the recipes in this book, begin by eating a low-histamine diet for about four weeks. This is usually long enough to see if you gain any relief from your symptoms. During those first few weeks, be careful to avoid the 'treats' that are generally only permitted in moderation (see 'The Right Ingredients.')

Don't depend too much on any one thing: You should aim for variety.

If you start feeling some improvement, then you can experiment to decide how strictly you need to follow the diet to relieve *your* symptoms. It could be that you only need to follow a low-histamine diet some of the time. You may be fortunate, and simply eating low-histamine a few times a week may be enough for you. If your symptoms start to return, you'll then know to pay particular attention to further reducing your histamine intake. Eventually, you'll find the balance that works for you.

Others, (like me!) find that to control their symptoms effectively they need to follow the diet pretty much 100% of the time. That's exactly why I designed the recipes in this book to be as tempting and easy to prepare as possible. I felt that there just had to be plenty of meals that people could happily imagine themselves eating longer-term.

When I short-listed the recipes for this book I started with over 2000. But only those that I felt people would really crave actually made it into this edition. The recipes all had to pass other tests too. They had to be reasonably quick to make, be economical, and only use ingredients that you could generally buy from most supermarkets or high street health stores.

I've heard it said that it takes 16 times of repeating a task before it becomes a habit, and some say it takes a month of practicing something before you can do it without thinking about it. It just so happens that four weeks is the length of time recommended to try the diet to see if you notice improvements. Surely that must be worth a go?

Snacks & Light Meals

'Rice Salad'

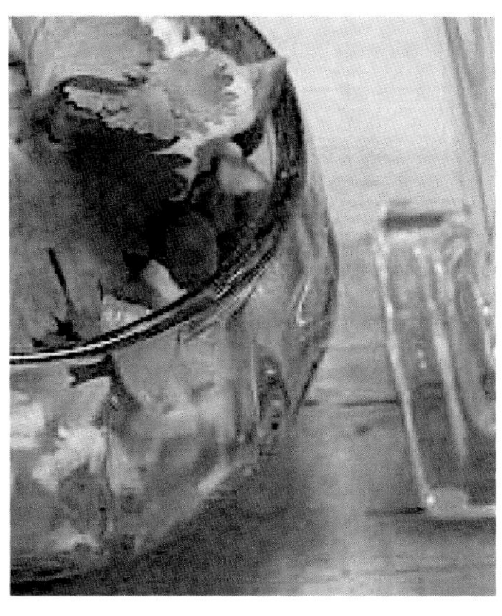

Ingredients

For 2 or 4 people -

125g or 250g	Brown rice
1 or 2	Carrots
1 or 2	Red onion
100g or 200g	Green peas
50g or 100g	Sunflower seeds
3 or 6cms	Fresh ginger
1 or 2	Red apple
125 or 250ml	Apple juice
15ml or 30ml	Olive oil

A handful of fresh basil to serve.

Method

Boil water, and cook rice according to pack instructions.

Five to ten minutes before the end of the rice cooking time prepare the vegetables. Do not take them out of the fridge or freezer too early.

Working quickly so the vegetables remain crisp, chop carrots into small chunks and finely dice onion. Place them with the peas and seeds in a steamer (or colander) over the boiling rice for no more than 2-3 minutes until they just start to soften.

Prepare ginger by finely dicing. Then sprinkle with sea salt, and crush with the back of a knife.

Mix apple juice, oil, ginger and herbs in a bowl. Cut apple into small cubes and stir into the apple juice dressing.

When the rice is cooked and the seeds and vegetables are ready, mix them together and rinse through with cold water to cool quickly. Do not leave on one side to cool slowly.

Drain the rice mix and stir well into the apple dressing. Season to taste with sea salt and black pepper.

Eat immediately. Do not be tempted to leave cooked rice to stand.

Hints & tips

Be careful when cooking rice. Always wash the rice and add a few basil leaves to the water during cooking. Make sure that all other food preparation is done while the rice cooks.

The vegetable alternatives are plenty - try adding courgette, celery, baby sweetcorn, beetroot, leek or cucumber. Vary the fresh herbs too!

If using fresh poultry (organic if possible and not stored even for one day) saute finely cubed pieces and stir into the apple juice dressing before adding the rice. **Make sure the meat is fully cooked before serving.**

'Sausage Rolls'

Ingredients

For 2 or 4 people -

250g or 500g	Puff pastry - store bought or (see recipe.)
125g or 250g	Red lentils
1 or 2	Red onion
1 or 2	Clove garlic
60ml or 120ml	Oats - ground
15ml or 30ml	Almond milk

A handful of fresh herbs.

Try replacing the red lentils with crushed mashed parsnip and feta cheese or puy lentils and mint.

Method

Firstly, prepare the puff pastry following the recipe in this book.

Wrap in cling film and leave to rest in the fridge. Alternatively, use frozen pastry and defrost at room temperature instead. Allow 25 minutes.

While the pastry is in the fridge boil a kettle of water. Cover red lentils with 400ml water, bring to the boil again then simmer for 20 minutes.

Dice onion finely. Prepare garlic by finely dicing then sprinkle with sea salt, crush with the back of a knife.

Drain the red lentils well, add and stir in the onion, garlic, oats and herbs, season. Leave to cool. Mould into 3 long thin sausage shapes.

Freeze any red lentil 'stock' to make light sauces and gravies in future.

Take pastry from the fridge and roll out on a floured surface as thick as a £1 coin. Cut pastry into 3 rectangles, lay sausages along the centre. Brush the sides of the pastry with milk.

Roll the pastry over the sausages, pressing together to seal. Cut to size, place (on the seam) on a baking tray and brush again with the milk.

Put in oven at 180°c for 20 mins.

Hints & tips

Making double the pastry quantity and freezing half makes this a quick comfort meal. Puff pastry should be stacked when frozen - not rolled into a ball! Use to top pie fillings.

Even better, 'sausage rolls' can easily be assembled then frozen. Simply add 5 minutes onto the cooking time when putting into the oven!

If using fresh poultry (organic if possible and not stored even for one day) saute finely cubed pieces and use only half the lentils. When cooked, stir into the lentil filling. **Make sure the meat is fully cooked before serving.**

'Breakfast Porridge'

Ingredients

For 2 or 4 people -

250 or 500ml	Quinoa flakes
½ or 1 litre	Apple juice
Or	
250 or 500ml	Millet flakes
½ or 1 litre	Apple juice
Or	
250 or 500ml	Rolled oats
½ or 1 litre	Apple juice
250 or 500ml	Filtered water
Or	
250 or 500ml	Rolled oats
½ or 1 litre	Almond milk
250 or 500ml	Filtered water

Method

If you haven't made porridge before and think it takes too long to make, and is too much hassle - don't worry!

Usually by the time you've had your morning drink, the porridge will be cooked and cooled enough to eat.

You can easily make a portion for one person by dividing the quantities.

For the quinoa and millet porridge, pour the flakes into a pan and stir in the apple juice.

Bring the porridge to the boil and then simmer for 2 minutes, stirring. Pour into a bowl and allow to cool a little before eating.

The rolled oats take a little longer to cook as they're thicker and absorb more water.

For the oat porridge, pour the oats into a pan and stir in the apple juice (or almond milk) with the water.

Bring to the boil. However, this time, cover and simmer for five minutes. Stir and remove from the heat.

Remember, to allow the porridge to cool slightly before eating.

Hints & tips

Sometimes Millet is sold more finely ground than flakes. If so, add an extra 250-500ml of water and cook on the hob for another 5 minutes. For the round grains, cook for 10 mins.

For extra 'zing', grate apple into the apple juice porridge before serving. For crunch, sprinkle the milk porridge with flaked almonds or seeds.

'Store-cupboard Supper'

Ingredients

For 2 or 4 people -

200g or 400g	Rice pasta
	Or
200g or 400g	Corn pasta
	Or
200g or 400g	Gluten pasta
	Or
200g or 400g	Brown rice
	Or
2 or 4	Sweet potatoes
100g or 200g	Carrots
100g or 200g	Celery sticks
100g or 200g	Green peas
30ml or 60ml	Olive oil

A handful of fresh basil.

Method

Fresh vegetables should be bought as soon after picking as possible. Plan any meals requiring fresh vegetables within a day or two of purchase.

But it isn't always possible to go shopping every other day. And there are times when you just don't have time to peel and chop them either.

Over time I've learnt to seek out frozen organic vegetables (such as peas and sweetcorn) from the supermarket. I also peel and chop carrots and celery (plus others) into small chunks to freeze on the day that I buy them.

These quick supper meals use those frozen vegetables, steamed over the pasta, rice or potato pan as they cook on the hob.

Boil kettle. Cover corn/gluten pastas, rice or peeled and cubed potato. To avoid sticking, pour cold water only over the rice pasta.

Cover the pan with a colander and add the frozen vegetables. Cover with the pan lid. Bring the pan to the boil and simmer for 5 minutes. Remove from the heat. Stir in herbs, oil and season.

Nb. Gluten pasta takes around 15 mins and rice takes 40 mins to cook. So vegetables should be steamed 5 mins from the end of cooking time.

Hints & tips

Choose these quick and simple meals for when you don't have long to prepare a full meal. They can also be served for lunch - simply add a 100g portion of white beans per person.

As always, try to vary the herbs - the robust herbs (for example, rosemary, sage and thyme) should be added to the vegetables as they steam.

If using fresh poultry (organic if possible and not stored even for one day) saute small cubed pieces while the pasta cooks. When cooked, stir into the pasta and vegetables. **Make sure the meat is fully cooked before serving.**

'Paté & Crispbreads'

Ingredients
For 2 or 4 people -

1 or 2 large	Carrot
1 or 2 sticks	Celery
100g or 200g	Green peas
100g or 200g	Sweetcorn
15ml or 30ml	Olive oil
20g or 40g	Fortified dairy-free spread*

A handful of fresh mint or basil.

Or -

125g or 250g	Puy lentils
1 or 2	Red onion
15ml or 30ml	Olive oil
20g or 40g	Fortified dairy-free spread*

A handful of fresh rosemary.

Method

For the vegetable paté, finely chop the carrot and celery. Place all the vegetables in a pan and cover with water. Bring to the boil and then simmer for 3 minutes.

Remove from heat and add ½ torn herbs, fortified dairy-free spread* and olive oil. Stir through, season with sea salt and black pepper.

For the lentil paté, boil the kettle and cover puy lentils with 400ml water. Bring to the boil again then simmer for 30 minutes.

Finely chop and add herbs half way through the cooking. Dice onion finely. Fry gently in the oil for 5 minutes, stirring, until soft.

Once cooked, stir through the fortified dairy-free spread* and season with sea salt and black pepper.

To serve both -

Blitz to a smooth or rough paste using a hand-held blender. Be careful to cover the pan with a cloth or use a blender with a covered base unit.

Spread paté onto the crispbreads. Top with ½ herbs and serve warm straight away or freeze to use later.

Hints & tips

Vary the 'crispbreads' - wholegrain rice cakes, corn cakes, oatcakes or rye crispbread (max 2 per day.)

The vegetable paté tastes nice with many soft herbs. The lentil paté can be made with other robust herbs.

Replace the puy with green, red or brown lentils - simply reduce the cooking time to 20 minutes.

If using fresh poultry (organic if possible and not stored even for one day) saute finely cubed pieces and use only half the lentils. When cooked, stir into the lentil topping. **Make sure the meat is fully cooked before serving.**

'Mixed Lentil Salad'

Ingredients

For 2 or 4 people -

65g or 125g	Puy lentils
1 or 2 sprigs	Fresh rosemary
65g or 125g	Green lentils
65g or 125g	Red lentils
1 or 2 medium	Carrots
100g or 200g	Green peas
1 or 2	Red onion
1 or 2 sticks	Celery
15ml or 30ml	Rapeseed oil
1 or 2 cloves	Fresh garlic

Stir through pasta, millet, cous-cous, quinoa or rice as a simple supper.

Method

A key part of this salad is that the lentils should keep their shape and colour. As a result, they are cooked in separate pans for different times.

To begin cover puy lentils with filtered water, bring to the boil then simmer for 30 mins. Finely chop rosemary and add to the pan. Top the water up after 10 mins and stir.

After the 10 mins, add green lentils to another pan. Cover with water, bring to a boil, simmer for 15 mins.

Meanwhile, cut the carrots into small pieces. Place with the peas in a colander or steamer over the puy lentils as they cook for the last 10 mins.

Place red lentils in a third pan and again cover with water, bring to the boil and then simmer for 5-10 mins until soft to the bite but not mushy.

Finely dice the red onion and celery and fry gently for 2 mins. Prepare garlic by finely dicing. Sprinkle with sea salt, and crush with the back of a knife. Add to the hot pan for 1 min.

Drain the lentils and retain the cooking liquors for 'stock'. Stir the lentils, rosemary and vegetables into the onion and garlic pan.

Season with unrefined sea salt and ground black pepper to taste.

Hints & tips

Also serve this dish hot as a side order, lasagne or pastry filling. Vary the vegetables - try leek or courgette. Sometimes a little fresh chilli!

For picnics in place of a rice, bean or pasta salad; Cook and drain the lentils and stir through apple juice, diced apple, finely chopped mint and onions with crushed ginger.

If using fresh poultry (organic if possible and not stored even for one day) saute finely cubed pieces and use only half the lentils. When cooked, stir into the lentil salad. **Make sure the meat is fully cooked before serving.**

'Pesto Pasta'

Ingredients

For 2 or 4 people -

150g or 300g	Wholegrain penne pasta
1 or 2	Red onion
100g or 200g	Sunflower seeds
15ml or 30ml	Rapeseed oil
1 or 2 cloves	Fresh garlic
4 or 8 handfuls	Fresh basil (60g or 120g packs)
30ml or 60ml	Olive oil

Try replacing the sunflower seeds with pumpkin or sesame. Alternatively, use crushed almonds.

Method

Boil the kettle and pour boiling water over the pasta. Cook according to packet instructions - usually for around 15 minutes.

While the pasta cooks, finely dice the onion and gently fry (with the sunflower seeds) in the rapeseed oil for 2 minutes.

Prepare garlic by finely dicing. Then sprinkle with sea salt, and crush with the back of a knife.

Stir the garlic into the onions and seeds and cook for another minute.

At the last moment while the pan is on the heat, tear and stir through the basil until just slightly wilted.

Remove from heat and stir through the olive oil. Season with sea salt and black pepper.

Simply put the basil mixture in a food processor if you have one and blend to the consistency you prefer.

Otherwise, pour the basil mixture into a pestle and mortar and carefully grind to a rough paste. A little extra sea salt increases the friction and makes this easier to do.

Drain the pasta once cooked and stir the pesto through while still hot.

Hints & tips

Alternate penne with fusilli or spaghetti. Pesto also tastes really good poured over sweet potatoes or roast vegetables. Even in a lasagne!

Try adding a little pesto to olive oil to drizzle over salads or turn into a dip for crudites, nachos or vegetable crisps by adding another 15ml or 30ml oil. Also try replacing the basil with coriander or rocket.

'Roasted Snack Mix'

Ingredients

For 2 or 4 people -

65g or 125g	Green split peas
65g or 125g	Yellow split peas
½ or 1 litre	Filtered water
125g or 250g	Chickpeas (drained)
30ml or 60ml	Rapeseed oil
2 or 4 sprigs	Fresh rosemary
10ml or 20ml	Unrefined sea Salt
65g or 125g	Green peas
65g or 125g	Sunflower seeds

Caution! This mix is very crunchy!

Method

Boil the kettle. If the green and yellow split peas are the same size, place together in a large saucepan. If one is much larger than the other, place in two separate pans and start to cook the large peas 5 mins sooner.

Cover green split peas with boiled filtered water, bring to the boil, then simmer for 20 minutes. Top the water up a little after 10 minutes and then again after another 5.

When the split peas are al dente but not too soft remove from heat and drain well. Retain the cooking liquid to use as a light 'stock' in future.

Preheat oven to 175°c and place two baking trays in the oven to heat up.

Rinse the chickpeas and drain well. It is important that they are not too wet when they go in the hot oven.

Mix the split peas and the chickpeas in a bowl and pour over 2/3rds of the oil, salt and rosemary. Pour the oiled mix onto one of the baking trays in a single layer. Put in oven for 45 mins.

Meanwhile, mix the green peas and seeds in the oiled bowl and add the remaining oil, salt and herbs. Put on the second tray and then in the oven.

Shake the trays every 10 min or sooner until they are golden brown.

Hints & tips

Caution! This mix is very crunchy! For a softer bite, roast for a shorter time and eat as soon as they cool.

For a change try mint, ginger, black pepper and occasionally fresh chilli!

Alternatively, try a variety of different lentils or seeds. Remember to check them at least every 10 mins.

Rosemary &
CAUTION! Very

'Porkie Pies'

Ingredients

Makes 2 or 4 individual pies -

250g or 500g	Shortcrust pastry - store-bought (or see recipe.)
65g or 125g	Puy lentils
½ or 1	Onion
½ or 1	Carrot
½ or 1 stick	Celery
15ml or 30ml	Rapeseed oil
1 or 2	Clove garlic
60ml or 120ml	Oats - ground
15ml or 30ml	Almond milk

A handful of fresh rosemary. *You need 2 (or 4) greased ramekins.*

Method

Firstly, prepare the shortcrust pastry following the recipe in this book. Wrap in cling film and leave to rest in the fridge. Alternatively, use frozen pastry and defrost at room temperature instead. Allow 25 minutes.

While the pastry is in the fridge boil a kettle of water. Cover puy lentils with ½ (or 1 litre) water, bring to the boil again, then simmer for 30 mins.

Dice onion, carrots and celery finely. Fry gently for 5 minutes, stirring, until soft. Finely chop and add herbs.

Prepare garlic by finely dicing then sprinkle with sea salt, crush with the back of a knife. Stir into the onions.

Drain the puy lentils (freeze any puy lentil 'stock' for gravies) and roughly mash with a fork. Add and stir in the vegetables, garlic and oats. Season.

Divide pastry into 2/3rd and 1/3rd balls - 1 of each per person. Roll out large and small circles to 2-3mm thick. Press the large circles into the ramekins. Fill with the lentil mix.

Press the smaller circles over the top of the pies, crimp the edges, brush with milk and prick with a fork. Put in oven at 180°c for 25 mins. Also put a separate baking tray in the oven.

Cool pies slightly then run a sharp knife gently around the tops to loosen. Tip pies over to remove from ramekin. Place on the hot baking tray, return to oven for 20 mins.

Hints & tips

Serve cold with salad leaves, sweet potato or parsnip wedges and 'chutney'. Serve hot with 'bread sauce' and 'gravy' or swede 'mash' and peas (see recipes.)

Make double quantity and freeze!

If using fresh poultry (organic if possible and not stored even for one day) saute finely cubed pieces and use only half the lentils. When cooked, stir into the lentil filling. **Make sure the meat is fully cooked before serving.**

'Burger in a Bun'

Ingredients

For 2 or 4 people -

125g or 250g	Puy lentils
1 or 2 sprigs	Fresh rosemary
400 or 800ml	Filtered water
1 or 2	Red onion
15ml or 30ml	Rapeseed oil
1 or 2 cloves	Fresh garlic
60ml or 120ml	Oats - ground
For the salsa -	
2 or 4 handfuls	Fresh coriander
2 or 4	Spring onions
½ or 1 small	Red apple
10ml or 20ml	Apple juice
10ml or 20ml	Rapeseed oil

Salad, chips and soda bread to serve.

Method

Boil a kettle of water. Cover puy lentils with the water, bring to the boil again then simmer for 30 mins. Finely chop rosemary and add to the pan.

Dice onion finely. Heat oil in a pan and cook the onion, stirring, for two minutes. Prepare garlic by finely dicing then sprinkle with sea salt, crush with the back of a knife. Add the garlic for a further minute.

Drain the puy lentils and retain the water. Freeze any puy lentil 'stock' to make sauces and gravies in future.

Roughly mash the lentils and rosemary. Stir in the onion, garlic and oats. Grease an oven proof tin.

Season and mould into burger patties - either 2 small or 1 large per person. Cook in the oven for 20 (or 30) mins, turning over to brown each side.

For the salsa, finely chop herbs and spring onion then dice but don't peel the apple. Add to a small jar with the juice and oil. Season with sea salt and black pepper. Shake well.

Serve in a toasted sesame seed soda bread bun (see recipe.) Top with salsa or mayo (see recipes) or slices of fresh goats cheese. Side orders could include sweet potato wedges or swede 'chips' and a fresh salad.

Hints & tips

Burger combinations are plenty! Try different lentils or 'bean burgers', add fresh chilli for 'spicy burgers', curry leaves and ginger for 'curry burgers', add diced mixed vegetable.

Add variety with torn fresh herbs. Whatever you try use a binder such as organic egg yolk, oats or flour.

For ease, toast frozen soda bread.

If using fresh poultry (organic if possible and not stored even for one day) saute finely cubed pieces and use only half the lentils. When cooked, stir into the lentil mix. **Make sure the meat is fully cooked before serving.**

'Vietnamese-Style Wraps'

Ingredients

For 2 or 4 people -

125g or 250g	Brown rice
½ or 1 litre	Filtered water
1 or 2 sprigs	Fresh basil
125g or 250g	Green lentils
1 or 2 sticks	Fresh lemongrass
1 or 2	Red onion
15 or 30ml	Sesame oil
1 or 2 cloves	Fresh garlic
3 or 6 cms	Fresh ginger
¼ or ½ whole	Cucumber
1 or 2 medium	Carrot
1 or 2 sticks	Celery
4 or 8 leaves	Little gem or romaine lettuce

Method

Wash the rice at least twice to rinse away the starch. Add rice to a pan and cover with water. Add a sprig of basil then bring to a boil for 10 mins.

Boil a second pan of water. Strain the rice and basil - put in a colander on top of this pan. Push a few holes with chopsticks to touch the colander.

Place a lid over the colander but not touching the rice for 30 mins. When cooked, fluff the rice up with a fork.

Meanwhile, boil a kettle of water. Cover green lentils with water, bring to the boil then simmer for 20 mins.

Remove the outer layers of the lemongrass and hit several times with a rolling pin to bruise it. Add to the pan of lentils as it simmers. Dice onion finely. Heat oil in a pan and cook the onion, stirring, for two minutes.

Prepare garlic and ginger by finely dicing then sprinkle with sea salt, crush with the back of a knife. Add to the pan for a further minute.

Drain the green lentils and freeze any lentil 'stock'. Stir in the onion, garlic and ginger - remove the lemongrass.

Cut the cucumber, carrot and celery into thin strips. Serve spooned with the mix into the lettuce leaves, ready for your guests to wrap.

Hints & tips

Lettuce wraps are very refreshing. However, as an alternative try using homemade flatbread or pancakes instead (see recipes.)

Try this method of cooking rice - so that it can be eaten with chopsticks, Vietnamese-style rice grains should be slightly sticky yet separate. Always add basil during cooking!

If using fresh poultry (organic if possible and not stored even for one day) saute finely cubed pieces and use only half the lentils. When cooked, stir into the lentil mix. **Make sure the meat is fully cooked before serving.**

'Pad Thai'

Ingredients

For 2 or 4 people -

100g or 200g	Wide ribbon noodles - egg free or organic free range if possible
30ml or 60ml	Sesame oil
2 or 4	Spring onions
125g or 250g	Green beans
2 or 4 cloves	Fresh garlic
3 or 6 cms	Fresh ginger
100 or 200ml	Apple juice
150g or 300g	Beansprouts
50g or 100g	Sesame seeds (or crushed almonds)
2 or 4 handfuls	Fresh coriander

Alternatively, replace sesame seeds with toasted crushed almonds.

Method

Boil the kettle and cook noodles according to packet instructions, usually for around 10 minutes. Once cooked, drain well and stir in ½ of the sesame oil to prevent sticking.

As the noodles cook, cut the spring onions into fine matchsticks. Working quickly so the vegetables remain crisp, top and tail the green beans (then cut in half) and add to a bowl of cold water.

Prepare garlic and ginger by finely dicing. Then sprinkle with sea salt, and crush with the back of a knife.

Once all ingredients are prepared, heat the remaining oil in a wok (or large frying pan.) Add the spring onions and stir to coat in oil.

Quickly stir the garlic and ginger into the wok. Do not allow to burn!

Drain the green beans well and add to the wok. Cook for a minute before adding the noodles. Add the sesame seeds and beansprouts. Stir and then pour in the apple juice.

Turn the heat up to high and cook for another minute, continuing to stir. Tear most of the coriander into the wok and season to taste. Stir.

Serve topped with the remaining herbs and spring rolls (see recipe.)

Hints & tips

This dish uses few vegetables, but you can try - chopped fresh green chilli, pak choi, or kaffir lime leaves.

Also, make a very thin egg omelette by cracking two egg yolks into a small greased frying pan (skillet) and sprinkle with sesame seeds. Turn onto plate, cut into thin strips. Alternatively, use scrambled egg yolk.

If using fresh poultry (organic if possible and not stored even for one day) cut into thin slices and add to the wok before the vegetables. When cooked, add the spring onions. **Make sure the meat is fully cooked before serving.**

'Sweet & Savoury Crepes'

Ingredients

For 2 or 4 people -

30ml or 60ml	Rapeseed oil
1 or 2	Leeks
125g or 250g	Green beans
100g or 200g	Green peas
50g or 100g	Sunflower seeds
2 or 4 sprigs	Fresh basil to serve
Or -	
6 or 12cms	Fresh ginger
1 or 2 whole	Mango
120 or 240ml	Apple juice
With -	
90g or 180g	Brown flour
1 or 2	Organic egg yolk
200 or 400ml	Almond milk
20g or 40g	Butter

Method

Preheat the oven to 175°c. **For the savoury filling** - slice the leeks and beans and toss all savoury ingredients in oil. Season. Add to a roasting tin and cook for 20 mins, shake after 10.

For the sweet filling - peel and cut the mango into thin slices. Prepare the ginger by finely dicing and crush with the back of a knife. Add to a roasting tin and pour over apple juice. Cook for 15 minutes.

Sift the flour (and a pinch of sea salt for savoury crepes, or 15 (or 30ml) glucose for sweet) into a bowl.

Make a well in the centre of the flour and pour the egg yolk into it. Whisk the eggs and flour together - be careful to mix with all the flour. Gradually stir in the milk and keep whisking until all of the lumps have disappeared and the batter is cream-like.

Melt a knob of butter (approx 5g) in a frying pan. Using a cup or ladle, pour in 70ml of batter mix and swirl around the pan to coat the base.

Cook for 2 mins or until the bottom side browns. Loosen and turn over. Cook the second side until brown - it will cook quicker than the first.

Repeat for each crepe - you should make 2 per person. Remember to melt a knob of butter each time.

Hints & tips

Crepes are thinner than pancakes. Mix crushed almonds, grated apple, seeds or herbs into the crepe mix.

Try using crepes in place of wraps for enchiladas, as part of a 'boxty' or cannelloni dish (see recipes.) Experiment with different fruit or savoury ingredients - even lunchtime or breakfast 'sandwich' fillings!

If using fresh poultry (organic if possible and not stored even for one day) slice thinly and toss in the seasoned oil. Roast in the oven with the other savoury ingredients. **Make sure the meat is fully cooked before serving.**

'Quesadillas'

Ingredients

For 2 or 4 people -

1 or 2	Sweet potato
5 or 10ml	Almond milk
20g or 40g	Butter
120g or 240g	Brown flour
1 or 2 sprigs	Fresh sage
45ml or 90ml	Rapeseed oil
1 or 2	Red onion
1 or 2 cloves	Fresh garlic
1 or 2	Red, green, orange or yellow pepper
1 or 2 small	Fresh chilli
200g or 400g	Haricot beans
1 or 2 handfuls	Fresh basil

Method

Wash and peel the sweet potatoes. Roughly cut into chunks and put into a pan on the hob. Cover with filtered water, bring to the boil for 10 mins.

Once cooked, drain the potatoes and mash with milk and butter. Mix in the flour, finely chop sage and season with a pinch of sea salt. Put plenty of flour on your workspace and rolling pin. Knead the dough for 2-3 mins. Mould into 4 (or 8) balls and roll all into circles 20 cm wide.

Heat 5ml of oil in a frying pan and lay the first flatbread into the pan. Cook until lightly brown before turning over and browning on the other side. Repeat until all are cooked - this will take around 2-3 mins each.

Meanwhile, preheat oven to 220°c. Quarter onion, slice pepper, season and toss in oil. Roast for 15 minutes.

Prepare garlic by finely dicing. Sprinkle with sea salt, and crush with the back of a knife. Finely chop the chilli. Add both to the oven tin for 1 min.

Separate the pepper and put to one side. Blitz the beans, onion, garlic and chilli until smooth. Spread 2 (or 4) of the flatbreads evenly with bean pate and top with the roasted peppers. Press the other 2 (or 4) flatbreads on top to make a sandwich. Cut into quarters, serve with salad.

Hints & tips

Also known as Sincronizada, fill flatbreads with refried beans, pea guacamole, feta or fresh salsa (see recipes.) Or at brunch, try scrambled eggs and homemade baked beans.

Vary the flatbreads (roti, lefse) with parsnip, swede or beetroot mash. Make double quantities and freeze the extra once cooked. Place a piece of kitchen film or foil between each.

If using fresh poultry (organic if possible and not stored even for one day) slice thinly and toss in the seasoned oil. Roast in the oven with the peppers and onions. **Make sure the meat is fully cooked before serving.**

'Tempura'

Ingredients
For 2 or 4 people -
<u>Savoury Tempura -</u>

1 or 2	Red, green, orange or yellow pepper
¼ or ½ whole	Broccoli
½ or 1 large	Sweet potato

<u>Sweet Tempura -</u>

1 or 2	Apple
1 or 2 hard	Pear
½ or 1 whole	Mango

<u>Tempura batter -</u>

1 or 2	Organic egg yolk
240ml or 480ml	Carbonated water
100g or 200g	Brown flour
Approx. 500ml	Rapeseed or sesame oil

Method

Be careful when cooking with hot oil.

Use ice cold water for the batter. Put a bottle of carbonated water in the fridge an hour before you start.

Wash and chop the fillings into rough chunks. Depending on your preferred taste; either keep them raw (not for root vegetables,) blanch them or toss in oil plus herbs and roast in a hot oven (200°c) for 20 minutes.

Either way, make sure any excess water has been drained away, and score watery fruit and vegetables with a knife to avoid them bursting. Roll lightly in a little plain flour.

Pour the oil into a small pan. Heat the oil while you prepare the batter (don't make in advance.) Whisk the egg yolk in a bowl. Stir in the cold water. Sift the flour into the bowl.

Mix the batter loosely for a few seconds with a fork or chopsticks if available. Don't over mix, the batter should be lumpy and freshly made.

Heat the oil into a small pan. Drip a small amount of batter into the oil - if the batter quickly rises to the top, it's ready to use. Coat a piece of filling in the batter mix - carefully lower into the oil. Fry for 2 mins until golden and crispy. Remove with slotted spoon. Repeat for each piece.

Hints & tips

Other fillings could include: courgette, carrot, green beans, cauliflower, peach or apricot.
Tempura is best eaten when freshly made. For a more substantial meal, serve alongside noodles or rice dishes. (For dips or coulis see recipes.)

Sprinkle savoury tempura with a little sea salt and sweet with glucose.

'Hummus & Pitta Bread'

Ingredients
For 2 or 4 people -

125g or 300g	Wholegrain Self Raising flour
2.5ml or 5ml	Unrefined sea salt
125 or 250ml	Filtered water
15ml or 30ml	Olive oil
Plus -	
60ml or 120ml	Sesame seeds
30ml or 60ml	Rapeseed oil
Or -	
80ml or 160ml	Light tahini
With -	
2 or 4 cloves	Fresh garlic
60ml or 120ml	Olive oil
200g or 400g	Chickpeas
60 or 120ml	Apple juice

Method

Sieve the flour and salt into a bowl. Warm the water and stir to mix into the flour. Add the olive oil and mould with your hands into a dough.

Lightly flour your workspace and knead for 2-3 mins to form a flexible dough. Divide the dough into 4 (or 8) and roll into small balls. Wrap in film while you prepare the hummus.

Homemade tahini is more coarse . Omit the next step if using canned. Preheat the oven to 170°c. Pour the sesame seeds into an oven tin. Roast for 8 mins, shaking often. Cool slightly. Add to a pestle and mortar with the oil and a pinch of coarse sea salt. Pound for 5 mins or until a semi-paste. Put into a blender.

Prepare garlic by finely dicing, sprinkle with sea salt, crush with the back of a knife. Gently fry in olive oil.

Drain the chickpeas and add almost all to the blender plus apple juice and a pinch of unrefined sea salt. Blitz until smooth, gradually pouring in the garlic and oil. Serve drizzled with oil and remaining chickpeas.

Increase the oven to 250°c. On the floured surface, roll the dough balls out to approx. 10 cm wide circles. Lightly oil a baking tray, place the dough in the oven for 10 mins. You may need to cook pitta in batches.

Hints & tips

Try adding fancy toppings to the 'Hummus' - use basil pesto, roasted peppers or chutneys (see recipes.)

'Pitta Bread' can be stuffed with several fillings - including; burgers and salad, mini 'Neatballs' and sauce, roast vegetables and pesto - or even many of your breakfast and lunch-time fillings (see recipes.)

'Asian-Style Broccoli'

Ingredients

For 2 or 4 people -

40g or 80g	Flaked almonds
30ml or 60ml	Sesame oil
20g or 40g	Sesame seeds
½ or 1 whole	Broccoli
250g or 500g	Brussels sprouts
3 or 6cms	Fresh ginger
1 or 2 cloves	Fresh garlic
½ or 1 whole	Fresh chilli
10ml or 20ml	Agave nectar
100 or 200ml	Apple juice or light 'stock'
2 or 4	Spring onions
1 or 2 handfuls	Fresh coriander

Method

Preheat the oven to 175°c.

Toss the almond flakes in 10ml (or 20ml) oil and season with a pinch of unrefined sea salt and ground black pepper. Place in an oven tin and roast for 10 mins. Then add the sesame seeds and shake the tin to coat in oil. Roast for a further 2-3 mins.

Meanwhile, cut the broccoli into florets and then in half again. Peel the sprouts and cut into quarters.

Prepare ginger and garlic by finely dicing. Then sprinkle with sea salt, and crush with the back of a knife. Finely chop the fresh chilli and put in a small bowl. Stir in the agave syrup.

Heat the remaining oil in a wok (or saucepan) and turn heat to high. Stir-fry the broccoli and sprouts for 2 mins until they just start to soften.

Add the ginger paste to the wok and stir well to combine. Pour in the juice or stock, stir, cover for 5 mins.

Finely slice the spring onion and add to the wok, simmer until the sauce reduces. By now the almonds should be ready. Remove from the oven and stir into the wok, tear and add herbs.

Serve as a simple light lunch with rice or as a side order alongside your favourite Asian dish (see recipes.)

Hints & tips

Try replacing the broccoli with cauliflower, and the sprouts for leeks.

Alternatively, use this recipe as a base for a main meal - add mixed peppers, beansprouts and pak choi.

This side dish also adds a delicious 'zing' when served with many traditional family meals such as the Sunday roast or with a deep-filled pie.

'Refried Bean Burrito'

Ingredients

For 2 or 4 people -

120g or 240g	Brown flour or corn flour
30g or 60g	Butter
70ml or 140ml	Filtered water
2 or 4 large	*Carrots*
1 or 2	*Celery stick*
125 or 250ml	*Beetroot juice*
125 or 250ml	*Light 'stock'*
1 or 2	Red onion
15ml or 30ml	Rapeseed oil
1 or 2	Red peppers
200g or 400g	Kidney beans
1 or 2 cloves	Fresh garlic
1 or 2 medium	Fresh chilli

Method

Be careful when using steam!

Sieve ½ the flour and a pinch of salt into a bowl. Cut the butter into cubes and rub into the flour (using your fingers) to create breadcrumbs.

Warm the filtered water and stir into the bowl. Add remaining flour and bring together to make a dough. On a floured surface, knead the dough for 5 mins until flexible. Wrap in film while you prepare the beans.

To make the 'Faux Mato', finely dice the carrots and celery, cover with the beetroot juice and 'stock'. Bring to the boil then simmer for 30 mins.

Dice the onion, fry gently in ½ oil for 2 mins. Chop the pepper and stir into onion along with the beans. Prepare garlic by finely dicing then sprinkle with sea salt, crush with the back of a knife. Finely chop chilli, stir with garlic into the oil for 1 min. Season.

Remove 'Faux Mato' from the heat. Stir through the beans mix and blitz with a hand blender to a chunky texture. Simmer uncovered for 15 mins.

Split dough into 4 (or 8) and roll into thin circles. Heat a large pan - dry fry the tortilla until brown spots form on both sides. Place a cooling rack over a pan of boiling water, steam each tortilla for 4 mins.

Divide the beans between tortillas - fold in the bottom, then each side. Wrap in foil to 'take out', add herbs.

Hints & tips

Serve Burritos with sweetcorn salsa, pea guacamole or feta. Also try serving refried beans with nachos or rice. Alternative fillings - rice, fahita vegetables - even breakfast ingredients!

A 'wet Burrito' is served smothered in a pepper sauce (see 'Calzone' recipe) - simply add extra fresh chilli.

‘Granola & Muesli’

Ingredients -

For 2 or 4 people -

250 or 500ml	Rolled oats
250 or 500ml	Apple juice
2 or 4	Apple
2 or 4	Peaches
40g or 80g	Flaked almonds
10g or 20g	Glucose powder
30ml or 60ml	Rapeseed oil
30ml or 60ml	Agave nectar

Optional for the Muesli -

250 or 500ml Almond milk

Method

For the Granola -

Preheat oven to 175°c.

Stir oats and apple juice together in an ovenproof tin. Place in the oven - uncovered - for 5 minutes.

Then chop the apple into small chunks and add to the pan - return to the oven for another 5 minutes.

While the oats and apples begin to cook, prepare the peaches (or other softer fruit) - cut into small pieces.

Stir the peaches, almonds and oil into the tin - stirring and turning the oats over in small clumps. Put back in the oven for 5 more minutes.

Finally, stir the glucose and agave into the tin and cook for 2 mins.

For the Muesli -

Preheat the oven to 175°c. Place the almonds in an oven proof tin and roast for 10 mins. Allow to cool.

Chop the apple and peaches and add to a bowl. Stir in the oats, almonds and glucose and mix together well.

Top with the apple juice or almond milk and a drizzle of agave nectar.

Hints & tips

Try replacing apple with pear and add to oven tin along with the oats.

Other fruit options include - apricot, rhubarb, mango, melon or figs.

Vary the nutty texture by using a mixture of seeds, such as sunflower or pumpkin. Other grains to try include - millet or quinoa flakes.

'Simple Pasta Sauce'

Ingredients -

For 2 or 4 people -

300ml or 600ml	Filtered water
100g or 200g	Red lentils or yellow split peas
1 or 2 small	Sweet potato
1 or 2	Carrots
30ml or 60ml	Rapeseed oil
1 or 2	Red onion
1 or 2	Red pepper
1 or 2 cloves	Fresh garlic
1 or 2 sprigs	Fresh basil
250ml or 500ml	Root vegetable stock or light 'stock'

Method

Boil a kettle of water. Cover lentils with the water, bring to the boil then simmer uncovered for 20 mins.

Meanwhile, preheat oven to 200°c. Wash and cut the sweet potato and carrots into chunks, toss in the oil. Season with unrefined sea salt and ground black pepper. Pour into an oven proof tin and roast for 25 mins.

After 10 minutes, quarter the red onion and stir into the tin. After another 2-3 minutes, cut the pepper into 1 inch pieces and add to the pan. Coat in oil. Return to the oven.

Prepare garlic by finely dicing, sprinkle with sea salt and crush with the back of a knife. Add to the pan.

Remove the tin from the oven before the garlic is allowed to burn. Tear the basil into the pan to warm.

Drain the lentils. Pour into a blender along with the the roast vegetables and root vegetable stock. Alternatively, combine ingredients in one pan and blitz with a hand blender. Season to taste. Return to the heat to a gentle simmer before serving.

For a quick supper, serve this sauce with oversized pasta, and optional crumbled feta cheese. For children, blitz the sauce until very smooth and add to small pasta rings or shapes.

Hints & tips

Use this simple sauce to accompany 'Gnocchi' or filled 'Ravioli' (see recipes). Also suitable for pizza bases when using less stock. Make double quantities as this sauce freezes well.

For a more 'tangy' sauce include roasted courgette or celery and replace the pepper with beetroot. Add some chopped fresh chilli to the oven tin to give a little extra bite!

'Mixed Bean Pasta Salad'

Ingredients -

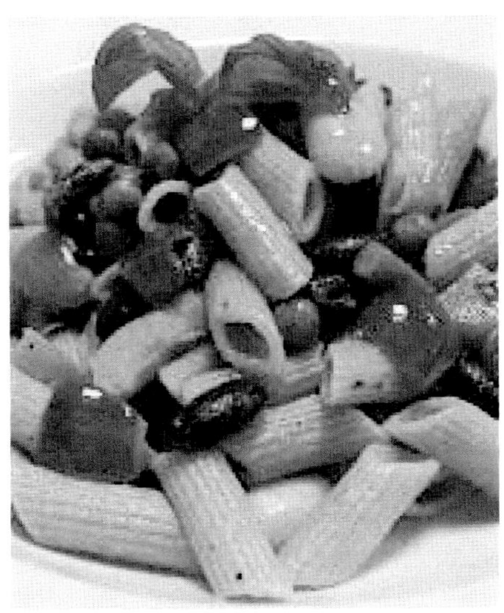

For 2 or 4 people -

150g or 300g	Wholegrain fusilli or penne
1 or 2 medium	Carrot
40g or 80g	Green beans
50g or 100g	Green peas
1 or 2	Red onion
15ml or 30ml	Rapeseed oil
2 or 4	Spring onions
½ or 1 whole	Red pepper
1 or 2 cloves	Fresh garlic
100g or 200g	Kidney beans
100g or 200g	Butter beans
2 or 4 sprigs	Fresh basil
15ml or 30ml	Olive oil

Method

Boil kettle. Put pasta in a large saucepan and cover with boiling water. Cook according to packet instructions, usually for 15 minutes.

Meanwhile, cut the carrots into small pieces. Place in a colander or steamer over the pasta as it cooks for the last 10 mins. As the carrots steam, cut the green beans into 1cm lengths and add to the colander.

Roughly chop the onion into chunks and fry gently in oil for 2-3 mins until it begins to soften. Cut the spring onion into ½cm lengths and add to the pan. Stir to coat in oil.

For the last 5 minutes pasta cooking time, add the peas to the carrots and green beans. Chop the pepper into small chunks and add to the colander for 1-2 mins to slightly soften.

Prepare garlic by finely dicing. Sprinkle with sea salt and crush with the back of a knife. Stir into the pan with the onions for 1-2 mins.

Drain the beans and stir into the onion pan to warm through. Tear the basil into the pan and remove from the heat. Once steamed, mix the vegetables with the beans and onion. Drain the pasta and stir into the mixed beans and vegetables. Season to taste and drizzle with olive oil.

Hints & tips

To make this meal even more substantial, add crumbled feta or melt goats cheese over the top. Delicious.

In place of the pasta, serve the mixed beans and vegetables in home-made pitta bread (see recipe.) Or as a delicious topping for baked sweet potatoes - wrap them in foil first to keep the skin lovely and soft!

'Popcorn'

Ingredients

For 2 or 4 people -

45ml or 90ml Rapeseed oil
75g or 150g Popping corn

With -
60g or 120g Glucose powder
60ml or 120ml Apple juice
Or -
60g or 120g Butter
3 or 6 cms Fresh ginger
Or -
5ml or 10ml Unrefined sea salt
90ml or 180ml Olive oil

Method

Prepare toppings before making the popcorn if you want to eat it warm.

Pour oil into large saucepan, turn the heat to medium-high. You may need two batches. Put one popping corn kernel in the oil, cover with a lid and listen for the kernel to pop.

Once it pops, remove pan from the heat and take out the one piece of popcorn. Pour all remaining kernels in the pan, stir to coat in oil, cover with a lid and put back on the heat.

Listen for the sound of the corn popping. Once it slows down, remove from heat - don't wait for every kernel to pop as they will start to burn.

For the sticky apple sauce - Pour both the glucose and apple juice in a small pan and turn the heat to low. Stir and allow to reduce for 3-4 mins.

For the buttered ginger sauce - Prepare ginger by very finely dicing, then sprinkle with glucose and crush with the back of a knife. Melt the butter in a small pan, add ginger and warm through until ginger softens.

For the savoury sea salt topping - Warm oil in a pan and stir in the sea salt. Toss the popcorn into the pan to coat in oil. Stir well to divide the salt evenly between the popcorn.

Hints & tips

Remember that popcorn and sauces can be very hot, especially glucose!

Other toppings could include - warm through some homemade glucose jam or carob sauce (see recipes.)

Savoury popcorn can also be used as a topping for salads - try fresh garlic butter or ground black pepper.

'Gnocchi'

Ingredients -

For 2 or 4 people -

<u>Sweet Potato Gnocchi -</u>

500g or 1kg	Sweet potato
200g or 400g	Brown flour

Organic fresh basil, crushed garlic, olive oil & butter to serve.

<u>Gnocchi alla Romana -</u>

285 or 570ml	Almond milk
100g or 200g	Semolina
75g or 150g	Feta cheese
1 or 2	Organic egg yolks

Organic butter and homemade sauce (see 'Hints & Tips') to serve.

Method

For the Sweet Potato Gnocchi -
Boil kettle. Peel and dice the sweet potato, add to a pan and cover with water. Bring to the boil for 10 mins until soft. Retain and freeze any cooking liquor for future stocks. Put the potato back in the pan for 2 mins on a low heat to 'dry out' the water.

Mash the potatoes until very smooth. Put in a bowl with the flour and a good pinch of unrefined sea salt and ground black pepper. Mix well with a spoon to make a dough. Knead the dough lightly for 2-3 mins on a floured surface before rolling out into a 'sausage' shape 1cm wide.

Cut the 'sausage' into 2cm pieces and press each against your thumb - gently push the prongs of a fork against the rounded side. Cook in batches in a pan of boiling water for 1-2 mins until they rise to the top.

For the Gnocchi alla Romana -

Simmer the milk with a pinch of unrefined sea salt and black pepper. Pour the semolina in a slow stream. Keep stirring until you can stand the spoon in the mixture. Beat in the eggs and crumbled feta cheese. Allow to cool.

Preheat the oven to 200°c. Form the mixture into small but rough balls. Put them in a single layer in an oven tin, pour the sauce around (below.)

Hints & tips

Serve the 'Gnocchi alla Romana' roasted with a 'Simple Pasta Sauce', 'Faux Mato', 'Ketchup' or 'Pesto' (see recipes.) Simply prepare the 'Gnocchi' and the sauce, add to an ovenproof tin and dot with butter. Roast uncovered for 45 mins. Try melted goats cheese to serve.

In place of 'Sweet Potato Gnocchi', try parsnip, swede or beetroot mash.

'Flapjacks & Oat Cookies'

Ingredients -

For 2 or 4 people -

<u>For the flapjacks -</u>

20g or 40g	Butter
20g or 40g	Fortified dairy-free spread*
50g or 100g	Glucose powder
50g or 100g	Ground almonds
90g or 180g	Rolled oats

<u>For the oat cookies -</u>

75g or 150g	Wholegrain Self-Raising flour
50g or 100g	Rolled oats
75g or 150g	Glucose powder
75g or 150g	Butter
15ml or 30ml	Agave nectar

Method

For both preheat oven to 180 °c.

For the flapjacks - Grease an oven dish. Gently melt the butter and fortified dairy-free spread* in a large saucepan. Add the glucose and stir over a low heat until dissolved.

Bring to a rolling boil and continue to heat for a minute without stirring. Remove from the heat and mix in the ground almonds and rolled oats.

Pour the mix into the oven dish, and press down evenly. Bake in the oven for 15 mins until lightly golden. Cut into squares while still warm but do not remove from the dish until cool.

For the oat cookies - Grease one (or two) large oven trays. Sieve the flour into a bowl and stir in the oats and glucose. Gently melt the butter in a saucepan. Add the agave and stir over a low heat until well combined.

Pour the butter and agave into the bowl and stir until all ingredients are combined. Use your hands to bring the mixture together as a dough.

Lightly flour your workspace. Divide the dough into 8 (or 16) and roll into balls. Put onto the baking tray(s) allowing space between them as the cookies will spread as they cook.

Flatten the balls slightly with your hands. Bake for 15 mins until golden brown. Remove from oven and put on a cooling rack until firm.

Hints & tips

For the flapjacks replace the glucose with agave nectar and ground almonds with almond or seed butter.

For both flapjacks and oat cookies, try adding carob frosting (see recipe) and grated apple or pear to the mix.

Eat the biscuits within a day or two.

'Panini & Winter Coleslaw'

Ingredients -

For 2 or 4 people -

125g or 300g	Wholegrain Self Raising flour
125 or 250ml	Filtered water
30ml or 60ml	Olive oil
¼ or ½ whole	Red cabbage
50ml or 100ml	Apple juice
15 or 30ml	Agave nectar
1 or 2 small	Red onion
1 or 2	Carrots
1 or 2 hard	Pear
1 or 2 portions	Green pepper pesto (see recipe)
100g or 200g	Cannellini beans
2 or 4 sprigs	Fresh basil

Method

Sieve the flour and tsp salt into a bowl. Warm the water and stir to mix into the flour. Add ½ olive oil and mould with hands into a dough.

Lightly flour your workspace and knead for 2-3 mins to form a flexible dough. Divide the dough into 2 (or 4), roll into small balls. Wrap in film.

Preheat the oven to 250°c. On the floured surface, roll the dough balls out to fit the base of a small loaf tin. Lightly grease the loaf tin, add the dough and bake for 11-13 mins.

While the dough bakes, shred the red cabbage and add to a bowl. Pour in the apple juice and agave - mix well. Finely chop the red onion and cut the carrot into thin matchsticks - add both to the bowl, coat well in juice. At the last moment before serving, cut the pear into thin wedges and add to the mixture. Season to taste.

While warm, slice in ½ along the length of the bread. Mix together pesto, beans and torn basil, season. Spoon onto the bread. Do not over-fill! Replace the top ½ of the bread.

Wrap in foil and press together with your hands. Remove from foil. Brush both sides with ½ olive oil. Place on a hot grill or frying pan until lightly brown, repeat on the other side.

Caution! Contents may be hot!

Hints & tips

Traditionally, panini are made from a yeasty focaccia or ciabatta dough.

Panini are popular toasted sandwiches and taste delicious with many different fillings. Try - roast peppers, onion, courgette and garlic with crumbled feta, spreadable goats cheese or buffalo mozzarella. Even try carob frosting (see recipe) with sliced apple, pear and almonds!

If using fresh poultry (organic if possible and not stored even for one day) saute small cubed pieces in place of the beans. When cooked, stir into the pesto mix. **Make sure the meat is fully cooked before serving.**

'Crunchy Pancakes'

Ingredients -

For 2 or 4 people -

65g or 130g	Puy lentils
400 or 800ml	Filtered water
1 or 2 large	Carrot
1 or 2	Red onion
15ml or 30ml	Rapeseed oil
60g or 120g	Green peas
1 or 2 cloves	Fresh garlic
1 or 2 handfuls	Fresh basil
60g or 120g	Brown flour
1 or 2	Organic egg yolk
200 or 400ml	Almond milk
20g or 40g	Butter
100g or 200g	Homemade soda breadcrumbs
1 or 2	Organic egg yolk

Method

To make the 'mince' cover puy lentils with filtered water. Bring to the boil then simmer for 30 mins. Top the water up a little after 20 mins.

Meanwhile, cut the carrot and onion into small pieces. Add to a saucepan with the oil and fry gently. Cover pan with lid - stirring occasionally for 10 mins until carrots start to soften.

After the 10 mins cooking time, add the peas to the pan. Stir to coat in oil. Prepare garlic by finely dicing then sprinkle with sea salt, crush with the back of a knife. Stir into the pan for a minute. Remove from heat.

Tear the basil into the pan and add a good pinch of unrefined sea salt and ground black pepper. Stir the vegetable ingredients into the lentils. Cover and simmer for 10 mins while you prepare the pancakes -

Make the pancakes following the method in the 'Sweet & Savoury Crepes' recipe. Once ready, brush one side of each with egg yolk.

Preheat the oven to 200°c. Dust a board with breadcrumbs and press the pancakes egg side down. Add 30ml of filling in the centre of each pancake. Roll the same way as a 'Chimichanga' using egg to seal instead of oil. Place on a baking tray and sprinkle with remaining crumbs.

Put in oven for 12 mins until crunchy.

Hints & tips

Serve this family favourite with 'Posh Baked Beans' & 'Ketchup'.

Alternatively, in place of the pancakes - wrap the filling in homemade tortilla wraps, filo pastry or cooked lasagne sheets. Add chopped fresh herbs, garlic or chilli to the crumbs.

If using fresh poultry (organic if possible and not stored even for one day) saute finely cubed pieces and use only half the lentils. When cooked, stir into the lentil mix. **Make sure the meat is fully cooked before serving.**

'Rice & Peas'

Ingredients

For 2 or 4 people -

125g or 250g	Brown rice
250 or 500ml	Almond milk
500 or 1 litre	Filtered water
1 or 2 small	Fresh scotch bonnet chilli
30ml or 60ml	Rapeseed oil
125g or 250g	Green split peas
1 or 2	Red onion
2 or 4 cloves	Fresh garlic
1 or 2 sprigs	Fresh sage

Halve the quantities when serving as a side order.

Method

Lightly fry the rice on the hob with 15ml (or 30ml) oil. Cover rice with almond milk and ½ water. Add a sprig of basil. Stir once. Return to boil, cover and simmer for 30 mins.

Wash the scotch bonnet - but keep it whole - do not chop it into pieces! Put the scotch bonnet on top of the liquid in the pan. Cover the pan tightly until the rice has cooked.

Meanwhile, boil kettle. Cover split peas with ½ the water, bring to the boil, then simmer for 20 mins. Top the water up a little after 10 mins.

As the rice and peas cook, roughly chop the onion and fry gently in a pan in 15ml (or 30ml) rapeseed oil.

Prepare garlic by dicing. Sprinkle with sea salt, crush with the back of a knife. Add to the oil for a minute.

Tear the sage into small pieces and stir into the onion and garlic.

Once the peas have cooked, drain and freeze any cooking liquor to use as light 'stock' in future. Stir together with the onions and garlic.

Remove basil and scotch bonnet once the rice is ready and liquor absorbed. Stir together with the peas. Serve as a snack lunch or as a side order.

Hints & tips

Beans are known as peas in Jamaica, hence the name 'rice and peas.' This recipe uses split peas in place of pigeon peas. Also try using red kidney beans or yellow split peas.

Also replace spring onions (scallions) for the red onion, Jalepeno peppers in place of scotch bonnet and Thyme, bay leaf or garnish with coriander in place of the sage.

'Cooked Breakfast'

Ingredients

For 2 or 4 people -

<u>For the sausages -</u>

2 or 4	Homemade sausages (see 'Bangers & Mash' recipe)

<u>For the hash browns -</u>

2 or 4 small	Parsnips
1 or 2	Red onion
25g or 50g	Butter
25g or 50g	Wholegrain flour
15ml or 30ml	Rapeseed oil

<u>For the scrambled egg -</u>

2 or 4	Organic egg yolk
60 or 120ml	Almond milk
20g or 40g	Butter

Method

For the sausages -

Prepare the sausages following the method for the 'Bangers & Mash' recipe. For breakfasts and brunch I use sausages that I've prepared extra for an evening meal and frozen.

Cook in a hot oven (250°) for 20 minutes, turning twice to brown each side. If using frozen sausages, allow an extra 10 mins cooking time.

For the hash browns -

Peel and grate the parsnips. Using either a clean tea towel (with no noticeable detergent odours) or your hands, squeeze out as much liquid as possible. Place the parsnip in a bowl.

Finely slice the onion, melt butter and stir into the bowl. Sieve the brown flour and stir also. Season.

Divide mix into 2 (or 4) and grease a ramekin. Press the mix tightly into the bottom. Tip upside down out on an oiled frying pan. Fry for 5 mins, then put pan in oven for 10 mins.

For the scrambled egg -

Once the hash browns are in the oven, mix the egg and milk with a fork. Melt ½ butter into the pan and pour in the egg mix. Stir gently over a low heat. When eggs are ready, stir through remaining butter. Season.

Hints & tips

As I'm already grinding some oats (in the food processor) for the sausages, I grind extra and roll the breakfast sausages in to coat before cooking.

Try serving this breakfast with toasted soda bread and butter or a good dollop of ketchup (see recipes.) Spice up the hash browns by using a little chopped fresh chilli or garlic.

If using fresh poultry (organic if possible and not stored even for one day) saute finely cubed pieces and use only half the lentils. When cooked, stir into the lentil mix. **Make sure the meat is fully cooked before serving.**

'Frittata'

Ingredients -

For 2 or 4 people -

1 or 2 medium	Sweet potato
½ or 1 whole	Swede
30ml or 60ml	Rapeseed oil
1 or 2	Red onion
1 or 2	Red pepper
75g or 150g	Brussels sprouts
1 or 2 cloves	Fresh garlic
2 or 4 sprigs	Fresh sage
3 or 6	Organic egg yolks
125g or 250g	Mascarpone cheese (uncultured)
50ml or 100ml	Almond milk

Method

Do not take vegetables out of the fridge too early. Work quickly so the vegetables remain crisp and fresh. Dice the sweet potato and swede, toss in ½ rapeseed oil and season. Add to an oven proof tin and roast in the oven at 220°c for 15 minutes.

Meanwhile, dice the onion and red pepper and stir into the roast vegetables. Return to the oven for a further 5 minutes. Peel and quarter the sprouts, add to the tin, stirring well to coat in oil.

After 5 mins, prepare garlic by finely dicing. Then sprinkle with sea salt, and crush with the back of a knife. Stir the garlic into the vegetables and tear the sage into small pieces. Cook for another 2-3 mins.

Beat the eggs in a bowl and mix with the mascarpone and milk. Season.

Reduce the oven to 200°c. Gently heat 1 (or 2) small oven proof saucepan(s) on the hob, brush with the remaining oil. Add the roasted vegetables to the pan(s) and pour over the egg mix. Swirl to make sure the base is well covered.

Heat for 8-10 mins until the egg begins to set. Then carefully add the pan to the oven for 12 mins to cook or until the top turns golden brown.

Hints & tips

Like a 'Bubble & Squeak' add many different vegetables to the frittata, try - spring greens, peas, sweetcorn, parsnip, carrots, courgette, broccoli, cauliflower, red cabbage, mangetout, babycorn, leek or celery.

Also vary the fresh herbs - and for extra bite stir through a little finely chopped fresh chilli (deseeded!)

If using fresh poultry (organic if possible and not stored even for one day) cut small cubed pieces and toss in the seasoned oil. Roast in the oven with the sweet potato. **Make sure the meat is fully cooked before serving.**

'Samosas'

Ingredients -

For 2 or 4 people -

65g or 125g	Red lentils
1 or 2	Red onion
1 or 2 small	Sweet potato
15 or 30ml	Rapeseed oil
1 or 2 cloves	Fresh garlic
3 or 6 cms	Fresh ginger
40g or 80g	Green peas
1 or 2 handfuls	Fresh coriander leaves & stalks
2 or 4 sheets	Filo pastry - de frosted (approx. 24cm by 50cm)
100g or 200g	Chickpeas

Optional -

1 or 2 finely chopped fresh chilli!

Method

Boil a kettle of water. Cover red lentils with 2 parts water, bring to the boil then simmer for 25 mins or until completely mushy and smooth.

While the lentils simmer, preheat oven to 200°c. Finely dice the onion and sweet potato. Toss in oil and season with unrefined sea salt and ground black pepper. Put into a oven tin and roast for 15 mins in total.

After 10 mins, prepare garlic and ginger by finely dicing, sprinkle with sea salt, crush with the back of a knife. Stir ½ into the tin for 2 mins.

Remove tin from the oven and stir in the peas and torn coriander. Lay the filo sheets on top of each other and cut into 2 rectangles lengthways. Lay the rectangles in lines facing away from you. Put a heaped tbsp of filling in the bottom corner of each strip.

Then roll the other corner of the filo over to the side to make a triangle. Turn the triangle up towards the top. Keep rolling and turning until you reach the end of the strip. Brush the last corner with oil and press down. Repeat until all strips are finished.

Grease a baking tray and place each 'Samosa' on its seam. Bake for 15 mins until light brown and crispy.

Meanwhile, drain the chickpeas and stir into the red lentils - along with the remaining garlic and ginger. Season to taste and simmer for 2 mins.

Hints & tips

Vary the 'Samosa' fillings - try adding carrot, parsnip, swede, leek, broccoli, cauliflower or courgette.

Try a sweet 'samosa' filling - known as 'Neuris' - use a mix of ground almonds, glucose, ginger and figs.

If using fresh poultry (organic if possible and not stored even for one day) saute finely cubed pieces, halve the other filling ingredients. When cooked, stir into the filling mix. **Make sure the meat is fully cooked before serving.**

'Feta & Watercress Tarts'

Ingredients -
For 2 or 4 people -

100g or 200g	Puff pastry - store bought or (see recipe.)
1 or 2 cloves	Fresh garlic
15ml or 30ml	Rapeseed oil
2 or 4 sprigs	Fresh mint
100 or 200ml	Double cream
2 or 4 handfuls	Watercress
100g or 200g	Fresh feta - (not matured.)
1 or 2	Organic egg yolks - beaten in a small ramekin

Method

Firstly, prepare the puff pastry following the recipe in this book. Wrap in cling film and leave to rest in the fridge. Allow 25 minutes. Alternatively, use frozen pastry and defrost at room temperature instead.

Meanwhile, prepare garlic by finely dicing, sprinkle with sea salt, crush with the back of a knife. Fry gently in the oil for 2 mins until soft - but don't let it burn. Allow to cool.

As it cools, tear mint into the oil and stir well to infuse. Once cool, add the double cream (no need to whip first) and watercress to the pan.

Return gently to the heat for 5-7 mins until the sauce has thickened. Take the pan from the heat and cool. Once cool, cut the feta into cubes and stir into the pan. Season. Preheat the oven to 200 c.

On a film surface, roll out the pastry to ¼ cm thick. Cut 1 rectangle per person approx. 15 x 10cm each.

Brush 1 (or 2) baking sheets with oil. Put the pastry on the tray(s) and mark 1cm in from the edge with a knife (but do not cut all the way through!) Divide the filling between the pastries, inside the border.

Brush the edges with the beaten egg yolk. Put tarts in the oven for 15 mins until golden, crispy and risen.

Hints & tips

Other flavour options include - fresh spreadable goats cheese, fresh basil pesto, spring greens, rocket, finely sliced roasted leek or spring onion.

Alternatively, fill the tarts with Buffalo mozzarella and caramelised red onion or 'Faux Mato' toppings.

Tasty with shortcrust or filo pastry.

'Deep Pan Pizza'

Ingredients -

For 1 or 2 pizzas -

2 or 4 large	*Carrots*
1 or 2 cloves	*Fresh garlic*
125 or 250ml	*Beetroot juice*
125 or 250ml	*Light 'stock'*
200g or 400g	Wholegrain Self Raising flour
30ml or 60ml	Olive oil
125 or 250ml	Filtered water
1 or 2 handfuls	Fresh basil
125g or 250g	Buffalo mozzarella

Method

To make the 'Faux Mato', finely dice the carrots and prepare garlic by finely dicing. Then sprinkle with sea salt, crush with the back of a knife. Cover with the beetroot juice and 'stock'. Bring to the boil and simmer uncovered for 40 mins. Meanwhile -

Sieve the flour into a mixing bowl and add a good pinch of unrefined sea salt. Make a well in the flour and add the oil, stirring well to combine.

Pour in the water to make a soft dough. If it feels sticky, add a little more flour. Lightly flour your workspace and knead the dough for 2-3 mins. Roll dough out to ½ cm thick. Dry fry the base on a medium heat for 2 mins each side until light brown spots form. Preheat oven to 190°c.

After its 40 minutes is up, remove the 'Faux Mato' from the heat.

Mash the mix carefully so not to splash until you get a finer texture, similar to that of a thick tomato puree. Tear ½ the basil into the pan. Season to taste and spread evenly over the pizza dough.

Tear the mozzarella into chunks and scatter over the faux mato base. Put in the oven for 18 mins until the base is crispy and the mozzarella melts. Once cooked, add the remaining basil on top of the pizza. Serve with dips.

Hints & tips

Use this simple 'Faux Mato' and mozzarella topping as the starting point for your favourite low histamine pizza recipes from this book. For example, add a little chopped fresh chilli and 'Neatballs' (see recipe.)

As with the other pizza dough bases, try making mini versions of this pizza to serve as finger food at parties.

If using fresh poultry (organic if possible and not stored even for one day) grill and slice or saute cubes before topping the pizza. Alternatively, adapt the 'Neatballs' recipe. **Make sure the meat is fully cooked before serving.**

'Rarebit'

Ingredients -

For 2 or 4 people -

½ or 1 whole	Homemade soda bread (see recipe) - cut into slices.
80ml or 160ml	Almond milk
15g or 30g	Butter
15g or 30g	Plain flour
1 or 2	Organic egg yolks
60g or 120g	Fresh spreadable goats cheese
80ml or 160ml	Apple juice

Method

Firstly, prepare the soda bread following the recipe in this book. As the bread cooks and cools prepare the 'Rarebit' topping. Alternatively, use frozen soda bread slices and defrost.

In a small pan, bring the milk to the boil then remove from the heat. In a larger pan, gently melt the butter then stir in the flour. Keep the heat low and keep stirring for 2-3 mins.

Slowly add the milk to the butter and flour 'roux'. Whisk each amount of milk into the roux before adding another. Repeat until all milk is used.

Again, remove pan from the heat as you whisk in the egg yolks and then return to the heat. Keep stirring.

Add cheese to the mixture and beat in to combine. Remove from heat.

Using your first smaller pan, add the apple juice and bring to the boil. Once thickened and reduced by ½, whisk the reduced juice into the cheese mixture. Season to taste.

Preheat the grill to medium (or the oven to high.) Divide the cheese mix evenly between the soda bread slices and spread thickly but evenly.

Grill or cook until lightly golden brown. Serve with watercress.

Hints & tips

Add a little 'bite' with a little crushed fresh garlic, finely chopped chilli or grated fresh horseradish. Also try adding a handful of chopped fresh herbs, spring onion or leek when you add the reduced juice.

Use the 'Rarebit' topping with mashed sweet potatoes as a filling to homemade pastry rolls or pasties.

'Sandwiches'

Ingredients -

For 2 or 4 people -

½ or 1 whole	Homemade soda bread (see recipe.)

Plus -

For Savoury Cottage Cheese -

1 or 2	Peppers
1 or 2	Leeks
15ml or 30ml	Rapeseed oil
200g or 400g	Cottage cheese

For Egg & Cress -

3 or 6	Organic hard-boiled eggs - yolk only
75ml or 150ml	Double cream - whipped
1 or 2 handfuls	Fresh cress

Method

Firstly, prepare the soda bread following the recipe in this book. As the bread cooks and cools -

For Savoury Cottage Cheese -

Preheat oven to 220°c. Wash and cut the peppers and leeks into small chunks, toss in the oil. Season with unrefined sea salt and ground black pepper. Pour into an oven proof tin and roast for 10 minutes. Check and shake the tin after 5 minutes.

After 10 mins, remove the tin from the oven and allow the vegetables to cool a little. Once cool, stir the cottage cheese through the vegetables.

For Egg & Cress -

Hard-boil whole eggs by placing in a pan and covering with cold water. Bring to the boil then turn off heat. Cover pan with a lid and leave eggs in the water for 15 mins. After 15 mins, add eggs to a second bowl of cold water. When cool, carefully peel the shell and whites away from the yolk.

In a cold bowl, lightly whip the cream with a whisk. Don't over-whip as cream will become grainy.

In a second bowl, mash the yolks with a fork and then stir in the cream and the fresh cress. Season to taste.

Hints & tips

Any remaining soda bread can be sliced and frozen - and then defrosted, toasted with uncultured butter or blitzed into breadcrumbs for using in another recipe in the future.

In place of the cottage cheese, try feta or fresh goats cheese served with a selection of roasted vegetables (see 'Polenta' recipe for ideas.)

If using fresh poultry (organic if possible and not stored even for one day) grill and serve either sliced with a salad or cubed and mixed with homemade mayo and sweetcorn. **Make sure the meat is fully cooked before serving.**

'Feta Salad'

Ingredients -

For 1 or 2 people -

50ml or 100ml	Olive oil
15ml or 30ml	Apple juice
2.5ml or 5ml	Glucose powder
1 or 2	Red onion
½ or 1	Red pepper
6 or 12cm	Cucumber
1 or 2 sprigs	Fresh mint
1 or 2 handfuls	Watercress
100g or 200g	Fresh feta - (not matured.)

Method

Firstly, in a small pan mix together the olive oil, apple juice, glucose and a pinch of unrefined sea salt and ground black pepper. Bring to a gentle heat, stirring, until the glucose dissolves. Remove from heat.

While the dressing cools, chop the red onion into small pieces, add to the pan. Stir to coat well in dressing.

Cut the pepper to the same size as the onion and add to the pan, stir. Once the dressing is cool, finely chop the cucumber and add to the pan.

Tear the mint into the pan and wash and drain the watercress. Dress your plate with the watercress garnish.

Only take the feta from the cold fridge when you are ready to use it. Cut into cubes approx. 1 cm wide.

Add the cubed feta to the pan and carefully mix together with all the ingredients to coat well in dressing.

Check the seasoning and add more if needed. At the last moment before serving, pour the feta salad and dressing onto the watercress leaves.

Serve with buttered homemade soda bread (see recipe) or oatcakes.

Hints & tips

Vary the feta salad by using different fresh herbs or finely chopped chilli. Add an extra crunch with croutons.

Another option is to vary the fresh cheese - try cubed paneer, halloumi or even torn buffalo mozzarella.

Also serve as a topping to a homemade pizza, a full fresh salad, baked jacket sweet potato or as a filling to homemade pitta bread (see recipes.)

The Right Ingredients

It can seem like a definitive list of low-histamine foods is hard to find. The food list I use has been scientifically approved, and it forms the basis for the recipes in this book. Then again, I've omitted a few key ingredients because many people with Histaminosis seem reluctant to use them. In case you want to try them for yourself, those foods are; lemons, bananas and egg white.

It's important to find your own tolerance level. At first, I had reactions from eating foods lower in histamine but high in folate; such as quinoa, chickpeas, broccoli, and cauliflower. Gradually, as my tolerance improved, I began using a broader selection of ingredients.

You may find you can't eat onions and garlic, for example. If so, try replacing them with fresh herbs and leek if you feel you tolerate those better. Be flexible - you'll often find alternatives that work just as well as the original.

Yet others may have a problem with too much calcium. That's why the milk I've used in the recipes is almond milk, even though cows' milk is allowed. If you prefer cows' milk, and it doesn't aggravate your symptoms, then use it. But do be aware that other foods besides dairy products also contain calcium. Ask your doctor for advice.

I use Unrefined Sea Salt. It enhances flavour and my GP tells me that it helps my low blood pressure. Don't use Refined Table Salt: That's had all the goodness processed out of it. People with intolerance to histamine don't often have high blood pressure - the opposite is often true - speak to your doctor to make sure. If you're concerned about your salt intake, replace it with fresh herbs and spices sometimes.

There are a few additional food 'rules' to be aware of: Choose organic foods wherever possible - especially if you buy pre-prepared salads that have been treated with sulphites; make sure that goats' and sheep's cheeses are fresh and without rind; and vegetables & fruit should be firm to hard - pears in particular contain more histamine as they ripen.

Glucose is less sweet than sucrose so you may prefer to add a little extra. It's more finely ground than sucrose yet if a certain texture is needed, I mention it in the recipe. It may also turn a darker brown as it caramelises, so keep a careful eye on your meals as they cook.

As you make progress, you may feel that your personal tolerance level improves. You could then occasionally try the recipes that include bicarb, carob, glucose and agave nectar. But remember, these are 'treats,' to enjoy only in moderation.

Main Meals

'Special Fried Rice'

Ingredients

For 2 or 4 people -

100g or 200g	Brown rice
2 or 4	Carrots
2 or 4	Leeks
2 or 4 cloves	Fresh garlic
3 or 6 cms	Fresh ginger
1 or 2	Red onion
75g or 150g	Green peas
30 or 60ml	Sesame oil
50g or 100g	Seeds - Sunflower or sesame

Handful fresh coriander to serve.

Method

Boil water, and cook rice according to pack instructions.

Fifteen minutes before the end of the rice cooking time prepare the vegetables. Do not take them out of the fridge or freezer too early.

Working quickly so the vegetables remain crisp, slice carrots into ribbons using either a vegetable peeler or mandolin. Be careful!

Cut the leeks into thin diagonals using a sharp knife. Place both vegetables in cold water to keep fresh.

Prepare garlic and ginger by finely dicing then sprinkle with sea salt and crush with the back of a knife.

Cut the onion into thin slices just as you are ready to use it.

Fry onions in the oil until clear then add garlic and ginger for 1 minute, stirring all the time.

Drain and add sliced vegetables, seeds and peas, stir for 2 minutes.

As soon as the rice is cooked, add to the vegetables, toss and serve while still hot.

Season and sprinkle with fresh herbs.

Hints & tips

Be careful when cooking rice. Always wash the rice and add a few basil leaves to the water during cooking. Make sure that all other food preparation is done while the rice cooks so that it can be used and eaten hot.

Add sliced baby sweetcorn, courgette ribbons, mange tout, green or haricot beans, mint or basil to serve.

If using fresh poultry (organic if possible and not stored even for one day) cut into thin slices and add to the wok before the vegetables. Once cooked, add the onions. **Make sure the meat is fully cooked before serving.**

‘Mince & Potato Pie’

Ingredients

For 2 or 4 people -

250g or 500g	Shortcrust pastry - see recipe
125g or 250g	Puy lentils
2 or 4 medium	Sweet potatoes
15ml or 30ml	Rapeseed oil
1 or 2 sticks	Celery
1 or 2 cloves	Fresh garlic
1 or 2	Red onion

A handful of fresh basil to serve.

Method

Firstly, prepare the short crust pastry following the recipe in this book.

Wrap in cling film and leave to rest in the fridge. Alternatively, use frozen pastry and defrost at room temperature instead. Allow 25 minutes.

While the pastry is in the fridge boil a kettle of water. Cover puy lentils with the water, bring to the boil then simmer for 30 minutes. After 10 minutes, add more water to cover. Stir.

While the lentils cook, wash and cube sweet potatoes, toss in oil and season with sea salt and pepper. Roast in a hot oven (250°c) for 15 minutes.

Chop celery and onion and add to the sweet potato for 5 minutes. Prepare garlic by finely dicing then sprinkle with sea salt and crush with the back of a knife. Add for a further minute.

Drain the lentils and retain all but a cup of the liquor and freeze the rest to make a stock for dark gravy.

Stir the vegetables through the lentils and season to taste. Pour into an ovenproof tin. Roll the pastry (see recipe) and cover the filling, pinch edges and pierce with a knife.

Turn oven down to 180°c. Bake for 25 minutes until the pastry browns.

Hints & tips

Making double the pastry quantity and freezing half makes this a quick comfort meal next time.

For thicker gravy, substitute puy for green or brown lentils and retain a little extra liquor.

In warm weather serve with a salad and parsnip wedges or crisps.

If using fresh poultry (organic if possible and not stored even for one day) saute finely cubed pieces and use only half the lentils. When cooked, stir into the lentil mix. **Make sure the meat is fully cooked before serving.**

'Bangers & Mash'

Ingredients

For 2 or 4 people -

125g or 250g	Red lentils
400 or 800ml	Filtered water
15 or 30ml	Rapeseed oil
1 or 2	Red onion
1 or 2 cloves	Fresh garlic
¼ or ½ litre	Defrosted puy 'stock'
60 or 125ml	Oats - ground
1 or 2 sprigs	Fresh basil
2 or 4	Sweet potatoes
15 or 30ml	Butter
15 or 30ml	Almond milk

Organic green peas and a handful of fresh basil to serve.

Method

Boil a kettle of water. Cover red lentils with the water, bring to the boil again then simmer for 20 mins.

Dice onion finely. Prepare garlic by finely dicing then sprinkle with sea salt, crush with the back of a knife.

Heat oil in a pan and cook the onion, stirring, for two minutes. Add the garlic for a further minute. Reduce the heat, pour over a little puy 'stock' and cover with a lid, simmering for 5 minutes to caramelise.

Preheat the oven to 220°c. Drain the red lentils and retain liquor. Stir in ½ the onion and garlic - plus oats and herbs. Season and mould into sausages. Cook in the oven for 20 mins, turning twice to brown each side.

Freeze any red lentil 'stock' to make light sauces and gravies in future.

Pour the remaining puy 'stock' into the onion and garlic. Continue to simmer gently. Season to taste.

Boil the kettle again. Wash and cube sweet potatoes, cover with the water, bring to the boil then simmer for 15 minutes.

Drain the potatoes, also freezing the stock. Mash potatoes with butter and almond milk. Season to taste.

Hints & tips

Red lentils and sweet potatoes cook very quickly and will go soft if they are cooked for too long.

For a darker sausage and a coarser texture, substitute red for green lentils. Experiment with fresh herbs!

In warm weather serve with a salad and parsnip wedges or crisps.

If using fresh poultry (organic if possible and not stored even for one day) saute finely cubed pieces and use only half the lentils. When cooked, stir into the lentil mix. **Make sure the meat is fully cooked before serving.**

'Sweet Potato Risotto'

Ingredients

For 2 or 4 people -

125g or 250g	Red lentils
125g or 250g	Brown rice
½ or 1 litre	Filtered water
2 or 4	Sweet potatoes
1 or 2	Red onion
1 or 2 cloves	Fresh garlic
15ml or 30ml	Rapeseed oil

Drizzle of olive oil and a handful of fresh basil or mint to serve.

Method

Boil a kettle of water. In an oven-proof tray, cover red lentils and rice with the water. Stir once.

Cover and place in the oven at 220°c. After 20 minutes, check the rice. Add more water to cover but do not stir. Put back in the oven.

Once the rice is back in the oven, dice the sweet potatoes, toss in oil and season. Add to an oven proof tin and roast in the oven for 15 minutes.

Then quarter the onion and stir into the sweet potatoes, and return to the oven for a further 5 minutes.

Prepare garlic by finely dicing. Then sprinkle with sea salt, and crush with the back of a knife.

Stir the garlic into the potatoes and cook for another minute.

By now, the rice and lentils should be cooked and the water absorbed. If not, cover the vegetables with foil and place at the bottom of the oven while you cook the rice a few minutes longer.

When the rice is cooked, remove from the oven and stir through the roast vegetables.

Hints & tips

Be careful when cooking rice. Always wash the rice and add a few basil leaves to the water during cooking. Make sure that all other food preparation is done while the rice cooks so that it can be used and eaten hot.

Sweet potatoes cook very quickly and will go soft if they are cooked for too long. Cover if it gets too brown.

'Garlic Kievs'

Ingredients

For 2 or 4 people -

1 or 2 cloves	Fresh garlic
25g or 50g	Butter
1 or 2	Onion
220g or 440g	Butter beans (drained weight)
60ml or 120ml	Brown flour
2 or 4	Sweet potatoes
30ml or 60ml	Rapeseed oil

2 handfuls of fresh basil - one for the garlic butter, the other for the kievs.

Method

Prepare garlic by finely dicing. Then sprinkle with sea salt, and crush with the back of a knife.

Fry garlic gently for 1 minute and remove from heat. Cut butter into chunks and mix together with garlic and a handful of torn basil.

Working quickly so that the butter doesn't melt, mould into a small sausage shape and wrap in cling film. Place in the freezer for 20 minutes.

Meanwhile, dice the onion and fry with ½ oil in the 'garlicky' pan. Add the drained butter beans and cook through for 2 minutes. Add torn basil, stir and remove from the heat.

Mash the flour into the butter beans and season with sea salt and black pepper. Mould into 2 (or 4) rounds, make a well in the centre of each.

While the kievs cool, cut the sweet potatoes into wedges, toss in remaining ½ oil and season.

Remove the butter from the freezer, divide and quickly roll into small balls. Place a garlic ball into the centre of each kiev, press holes closed.

Put the kievs and sweet potatoes in the oven at 220°c for 20 minutes. Serve with steamed green beans.

Hints & tips

Sweet potatoes cook very quickly and will go soft if they are cooked for too long. Cover if it gets too brown.

Yellow and green split peas are a good alternative to butter beans. Try adding thyme or rosemary instead.

In warm weather serve with a salad and vegetable crisps.

If using fresh poultry (organic if possible and not stored even for one day) cut a pocket into a skinned breast and fill with the garlic butter. Coat in breadcrumbs to seal. **Make sure the meat is fully cooked before serving.**

'Sloppy Joe Peppers'

Ingredients

For 2 or 4 people -

1 or 2 large	*Carrots*
1 or 2	*Celery stick*
65ml or 130ml	*Beetroot juice*
65ml or 130ml	*Light 'stock'*
65g or 130g	Green lentils
1 or 2	Red onion
15ml or 30ml	Rapeseed oil
1 or 2 cloves	Fresh garlic
1 or 2 medium	Fresh chilli
5ml or 10ml	Agave nectar
2 or 4	Red peppers - bell or pointed
2 or 4 small	Parsnips
15ml or 30ml	Rapeseed oil

Method

To make the 'Faux Mato', finely dice the carrots and celery, cover with the beetroot juice and 'stock'. Bring to the boil then simmer for 30 mins.

Meanwhile, cover green lentils with water, bring to the boil and simmer for 15 mins. Top up water if needed. Once the lentils have cooked, carefully drain and retain the cooking liquor. Add and stir the liquor into the 'Faux Mato' as it simmers.

Dice the onion. Fry gently in ½ oil for 2 mins then prepare garlic by finely dicing then sprinkle with sea salt, crush with the back of a knife. Finely chop the fresh chilli and stir with the garlic into the oil for 1 min.

Remove the 'Faux Mato' from the heat. Mash the mix carefully until you get a finer texture, similar to that of chopped, tinned tomatoes.

Stir lentils, agave and vegetables into the 'Faux Mato'. Slice around the stalk of the peppers, scoop out seeds, then stuff insides with lentil mix, replace the top. Wrap in foil.

Preheat oven to 220°c. Put peppers in oven for 20 mins until they soften. Slice parsnips thinly with either a peeler or mandolin. Toss in oil and a pinch of sea salt. Lay flat on a large baking sheet covered in foil - bake for 15 mins, turning to brown edges.

Hints & tips

Bell peppers are the easiest to stuff!

'Jalapeno poppers' are stuffed with mozzarella cheese, coated in egg yolk, then breadcrumbs and fried or baked. Or try stuffing with your favourite risotto or feta salad (see recipes.) Even try mashed sweet potato, caramelised onion, chilli and coriander. Try different coloured peppers.

If using fresh poultry (organic if possible and not stored even for one day) saute finely cubed pieces and use only half the lentils. When cooked, stir into the lentil mix. **Make sure the meat is fully cooked before serving.**

'Risotto Verde'

Ingredients

For 2 or 4 people -

30ml or 60ml	Rapeseed oil
125g or 250g	Brown rice
½ or 1 litre	Light 'stock'
125g or 250g	Green split peas
400 or 800ml	Filtered water
1 or 2 sticks	Celery
1 or 2	Onion
1 or 2 cloves	Fresh garlic
125g or 250g	Green beans
1 or 2 large	Courgette
100g or 200g	Green peas

A handful of fresh mint.

Method

Lightly fry the rice on the hob with ½ rapeseed oil. Add the stock to the rice a little at a time - enough to cover and do not allow to dry out - until all of the stock has been used.

Meanwhile, cover green split peas with filtered water, bring to the boil, then simmer for 20 minutes. Top the water up a little after 10 minutes and then again after another 5.

Then roughly chop the celery and onion. Fry gently in ½ the oil for 2 mins. Prepare garlic by finely dicing then sprinkle with sea salt, crush with the back of a knife. Finely chop herbs and stir both into the onions for 1 minute.

Once the split peas are al dente, drain and stir into the rice along with the onion, celery, garlic and herbs. Freeze cooking liquid for 'stock'.

Do not take vegetables out of the fridge too early. Work quickly so the vegetables remain crisp.

Cut the green beans diagonally into thirds and slice courgette into ribbons using a vegetable peeler or mandolin. Stir vegetables and peas into the rice.

Cook until vegetables are still a little crisp and the rice cooked. Season.

Hints & tips

Be careful when cooking rice. Always wash the rice and add a few basil leaves to the water during cooking.

Experiment with fresh herbs, and alternate with white beans. Also try other vegetables - leeks, sprouts, spring greens, broccoli, cabbage, mange tout, kale, courgette, and sprinkle with watercress or rocket.

‘Spaghetti Bolognese’

Ingredients

For 2 or 4 people -

2 or 4 large	*Carrots*
1 or 2	*Celery stick*
125 or 250ml	*Beetroot juice*
125 or 250ml	*Light ‘stock’*
125g or 250g	Green lentils
1 or 2	Red onion
1 or 2 cloves	Fresh garlic
150g or 300g	Wholegrain Spaghetti
100g or 200g	Green peas
15ml or 30ml	Rapeseed oil

A handful of fresh basil to serve.

Method

To make the ‘Faux Mato’, finely dice the carrots and celery, cover with the beetroot juice and ‘stock’. Bring to the boil and then simmer uncovered for 30 minutes.

Meanwhile, boil a kettle of water. Cover green lentils with the water, bring to the boil again then simmer for 20 minutes.

Slice onion and prepare garlic by finely dicing. Then sprinkle with sea salt, crush with the back of a knife.

Heat oil in a pan and cook the onion, stirring, for two minutes. Add the garlic for a further minute.

After the 30 minutes is up, remove the ‘Faux Mato’ from the heat. Mash the mix carefully so not to splash until you get a finer texture, similar to that of chopped, tinned tomatoes.

Boil the kettle again and pour boiling water over the spaghetti. Cook according to packet instructions.

Remove the lentils from the heat - most of the liquid will be absorbed. Stir through the garlic and onion and ‘Faux Mato’ sauce. Add the peas and simmer together for 5 minutes.

Season with sea salt and black pepper, add fresh basil and taste.

Hints & tips

A 750ml bottle of beetroot juice can be made into several servings of ‘Faux Mato’. Make a larger quantity and freeze in separate portions.

The ‘bolognese’ sauce also freezes well and can also be used with penne as an Al forno, in a lasagne with bechamel-style sauce, or even in a pie.

If using fresh poultry (organic if possible and not stored even for one day) saute finely cubed pieces and use only half the lentils. When cooked, stir into the lentil mix. **Make sure the meat is fully cooked before serving.**

‘Puff Pastry’

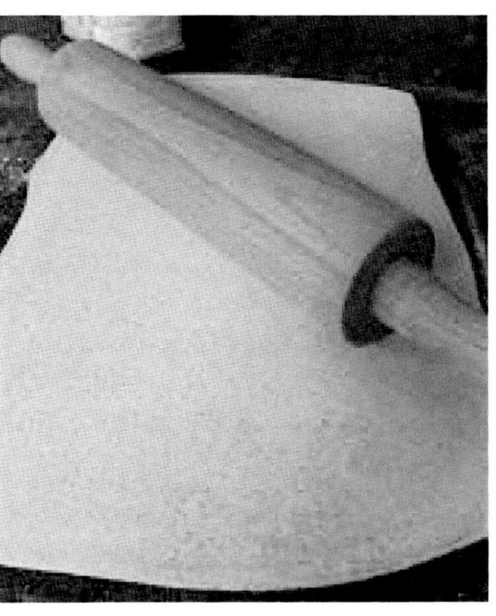

Ingredients

For 2 or 4 people -

(Makes approx. 250g or 500g pastry)
45g or 90g Brown flour
45g or 90g White flour
2mg or 4mg Unrefined sea salt
90g or 180g Butter
50 or 100ml Filtered cold water

<u>Sweet pastry ideas -</u> Sprinkle glucose, mint or finely crushed almonds into the pastry layers.
<u>Savoury pastry ideas -</u> Sprinkle a selection of fresh herbs, finely crushed seeds or crumble unripe goats cheese into the pastry layers.

Method

Sieve the flours and salt together. Chop the butter into small chunks, add to the flour and mix with a fork making large buttery ‘breadcrumbs’.

Make a well in the ‘crumbs’ and pour in 2/3rds of the water. Mix until you have a rough dough (add extra water if needed.) Mould into a smooth rectangle, cover with cling film and put in the fridge for 20 minutes.

Remove pastry from fridge and unwrap cling film. Cover with a second piece of film. Roll the dough in the same direction, until 3 times the width. You will get a marbled effect.

When heated, the butter in the dough melts, causing the layers to separate. The water in the butter turns to steam, puffing up the pastry with air bubbles that become trapped to form air pockets.

Fold the top third down to the centre, then the bottom third up and over that. Give the dough a quarter turn (to the left or right) and roll out again to three times the length.

Fold as before, cover with cling film and chill for at least 20 minutes before rolling to use.

Just before cooking pastry, prick with a fork in the centre (not sides.)

Hints & tips

Making double the pastry quantity and freezing half makes for a quick comfort meal. Puff pastry should be stacked when frozen - not rolled into a ball! Use to top favourite pies.

Store-bought puff pastry seems more ‘flaky’ than this homemade version. But when I do use the store-bought one, I miss the buttery nutty flavour.

'Shortcrust Pastry'

Ingredients

For 2 or 4 people -
(Makes approx. 250g or 500g pastry)

170 or 340g	Brown flour
1 or 2 pinches	Unrefined sea salt
40g or 85g	Butter
40g or 85g	Fortified dairy-free spread*
80 or 160ml	Filtered cold water

Sweet pastry ideas - Sprinkle glucose, mint or finely crushed almonds into pastry layers in place of sea salt.
Savoury pastry ideas - Sprinkle a selection of fresh herbs, finely crushed seeds or crumble unripe goats cheese into the pastry layers.

Method

Sieve the flour and salt (if using) together. Chop the butter and fortified dairy-free spread* into small chunks, add to the flour and mix with a fork making small fine 'breadcrumbs'.

Make a well in the 'breadcrumbs' and pour in 70ml (or 140ml) of the water. Mix until you have a rough dough (add extra water if needed.)

Mould into a smooth rectangle (or ball,) cover with cling film and put in the fridge for 25 minutes.

After 25 mins, remove pastry from fridge and unwrap the cling film. If you wish to add sweet or savoury ingredients, now is the time to sprinkle them onto the pastry.

When using robust herbs such as rosemary, blitz first in a blender so that they do not damage the pastry.

Cover with a second piece of film. Roll the dough between the two sheets of film, turning the pastry by 90 degrees regularly.

Be careful to adjust the film from time to time to keep the pastry covered.

Just before cooking pastry, prick with a fork in the centre (not the sides.) Brush with almond milk.

Hints & tips

Making double the pastry quantity and freezing half makes for a quick comfort meal. Freeze in a smooth rectangle - easier to store and also to roll! Use to top favourite pie fillings.

Pies and pasties can easily be assembled and frozen. Simply add 5 - 10 mins onto the cooking time when putting into the oven!

'Loaf Wellington'

Ingredients

For 2 or 4 people -

250g or 500g	Puff pastry - store-bought or (see recipe.)
65g or 130g	Puy lentils
½ or 1	Onion
15 or 30ml	Rapeseed oil
1 or 2 cloves	Fresh garlic
60 or 125ml	Oats - ground
5ml or 10ml	Almond milk

Two handfuls of fresh mint.

Serve with swede, carrot or sweet potato wedges, salad or organic peas.

Method

Firstly, prepare the puff pastry following the recipe in this book.

Wrap in cling film and leave to rest in the fridge. Alternatively, use frozen pastry and defrost at room temperature instead. Allow 25 minutes.

While the pastry is in the fridge boil a kettle of water. Cover puy lentils with ½ or 1 litre water, bring to the boil then simmer for 30 minutes.

Dice onion finely and fry gently in oil. Prepare garlic by finely dicing then sprinkle with sea salt, crush with the back of a knife. Fry for 1 minute.

Drain the puy lentils and lightly crush with a fork. Stir in the oats , onion and garlic. Season and mould into a long loaf shape. Leave to cool. Freeze any puy lentil 'stock' to make light sauces and gravies in future.

Take pastry from the fridge and roll out into a rectangle as thick as 3-4 mm on a floured surface. Lay ½ herbs on the pastry and then the loaf along the centre.

Roll the pastry over the loaf, wrap under the ends, pressing together to seal. Place (on the seam) on a baking tray and brush with milk. Prick pastry with a sharp knife.

Put in oven at 180°c for 25 mins.

Hints & tips

Make double the pastry quantity and freeze half to make a quick comfort meal next time. 'Loaf wellington' can be assembled and frozen. Simply add 15 mins onto the cooking time!

Try using a variety of 'neat loaf' - green split peas & basil, yellow split peas and sage, brown lentils & thyme, or chickpeas & coriander.

If using fresh poultry (organic if possible and not stored even for one day) saute finely cubed pieces and use only half the lentils. When cooked, stir into the lentil mix. **Make sure the meat is fully cooked before serving.**

'Roast Vegetable Lasagne'

Ingredients

For 2 or 4 people -

1 or 2	Sweet potato
1 or 2	Red onion
2 or 4	Leeks
2 or 4	Beetroot
30ml or 60ml	Rapeseed oil
50 or 100g	Butter
125 or 250ml	Brown flour
250 or 500ml	Almond milk
250 or 500ml	Filtered water
1 or 2 cloves	Fresh garlic
4 or 8 sheets	Lasagne
50g or 100g	Fresh goats cheese

A handful of fresh basil.

Method

Do not take vegetables out of the fridge too early. Working quickly so the vegetables remain crisp, peel and chop sweet potatoes, onions and leeks into large chunks.

Preheat oven to 220°c and place two tins in the oven to heat up. Peel and cut beetroot into large chunks. Be careful to avoid staining your clothes and workspace.

Add oil to the hot tins and stir the beetroot in one and the vegetables and herbs in the other. Season with sea salt and black pepper. Cover and place in the oven. After 20 mins, remove the covers for 10 more mins.

Meanwhile, to make the bechamel sauce, melt the butter and stir in the flour. Gradually add the milk and water. Finely chop and add herbs and simmer for 5 mins. Season, stir often.

After 30 minutes roasting. Prepare garlic by finely dicing. Then sprinkle with sea salt, crush with the back of a knife. Stir into the vegetables.

Add half of the roast vegetables to a dish and drizzle with bechamel. Add half of the lasagne sheets and then repeat. Stir the cheese into the remaining sauce and pour over the top.

Season. Put in the oven for 25 mins.

Hints & tips

You can vary the vegetables to roast. Try a selection of - courgettes, broccoli, cauliflower, carrots, parsnip, swede, babycorn or celery.

Add 'Faux mato' to the vegetables and add cannelini beans. Or feta.

In warm weather serve with a salad and vegetable crisps and wedges.

'Roast Beetroot Risotto'

Ingredients

For 2 or 4 people -

125g or 250g Brown rice
½ or 1 litre Light 'stock'
2 or 4 Beetroot
1 or 2 Red onion
1 or 2 cloves Fresh garlic
50g or 100g Sunflower seeds
15ml or 30ml Rapeseed oil
A handful of fresh rosemary.

Drizzle of Organic olive oil to serve.

Method

In an ovenproof tray, cover the rice with the light stock. Stir once.

Cover and place in the oven at 220°c. After 20 minutes, check the rice. Add boiled water to cover but do not stir. Put back in the oven.

Peel and roughly chop the fresh beetroot, toss in oil and season. Be careful to avoid staining your clothes and workspace. Add to an oven proof tin and roast in the oven for 25 minutes.

Quarter the onion and add to another roasting tin with oil, and place into the oven for a further 5 minutes.

Prepare garlic by finely dicing. Then sprinkle with sea salt, and crush with the back of a knife. Stir the garlic, rosemary and seeds into the onion and cook for another 3-4 minutes.

Once the beetroot is ready, the rice should be cooked and the water absorbed. If not, cover the vegetables with foil and place at the bottom of the oven while you cook the rice a few minutes longer.

When the rice is cooked, remove from the oven and carefully stir through the vegetables, leaving the beetroot until last.

Hints & tips

Be careful when cooking rice. Always wash the rice and add a few basil leaves to the water during cooking. Make sure that all other food preparation is done while the rice cooks so that it can be used and eaten hot.

Try replacing the seeds with cubes of feta or cooked butter beans - do not roast but stir through at the end.

'Jalousie'

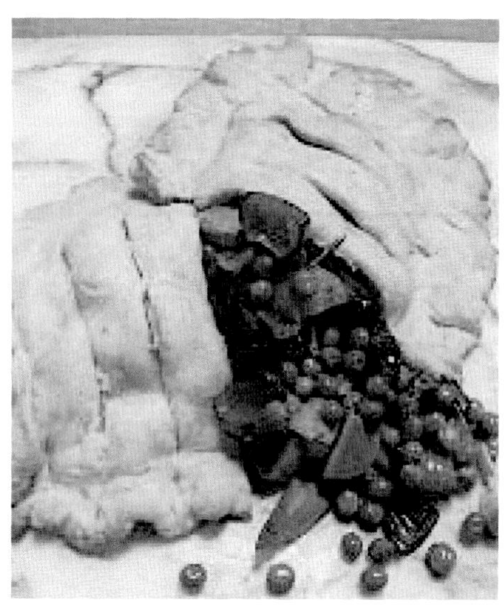

Ingredients

Makes 1 or 2 large pastries -

500g or 1kg	Shortcrust pastry - store-bought (or see recipe.)
2 or 4	Carrots
1 or 2	Onion
2 or 4 sticks	Celery
1 or 2 cloves	Fresh garlic
100g or 200g	Green peas
1 or 2	Leeks
15ml or 30ml	Rapeseed oil

A handful of fresh rosemary.

Method

Firstly, prepare the shortcrust pastry following the recipe in this book. Wrap in cling film and leave to rest in the fridge. Alternatively, use frozen pastry and defrost at room temperature instead. Allow 25 minutes.

Preheat oven to 220°c and place a tin in the oven to heat up. Working quickly so the vegetables remain crisp, peel and chop carrots, onions, celery and leeks into large chunks.

Add oil to the tin and stir in the vegetables and finely chopped herbs. Season with sea salt and black pepper. Cover and place in the oven. After 20 mins, remove the cover for 10 more mins.

Prepare garlic by finely dicing then sprinkle with sea salt, crush with the back of a knife. Mix together with the peas and stir into the vegetables.

Take pastry from the fridge and roll out on a floured surface to ½ cm thick. Cut pastry into 2 rectangles, one slightly larger than the other.

Spoon the vegetables into the centre of the small rectangle. Cut slits in the large rectangle leaving 1-inch. Brush the edge of the small rectangle with milk and then lay the larger on top. Seal edges and brush with milk. Put in oven at 180°c for 20 mins.

Hints & tips

Make double the pastry quantity and freeze half to make a quick comfort meal next time.

For a more filling main meal, stir white beans through the vegetables with the peas. Experiment with fresh herbs such as tarragon or sage, and try adding green beans, sweetcorn, courgette or cubes of sweet potato.

If using fresh poultry (organic if possible and not stored even for one day) cut into small pieces and toss in the seasoned oil. Roast in the oven with the carrots and onions. **Make sure the meat is fully cooked before serving.**

'Bubble & Squeak Pie'

Ingredients

For 2 or 4 people -

250g or 500g	Shortcrust pastry - store-bought (or see recipe.)
1 or 2	Sweet potato
½ or 1	Swede
30ml or 60ml	Rapeseed oil
1 or 2 sprigs	Fresh rosemary
1 or 2	Red onion
2 or 4	Leeks
1 or 2 cloves	Fresh garlic
100g or 200g	Green peas
200g or 400g	Kidney beans (drained)
15ml or 30ml	Almond milk

Method

Firstly, prepare the short crust pastry following the recipe in this book.

Wrap in cling film and leave to rest in the fridge. Alternatively, use frozen pastry and defrost at room temperature instead. Allow 25 minutes.

While the pastry is in the fridge, wash and cube sweet potato and swede - toss in ½ oil and season with sea salt and pepper.

Finely chop and add rosemary. Roast together in a hot oven (250°c) for 15 minutes until they start to brown.

Meanwhile, dice the onion and cut leeks into 1cm pieces. Stir into potatoes. Place in the oven for 5 mins.

Prepare garlic by finely dicing. Then sprinkle with sea salt, and crush with the back of a knife.

Stir the garlic (with the peas and beans) into the vegetables for 1 minute. Once cooked, roughly mash everything together with a fork. Turn oven down to 180°c.

Roll the pastry (see recipe) into a large circle. Place in the bottom of a round pie tin with the edges overlapping. Pile the mash in the centre and roughly fold the pastry up over the sides. Brush with milk, bake for 25 mins until golden brown.

Hints & tips

Traditionally a way to use up leftovers but worth making from scratch. For variety try adding cabbage, broccoli, cauliflower, sprouts, courgette, carrots, parsnips or chard.

Bubble & Squeak is delicious on its own without the pastry - simply fry the mash in a hot pan. Ideal with lentil loafs, burgers or sausages.

'Baked Macaroni'

Ingredients

For 2 or 4 people -

125g or 250g	Red lentils
400 or 800ml	Filtered water
2 or 4	Leeks
15ml or 30ml	Rapeseed oil
50 or 100g	Butter
125 or 250ml	Brown flour
250 or 500ml	Almond milk
250 or 500ml	Wholegrain Penne
1 or 2 cloves	Fresh garlic
100g or 200g	Green peas

A handful of fresh basil.

Method

Boil a kettle of filtered water. In a large pan, cover red lentils with the water, bring to the boil then simmer for 20 minutes.

Meanwhile, top and tail leeks but do not peel. Add to a roasting tin with oil, and place into the oven (at 220°c) for 15 minutes.

Cover pasta with the water, bring to the boil then simmer for 5 minutes (until part cooked.)

Meanwhile, to make the bechamel sauce, melt the butter and stir in the flour. Gradually add the milk and water. Finely chop and add herbs and simmer for 5 mins. Season to taste. Stir often.

Remove the leeks from the oven and carefully peel the outer layer. Cut into 1cm wide rings.

Prepare garlic by finely dicing. Then sprinkle with sea salt, and crush with the back of a knife.

Stir the garlic, part cooked pasta, leeks and bechamel sauce into the red lentils. Add the frozen peas.

Pour into an oven dish. Cover and cook at 220°c for 20 minutes. Remove cover - do not stir - and return to the oven for 10 minutes.

Hints & tips

Serve with a sprinkle of crushed almonds and one of the fresh salsa recipes featured in this book.

Try adding cubed feta or tear unripe goats cheese at the end of the cooking time. Other vegetables such as broccoli or cauliflower are very tasty too (think cauliflower cheese!)

Alternatively use a Carbonara sauce.

'Penne al Forno'

Ingredients

For 2 or 4 people -

2 or 4 large	*Carrots*
1 or 2 sticks	*Celery*
125 or 250ml	*Beetroot juice*
125 or 250ml	*Light 'stock'*
150g or 300g	Wholegrain Penne
1 or 2	Onion
1 or 2 cloves	Fresh garlic
220g or 440g	Cannelini beans (drained)
100g or 200g	Green peas
15ml or 30ml	Rapeseed oil

A handful of fresh basil to serve.

Method

To make the 'Faux Mato', finely dice the carrots and celery, cover with the beetroot juice and 'stock'. Bring to the boil and then simmer uncovered for 20 minutes. After 10 mins -

Boil a kettle. Cover pasta with the water, bring to the boil then simmer for 5 minutes (until part cooked.)

Dice onion and prepare garlic by finely dicing. Then sprinkle with sea salt, crush with the back of a knife.

Heat oil in a pan and cook the onion, stirring, for two minutes. Add the garlic for a further minute.

Drain the beans and stir into the onions and garlic, add the peas and cook through, stirring, for two minutes. Add the part cooked pasta and stir through. Season with sea salt and black pepper and add fresh herbs.

After the 30 minutes is up, remove the 'Faux Mato' from the heat. Mash the mix carefully so not to splash until you get a finer texture, similar to that of chopped, tinned tomatoes.

Stir the 'Faux Mato' into the pasta and check the seasoning. Pour into an oven dish. Cover and cook at 220°c for 20 minutes. Stir. Return to the oven (uncovered) for 10 minutes.

Hints & tips

A 750ml bottle of beetroot juice can be made into several servings of 'Faux Mato'. Make a larger quantity and freeze in separate portions.

Cooking the pasta 'Al forno' (means 'at oven') adds a deep flavour and roasted texture. However for speed, simply cook the pasta completely on the hob and stir into the sauce.

If using fresh poultry (organic if possible and not stored even for one day) saute small cubed pieces in place of the beans. When cooked, stir into the 'Faux Mato' mix. **Make sure the meat is fully cooked before serving.**

'Classic Lasagne'

Ingredients

For 2 or 4 people -

125g or 250g Puy lentils
400 or 800ml Filtered water
100g or 200g Carrot
50 or 100g Butter
60ml or 120ml Brown flour
250 or 500ml Almond milk
250 or 500ml Filtered water
1 or 2 cloves Fresh garlic
2 or 4 sticks Celery
1 or 2 Red onion
4 or 8 sheets Lasagne
15ml or 30ml Rapeseed oil
A handful of fresh rosemary.

Method

To make the 'mince' cover puy lentils with filtered water. Bring to the boil then simmer for 30 mins. Top the water up a little after 10 mins and then again after another 5.

Cut the carrots into small pieces. Place in a colander or steamer over the puy lentils as they cook for the last 5 minutes.

To make the bechamel sauce, melt the butter and stir in the flour. Gradually add the milk and water. Finely chop and add ½ herbs. Season and simmer for 2 mins. Stir often.

Prepare garlic by finely dicing then sprinkle with sea salt, crush with the back of a knife.

Roughly chop the celery and onion. Fry gently in the oil for 2 mins then stir in the garlic for 1 minute.

After the 20 minutes 'mince' cooking time, add and stir in the onion, garlic, celery, carrots and ½ herbs, season with sea salt and black pepper.

Add half of the 'mince' to a dish and drizzle with bechamel. Add half of the lasagne sheets and then repeat. Pour the remaining sauce over the top. Season and drizzle with oil.

Put in the oven at 220°c for 25 mins.

Hints & tips

Try experimenting with different fresh herbs, green or brown lentils.

For a family meal, serve with sweet potato wedges and peas. Alternatively, serve with swede 'chips' and garlic 'soda bread'.

In warm weather serve with a salad and vegetable crisps.

If using fresh poultry (organic if possible and not stored even for one day) saute finely cubed pieces and use only half the lentils. When cooked, stir into the lentil mix. **Make sure the meat is fully cooked before serving.**

'Shroomy Risotto'

Ingredients

For 2 or 4 people -

125g or 250g	Brown rice
½ or 1 litre	Light 'stock'
125g or 250g	Green lentils
400 or 800ml	Filtered water
2 or 4 cloves	Fresh garlic
2 or 4 sticks	Celery
2 or 4	Onion
15ml or 30ml	Rapeseed oil
25g or 50g	Butter

A handful of fresh basil.

Method

Lightly fry the rice on the hob with the rapeseed oil. Add the stock to the rice a little at a time - enough to cover and do not allow to dry out - until all of the stock has been used.

Meanwhile cover green lentils with filtered water, bring to the boil, then simmer for 20 minutes. Top the water up a little after 10 minutes and then again after another 5.

Do not take vegetables out of the fridge too early. Work quickly so the vegetables remain crisp.

Prepare garlic by finely dicing then sprinkle with sea salt, crush with the back of a knife. Finely chop herbs.

Roughly chop the celery and onion. Fry gently in the oil for 2 mins then stir in the garlic for 1 minute.

Once the lentils have cooked, stir them (cooking liquor and all!) into the rice with the the onion, celery, garlic and ½ herbs. Cook through, stirring, for 5 minutes until moist and creamy.

Remove from the heat and stir the butter through. Season with sea salt and freshly ground pepper.

Top with ½ fresh herbs and torn buffalo mozzarella (if preferred.)

Hints & tips

Be careful when cooking rice. Always wash the rice and add a few basil leaves to the water during cooking.

Experiment with fresh herbs such as sage or rosemary, and alternate with brown lentils. Like a mushroom risotto, usually this doesn't contain extra vegetables but do try small cubes of roast parsnip or swede.

'Poached Apple Spaghetti'

Ingredients

For 2 or 4 people -

150g or 300g	Wholegrain spaghetti
1 or 2	Apple
125 or 250ml	Apple juice
125 or 250ml	Light 'stock'
1 or 2	Red onion
15 or 30ml	Rapeseed oil
25g or 50g	Butter
1 or 2 cloves	Fresh garlic

A handful of fresh basil and a drizzle of olive oil to serve.

Method

Boil the kettle and pour boiling water over the spaghetti. Cook according to packet instructions - usually for around 15 minutes.

Do not take vegetables out of the fridge too early. Work quickly so the vegetables remain crisp.

While the pasta cooks, finely slice the apple and add to a pan. Pour over the apple juice and stock. Poach the apple uncovered over a gentle heat for 10 minutes.

Meanwhile, finely slice the onion. Heat the butter and oil until the butter melts. Gently fry the onion for 2 minutes.

Prepare garlic by finely dicing then sprinkle with sea salt, crush with the back of a knife.

Add the garlic to the onion, stirring, for a further minute.

Once cooked, stir the onions and garlic into the poached apple and juice. Season with unrefined sea salt and ground black pepper.

By this point, the spaghetti should also be ready. Drain carefully and stir into the sauce. Dress with torn basil and a drizzle of olive oil.

Hints & tips

To convert this to a more substantial meal - simply stir through a 100g portion of white beans, seeds, unripe goats cheese or feta per person.

Alternatively, replace the apple with very hard pears. Pears are low in histamine as long as they aren't ripe.

Try to experiment with fresh herbs!

'Lasagne Cannelloni'

Ingredients

For 2 or 4 people -
1 or 2 large *Carrots*
1 or 2 sticks *Celery*
65ml or 125ml *Beetroot juice*
65ml or 125ml *Light 'stock'*
4 or 8 sheets Lasagne
65g or 125g Green lentils
1 or 2 Red onion
15ml or 30ml Rapeseed oil
50 or 100g Butter
125 or 250ml Brown flour
250 or 500ml Almond milk
1 or 2 cloves Fresh garlic
A handful of fresh rosemary.

Method

To make the 'Faux Mato', finely dice the carrots and celery, cover with the beetroot juice and 'stock'. Bring to the boil and simmer for 30 mins.

Meanwhile cover green lentils with water, bring to the boil and simmer for 15 mins. Top up water if needed.

Boil a pan of water. Add 2 lasagne sheets, bring back to the boil, and cook until 'al dente'. Place in cold water. Repeat with remaining sheets.

Dice the onion, gently fry for 2 mins. Prepare garlic by finely dicing then sprinkle with sea salt, crush with the back of a knife. Add ½ herbs with the garlic to the onion, for a minute.

Mash the 'Faux Mato' carefully until you get a finer texture, similar to that of chopped, tinned tomatoes. Stir the onions, garlic, herbs and 'Faux mato' into the green lentils.

To make the bechamel sauce, melt the butter and stir in the flour. Gradually add the milk and water. Finely chop and add ½ herbs. Simmer for 2 mins. Season to taste, stir often.

Cut lasagne sheets in half. Spoon the 'bolognese' across the centre of each and roll - allowing a 2cm overlap. Place on the overlap in a oven proof tray. Pour over the bechamel sauce, cook at 220 c for 20 mins.

Hints & tips

Cook the lasagne sheets until 'al dente' - still with a bite. The sheets will be cooked again in the oven.

A 750ml bottle of beetroot juice can be made into several servings of 'Faux Mato'. Make a larger quantity and freeze in separate portions.

Try a watercress and ricotta filling!

If using fresh poultry (organic if possible and not stored even for one day) saute finely cubed pieces and use only half the lentils. When cooked, stir into the lentil mix. **Make sure the meat is fully cooked before serving.**

‘Roast Vegetable Spaghetti’

Ingredients

For 2 or 4 people -

1 or 2	Sweet potato
2 or 4	Carrots
150g or 300g	Wholegrain spaghetti
1 or 2	Red onion
1 or 2 sticks	Celery
1 or 2 cloves	Fresh garlic
220g or 440g	Chickpeas (drained)
15ml or 30ml	Rapeseed oil
15ml or 30ml	Olive oil

A handful of fresh mint.

Method

Do not take vegetables out of the fridge too early. Work quickly so the vegetables remain crisp.

Dice the sweet potatoes and carrots, toss in rapeseed oil and season. Add to an oven proof tin and roast in the oven at 220°c for 15 minutes.

Meanwhile, boil the kettle and pour boiling water over the spaghetti. Cook according to packet instructions - usually for around 15 minutes.

While the pasta cooks, dice the onion and celery and stir into the roast vegetables. Return to the oven for a further 5 minutes.

Prepare garlic by finely dicing. Then sprinkle with sea salt, and crush with the back of a knife. Stir the garlic (with the chickpeas) into the vegetables and cook for another minute.

Drain the spaghetti and put back in the pan. Add the roast vegetables, chickpeas and olive oil.

Tear the herbs into the pasta and season to taste. Stir well. Serve topped with the remaining roast vegetables from the pan.

Cook in oven at 180°c for 20 mins.

Hints & tips

Try greasing a muffin tin and ‘twirl’ the pasta mix onto a fork and place into each section. Bake as above.

Try a selection of - courgette, broccoli, cauliflower, parsnip, swede or beetroot. Or replace the spaghetti with noodles and fill with roast babycorn, carrots, onion and leeks. Stir through mangetout and seeds.

If using fresh poultry (organic if possible and not stored even for one day) cut into small pieces and toss in the seasoned oil. Roast in the oven with the sweet potatoes. **Make sure the meat is fully cooked before serving.**

'Biryani'

Ingredients

For 2 or 4 people -

2 or 4 sprigs	Fresh curry leaves
125g or 250g	Yellow split peas
125g or 250g	Brown rice
½ or 1 litre	Filtered water
2 or 4 large	Carrots
15ml or 30ml	Rapeseed oil
1 or 2	Red onion
2 or 4	Spring onions
100g or 200g	Green peas
1 or 2 cloves	Fresh garlic
3 or 6 cms	Fresh ginger

A handful of fresh coriander to serve.

Method

Boil a kettle of water and finely chop curry leaves. In an ovenproof tray, cover yellow split peas, curry leaves and rice with the water. Stir once.

Cover and place in the oven at 220°c. After 20 minutes, check the rice. Add more water to cover but do not stir. Put back in the oven.

Roughly chop the carrots, toss in oil and season. Add to an oven proof tin and roast in the oven for 15 minutes. Then quarter the onion and stir into the carrots, and return to the oven for a further 5 minutes.

Slice spring onions to ½cm and stir with the peas into to the vegetables.

Prepare garlic and ginger by finely dicing. Then sprinkle with sea salt, and crush with the back of a knife.

Stir the garlic and ginger into the vegetables and cook for 2 minutes.

By now, the rice should be cooked and the water absorbed. If not, cover the vegetables with foil and place at the bottom of the oven while you cook the rice a few minutes longer.

When the rice is cooked, remove from the oven and stir through the roast vegetables. Season to taste.

Hints & tips

Biryani differs from a pilaf in that the ingredients are cooked separately to the rice. Whereas for a pilaf, ingredients are cooked together.

Alternative vegetables include - cauliflower, broccoli, green beans and occasionally a little fresh chilli. Consider replacing the split peas with crushed almonds, chickpeas or seeds.

If using fresh poultry (organic if possible and not stored even for one day) cut into small pieces and toss in the seasoned oil. Roast in the oven with the carrots. **Make sure the meat is fully cooked before serving.**

'Roast Vegetable Tart'

Ingredients

For 2 or 4 people -

250g or 500g	Shortcrust pastry Store-bought or (see recipe.)
1 or 2 large	*Carrots*
1 or 2 sticks	*Celery*
65ml or 125ml	*Beetroot juice*
65ml or 125ml	*Medium 'stock'*
15ml or 30ml	Rapeseed oil
1 or 2 large	Sweet potato
1 or 2	Red onion
1 or 2 cloves	Fresh garlic
125g or 250g	Green beans
1 or 2 sprigs	Fresh mint
200g or 400g	Cannelini beans - drained

Method

Firstly, prepare the short crust pastry following the recipe in this book. Wrap in cling film and leave to rest in the fridge. Alternatively, use frozen pastry and defrost at room temperature instead. Allow 25 minutes.

Meanwhile, make the 'Faux Mato'. Finely dice the carrots and celery, cover with the beetroot juice and 'stock'. Bring to the boil and then simmer uncovered for 30 minutes.

Then wash and slice the sweet potato. Add to an oven proof tin and roast in the oven at 220°c for 10 minutes. slice the onion and stir into the potatoes. Place in the oven for 5 mins.

Prepare garlic by finely dicing. Then sprinkle with sea salt, and crush with the back of a knife. Top and tail the green beans and finely chop mint. Add it all to the hot tin for 1 minute.

Mash the 'Faux Mato' carefully until you get a finer texture, similar to that of chopped, tinned tomatoes.

Roll the pastry (see recipe) into a circle. Place in the bottom of a round pie tin with the edges slightly overlapping. Spoon the 'Faux Mato' to cover the base, add the beans then arrange the roast vegetables on top.

Turn the oven down to 180°c. Bake tart for 25 mins until golden brown.

Hints & tips

This tart filling can also be used as a pizza topping. Simply choose your base from the selection in this book!

Other vegetables can include - peas, carrots, sweetcorn or babycorn, parsnip, beetroot, courgette or leek.

Try replacing the 'Faux Mato' sauce with basil or coriander pesto.

If using fresh poultry (organic if possible and not stored even for one day) cut into thin strips and toss in the seasoned oil. Roast in the oven with the sweet potatoes. **Make sure the meat is fully cooked before serving.**

'Bonfire Night BBQ'

Ingredients

For 2 or 4 people -

2 or 4 medium	Sweet potato
4 or 8 medium	Homemade burgers and/or sausages (see recipe)
2 or 4	Red onion
2 or 4 sprigs	Fresh robust herbs - e.g. thyme, sage, rosemary or bay
50g or 100g	Butter
1 or 2 whole	Corn-on-cobs
1 or 2 sprigs	Fresh mint
30ml or 60ml	Apple juice
30ml or 60ml	Rapeseed oil

Method

The method below is based on using an oven. To cook this meal on a BBQ - make sure the coals are white hot topped with a few sprigs of robust herbs. Cooking times can be longer on the BBQ - make sure everything is cooked and piping hot before serving.

Jacket sweet potatoes are best wrapped in foil if you want to eat the skin. This keeps the skin soft - or it can go too hard. If do you like the skin crispy, cook in foil for all but the last few minutes and rub with salt.

Preheat the oven to 220 °c. Wash the sweet potatoes and score a cross into the top. Wrap in foil and place in the hot oven for 50 minutes.

If making the burgers from scratch, start them now to allow plenty of cooking time. Once shaped into patties, cook in the oven for 20-30 mins.

Don't peel the onions, cut a deep cross in the top. Push a sprig of robust herbs in each and add ½ butter. Wrap well in foil - cook for 15 mins. Cool then peel away the outer layer.

Boil a pan of water and add the corn on the cob for 2-3 minutes. Drain and top with the other ½ of the butter.

Finely chop mint - add to a jar with the juice and oil and shake well. Season with sea salt and black pepper.

Hints & tips

Make burgers and sausages in advance and freeze. If so, add a few extra minutes onto the cooking time.

In place of whole roasted red onion, slice and gently fry in rapeseed oil.

Try serving the mint sauce with hot mushy peas (see recipe) in mugs - it makes a delicious warming snack!

If using fresh poultry (organic if possible and not stored even for one day) saute finely cubed pieces and use only half the lentils. When cooked, stir into the lentil mix. **Make sure the meat is fully cooked before serving.**

'Moroccan-Style salad'

Ingredients

For 2 or 4 people -

1 or 2	Sweet potato
30 or 60ml	Rapeseed oil
1 or 2	Beetroot
½ or 1 litre	Light 'stock'
125g or 250g	Millet grains
2 or 4 sprigs	Fresh curry leaves
1 or 2	Red onion
1 or 2	Courgette
2 or 4	Spring onions
1 or 2 sprigs	Fresh mint leaves
100g or 200g	Sweetcorn
220g or 440g	Chickpeas
1 or 2 cloves	Fresh garlic
1 or 2 inch	Fresh ginger

Method

Preheat oven to 220°c and place two tins in the oven to heat up. Do not take vegetables out of the fridge too early. Work quickly so the vegetables remain crisp.

Dice the sweet potatoes, toss in rapeseed oil and season. Add to one oven proof tin and roast in the oven at 220°c for 10 minutes. Repeat with the beetroot (being careful to avoid staining) and place in the second tin.

Now place millet and stock in a pan and bring to the boil. Finely chop curry leaves and stir into the pan. Reduce to a simmer for 10-15 mins.

Meanwhile, dice the onion and courgette - add to the potatoes and roast for a further 5 mins. Slice spring onions to ½cm and finely chop mint. Stir with the sweetcorn and chickpeas into to the potatoes. Put in oven.

Prepare garlic and ginger by finely dicing. Sprinkle with sea salt, and crush with the back of a knife. Stir into the potatoes - cook for 2 mins.

When the millet is cooked and almost all of the stock is absorbed, remove both tins from the oven. Stir the roast vegetables into the millet.

Season to taste. Try serving with garlic soda bread or with a crisp salad.

Hints & tips

Couscous and quinoa can also be used in place of millet. However, couscous is cooked by pouring boiling stock over and leaving to absorb.

Use in place of rice or pasta - cook in light stock, add fresh herbs and season to taste. Herbs commonly used in Moroccan cookery include - basil, parsley, coriander and marjoram.

If using fresh poultry (organic if possible and not stored even for one day) cut into small pieces and toss in the seasoned oil. Roast in the oven with the sweet potatoes. **Make sure the meat is fully cooked before serving.**

'Posh Baked Beans Lasagne'

Ingredients

For 2 or 4 people -

2 or 4 large	*Carrots*
1 or 2 sticks	*Celery*
125 or 250ml	*Beetroot juice*
125 or 250ml	*Medium 'stock'*
1 or 2	Red onion
30ml or 60ml	Rapeseed oil
1 or 2 cloves	Fresh garlic
1 or 2 handfuls	Fresh basil
200g or 400g	Haricot beans - drain
50 or 100g	Butter
125 or 250ml	Brown flour
250 or 500ml	Almond milk
250 or 500ml	Filtered water
4 or 8 sheets	Lasagne

Method

To make the 'Faux Mato', finely dice the carrots and celery, cover with the beetroot juice and 'stock'. Bring to the boil and then simmer uncovered for 20 minutes. After 10 mins...

Finely dice the onion. Fry gently in the oil for 2 mins. Prepare garlic by finely dicing then sprinkle with sea salt, crush with the back of a knife. Stir the garlic into the pan for 1 min.

Turn off the heat and tear ½ the basil into the pan. Rinse and add the beans. Stir well and keep covered.

Mash the 'Faux Mato' carefully until you get a finer texture, similar to that of chopped, tinned tomatoes.

Stir the beans, onion and garlic into the 'Faux Mato'. Season to taste with sea salt and black pepper - remember that it can be quite sweet otherwise.

To make the bechamel sauce, melt the butter and stir in the flour. Gradually add the milk and water. Finely chop and add ½ herbs. Simmer for 5 mins. Season to taste, stir often.

Add half of the 'baked beans' to a greased oven dish and drizzle with bechamel. Add half of the lasagne sheets and repeat with the second layer. Finish by pouring the remaining bechamel over the top. Season. Put in the oven at 220°c for 25 mins.

Hints & tips

Top with torn unripe goats cheese.

'Posh Baked Beans' can become a regular staple - such as on toasted soda bread, on jacket sweet potatoes or as part of a cooked breakfast. To make an easy warming supper - simply add a few frozen mixed vegetables and serve as a filling to crepes or pitta bread (see recipe).

'Rice Gratin'

Ingredients
For 2 or 4 people -

125g or 250g	Puy lentils
1 or 2 sprigs	Fresh curry leaves
125g or 250g	Brown rice
½ or 1 litre	Light 'stock'
2 or 4 medium	Carrots
2 or 4 sticks	Celery
125g or 250g	Green beans
15ml or 30ml	Rapeseed oil
25g or 50g	Butter
100g or 200g	Sweetcorn
1 or 2	Red onion
1 or 2 cloves	Fresh garlic
30ml or 60ml	Soda bread breadcrumbs

Method

To begin cover puy lentils with filtered water, bring to the boil then simmer for 30 mins. Finely chop curry leaves and add to the pan. Top the water up after 10 minutes and stir.

As the lentils cook, wash and add rice to another pan. Cover with stock, add a sprig of basil to the pan then bring to a boil, then simmer for 30 mins.

Meanwhile, cut the carrots and celery into matchsticks and also top and tail the green beans. Gently heat the oil and butter and add the vegetables once the butter has melted. Fry gently for 5 mins. Stir in the sweetcorn.

Then cut the onion into thick slices. Add to the vegetables and stir to coat in oil and butter. Prepare garlic by finely dicing. Then sprinkle with sea salt, and crush with the back of a knife. Add to the pan for 1 minute.

Preheat the oven to 180°c. Drain the lentils and rice well and retain the lentil cooking liquor for 'stock'. Stir together into the vegetable pan. Season with sea salt and black pepper.

Grease an ovenproof dish. Pour the gratin mixture into the dish and top with the soda bread breadcrumbs.

Place in the oven, uncovered, for 15 minutes - or until the breadcrumbs turn golden brown. Serve while hot.

Hints & tips

For quick breadcrumbs - next time you make soda bread (see recipe), freeze a ½ or whole quarter portion to use as breadcrumbs in this recipe.

Or while the lentils cook, make fresh soda bread. Serve this gratin with warm buttered bread. Delicious!

Try courgette, seeds or goats cheese.

If using fresh poultry (organic if possible and not stored even for one day) saute finely cubed pieces and use only half the lentils. When cooked, stir into the lentil mix. **Make sure the meat is fully cooked before serving.**

‘Spaghetti & Neatballs’

Ingredients

For 2 or 4 people -

2 or 4 large	*Carrots*
1 or 2 sticks	*Celery*
125 or 250ml	*Beetroot juice*
125 or 250ml	*Light ‘stock’*
125g or 250g	Green lentils
1 or 2	Red onion
30ml or 60ml	Rapeseed oil
1 or 2 cloves	Fresh garlic
60ml or 120ml	Oats - ground
1 or 2 handfuls	Fresh basil
150g or 300g	Wholegrain spaghetti

Method

To make the ‘Faux Mato’, finely dice the carrots and celery, cover with the beetroot juice and ‘stock’. Bring to the boil and then simmer uncovered for 30 minutes.

Meanwhile, cover green lentils with water, bring to the boil and simmer for 15 mins. Top up water if needed.

Then finely dice the onion. Fry gently in the oil for 2 mins then prepare garlic by finely dicing then sprinkle with sea salt, crush with the back of a knife. Stir in the garlic for 1 minute.

Once the lentils have cooked, carefully drain and retain the cooking liquor. Freeze to use as a medium-weight ‘stock’ in future dishes.

Mash the onion and garlic plus oats and basil into the lentils. Season well and mould into small balls.

Preheat the oven to 220°c. Place the Neatballs on a greased tray - put in the oven for 15 mins, turning twice.

Meanwhile, cook spaghetti according to packet instructions - usually for 15 mins. Remove the ‘Faux Mato’ from the heat. Mash the mix carefully until you get a finer texture, similar to that of chopped, tinned tomatoes.

Stir the Neatballs into the ‘Faux Mato’ and season to taste. Serve hot.

Hints & tips

As is often the case, you can vary the lentils or beans used to make the Neatballs. Be adventurous and experiment with other fresh herbs - and occasionally a little fresh chilli!

For a ‘Sloppy Joe’-type pizza topping, simply thicken the Neatball sauce with a little corn flour and use to top your favourite pizza base!

If using fresh poultry (organic if possible and not stored even for one day) saute finely cubed pieces and use only half the lentils. When cooked, stir into the lentil mix. **Make sure the meat is fully cooked before serving.**

'Cottage Pie'

Ingredients

For 2 or 4 people -

1 or 2 medium	Swede
30ml or 60ml	Rapeseed oil
125g or 250g	Green lentils
1 or 2 sprigs	Fresh rosemary
2 or 4	Carrots
100g or 200g	Green peas
1 or 2	Onion
2 or 4 sticks	Celery
1 or 2 cloves	Fresh garlic
30ml or 60ml	Almond Milk
25g or 50g	Butter

Method

Wash, peel and cube the swede. Toss in ½ oil, season with sea salt and pepper. Roast in the oven (220°c) for 15 mins until it starts to brown.

Meanwhile, boil a kettle. Cover green lentils with the water, bring to the boil then simmer for 15 minutes.

Finely chop the rosemary and add to the lentils as they cook. Cut the carrots into small pieces. Place with the peas in a colander over the lentils as they cook for the last 10 mins.

Dice the onion and celery and fry gently in the remaining oil for 2 mins. Prepare the garlic by finely dicing. Then sprinkle the garlic with sea salt, and crush with the back of a knife. Add to the oil for a further minute.

Take the swede out of the oven and drain from the oil. Retain for later.

Mash together the swede with the milk and butter. Season to taste.

Drain the lentils and freeze all but a little 'stock'. Stir together with all of the vegetables. Grease an oven dish.

Pour the lentil mixture in the dish. Spoon the swede mash over the top and press down making a pattern with a fork. Drizzle with the oil.

Bake in the oven for 20 minutes.

Hints & tips

Traditionally, Shepherds Pie contains lamb mince and Cottage Pie contained any mince that wasn't lamb - commonly beef. However, both types of mince are aged and unsuitable for a low histamine diet.

In place of swede mash, try topping with parsnip or sweet potato mash - and crumble with goats cheese.

If using fresh poultry (organic if possible and not stored even for one day) saute finely cubed pieces and use only half the lentils. When cooked, stir into the lentil mix. **Make sure the meat is fully cooked before serving.**

'Spaghetti Carbonara'

Ingredients

For 2 or 4 people -

2 or 4	Sweet potato
15ml or 30ml	Rapeseed oil
150g or 300g	Wholegrain spaghetti or penne
1 or 2	Red onion
1 or 2 cloves	Fresh garlic
50 or 100g	Butter
125 or 250ml	Brown flour
250 or 500ml	Almond milk
250 or 500ml	Filtered water
200g or 400g	Butter beans - drained
2 or 4	Organic egg yolks
1 or 2 handfuls	Fresh basil

Method

Wash and slice the sweet potatoes into large chunky rounds - toss in oil and season with sea salt and pepper. Roast in a hot oven (250 °c) for 15-20 minutes until they brown at the edges. Turn part way through cooking.

Meanwhile, boil the kettle and cook pasta according to packet instructions, usually for around 15 minutes.

Dice the onion and gently fry in a pan for two minutes. Prepare the garlic by finely dicing. Then sprinkle the garlic with sea salt, and crush with the back of a knife. Add to the pan for a further minute.

To make the bechamel sauce, melt the butter and stir in the flour. Gradually add the milk and water. Finely chop and add the herbs. Simmer for 5 mins. Season to taste and stir often.

Stir the onions and garlic through the bechamel. Rinse the butter beans, add to the sauce and cook through for a minute. Season to taste.

Once the pasta has cooked, drain and stir the pasta into the sauce. Whisk the eggs with a fork and stir through the pasta. Do not add any more heat to the pan or the egg will scramble.

Serve along with the roast sweet potatoes, a salad or soda garlic bread.

Hints & tips

Try adding a little goats cheese crumbled over the pasta before serving. Maybe even a little fresh chilli!

Don't mock until you try pasta and roast potatoes. A guilty pleasure!

To make 'Patatas Bravas' top potatoes with your favourite spicy pasta sauce - potatoes are especially good with pesto or bolognese sauces.

If using fresh poultry (organic if possible and not stored even for one day) saute small cubed pieces in place of the beans. When cooked, stir into the bechamel sauce. **Make sure the meat is fully cooked before serving.**

'Noodle Stir Fry'

Ingredients

For 2 or 4 people -

100g or 200g	Wide ribbon noodles - egg free or organic free range if possible
30ml or 60ml	Sesame oil
1 or 2	Leeks
1 or 2	Carrots
½ or 1	Red pepper
90g or 180g	Babycorn
1 or 2	Red onions
2 or 4 leaves	Cabbage
1 or 2	Fresh lemongrass
2 or 4 cloves	Fresh garlic
6 or 12 cms	Fresh ginger
200g or 400g	Butter beans
2 or 4 handfuls	Fresh coriander

Method

Boil the kettle and cook noodles according to packet instructions, usually for around 10 minutes. Once cooked, drain well and stir in ½ of the sesame oil to prevent sticking.

As the noodles cook, working quickly so the vegetables remain crisp, slice the leeks, carrots and pepper into fine matchsticks. Cut the babycorn in half lengthways and the onion and cabbage into thin slices.

Remove the outer layers of the lemongrass and hit several times with a rolling pin to bruise it. Prepare garlic and ginger by finely dicing. Then sprinkle with sea salt, and crush with the back of a knife.

Heat the remaining oil in a wok (or large frying pan.) Add the lemongrass and stir to coat in oil. Quickly stir the red onion into the wok.

Add the garlic and ginger and then the leeks to the pan. Cook for 2 minutes before stirring in the carrots, pepper, babycorn and cabbage.

Once the vegetables have begun to soften, add the noodles and butter beans. Turn the heat up to high and cook for another minute. Stir.

Tear the coriander into the wok, remove the lemongrass. Season well.

Hints & tips

Unlike Pad Thai, you can stir fry an almost endless mix of vegetables!

Try - bamboo shoots, waterchestnuts, beansprouts, pak choi, fresh chilli, broccoli, courgette, mangetout, spring onion, kaffir lime leaves.

Replace noodles with rice (see special fried rice) and beans with seeds.

If using fresh poultry (organic if possible and not stored even for one day) cut into thin slices and add to the wok before the vegetables. When cooked, add the lemongrass. **Make sure the meat is fully cooked before serving.**

'Spaghetti & Neatballs'

Ingredients

For 2 or 4 people -

2 or 4 large	*Carrots*
1 or 2 sticks	*Celery*
125 or 250ml	*Beetroot juice*
125 or 250ml	*Light 'stock'*
125g or 250g	Green lentils
1 or 2	Red onion
30ml or 60ml	Rapeseed oil
1 or 2 cloves	Fresh garlic
60ml or 120ml	Oats - ground
1 or 2 handfuls	Fresh basil
150g or 300g	Wholegrain spaghetti

Method

To make the 'Faux Mato', finely dice the carrots and celery, cover with the beetroot juice and 'stock'. Bring to the boil and then simmer uncovered for 30 minutes.

Meanwhile, cover green lentils with water, bring to the boil and simmer for 15 mins. Top up water if needed.

Then finely dice the onion. Fry gently in the oil for 2 mins then prepare garlic by finely dicing then sprinkle with sea salt, crush with the back of a knife. Stir in the garlic for 1 minute.

Once the lentils have cooked, carefully drain and retain the cooking liquor. Freeze to use as a medium-weight 'stock' in future dishes.

Mash the onion and garlic plus oats and basil into the lentils. Season well and mould into small balls.

Preheat the oven to 220°c. Place the Neatballs on a greased tray - put in the oven for 15 mins, turning twice.

Meanwhile, cook spaghetti according to packet instructions - usually for 15 mins. Remove the 'Faux Mato' from the heat. Mash the mix carefully until you get a finer texture, similar to that of chopped, tinned tomatoes.

Stir the Neatballs into the 'Faux Mato' and season to taste. Serve hot.

Hints & tips

As is often the case, you can vary the lentils or beans used to make the Neatballs. Be adventurous and experiment with other fresh herbs - and occasionally a little fresh chilli!

For a 'Sloppy Joe'-type pizza topping, simply thicken the Neatball sauce with a little corn flour and use to top your favourite pizza base!

If using fresh poultry (organic if possible and not stored even for one day) saute finely cubed pieces and use only half the lentils. When cooked, stir into the lentil mix. **Make sure the meat is fully cooked before serving.**

'Cottage Pie'

Ingredients

For 2 or 4 people -

1 or 2 medium	Swede
30ml or 60ml	Rapeseed oil
125g or 250g	Green lentils
1 or 2 sprigs	Fresh rosemary
2 or 4	Carrots
100g or 200g	Green peas
1 or 2	Onion
2 or 4 sticks	Celery
1 or 2 cloves	Fresh garlic
30ml or 60ml	Almond Milk
25g or 50g	Butter

Method

Wash, peel and cube the swede. Toss in ½ oil, season with sea salt and pepper. Roast in the oven (220°c) for 15 mins until it starts to brown.

Meanwhile, boil a kettle. Cover green lentils with the water, bring to the boil then simmer for 15 minutes.

Finely chop the rosemary and add to the lentils as they cook. Cut the carrots into small pieces. Place with the peas in a colander over the lentils as they cook for the last 10 mins.

Dice the onion and celery and fry gently in the remaining oil for 2 mins. Prepare the garlic by finely dicing. Then sprinkle the garlic with sea salt, and crush with the back of a knife. Add to the oil for a further minute.

Take the swede out of the oven and drain from the oil. Retain for later.

Mash together the swede with the milk and butter. Season to taste.

Drain the lentils and freeze all but a little 'stock'. Stir together with all of the vegetables. Grease an oven dish.

Pour the lentil mixture in the dish. Spoon the swede mash over the top and press down making a pattern with a fork. Drizzle with the oil.

Bake in the oven for 20 minutes.

Hints & tips

Traditionally, Shepherds Pie contains lamb mince and Cottage Pie contained any mince that wasn't lamb - commonly beef. However, both types of mince are aged and unsuitable for a low histamine diet.

In place of swede mash, try topping with parsnip or sweet potato mash - and crumble with goats cheese.

If using fresh poultry (organic if possible and not stored even for one day) saute finely cubed pieces and use only half the lentils. When cooked, stir into the lentil mix. **Make sure the meat is fully cooked before serving.**

'Spaghetti Carbonara'

Ingredients

For 2 or 4 people -

2 or 4	Sweet potato
15ml or 30ml	Rapeseed oil
150g or 300g	Wholegrain spaghetti or penne
1 or 2	Red onion
1 or 2 cloves	Fresh garlic
50 or 100g	Butter
125 or 250ml	Brown flour
250 or 500ml	Almond milk
250 or 500ml	Filtered water
200g or 400g	Butter beans - drained
2 or 4	Organic egg yolks
1 or 2 handfuls	Fresh basil

Method

Wash and slice the sweet potatoes into large chunky rounds - toss in oil and season with sea salt and pepper. Roast in a hot oven (250 °c) for 15-20 minutes until they brown at the edges. Turn part way through cooking.

Meanwhile, boil the kettle and cook pasta according to packet instructions, usually for around 15 minutes.

Dice the onion and gently fry in a pan for two minutes. Prepare the garlic by finely dicing. Then sprinkle the garlic with sea salt, and crush with the back of a knife. Add to the pan for a further minute.

To make the bechamel sauce, melt the butter and stir in the flour. Gradually add the milk and water. Finely chop and add the herbs. Simmer for 5 mins. Season to taste and stir often.

Stir the onions and garlic through the bechamel. Rinse the butter beans, add to the sauce and cook through for a minute. Season to taste.

Once the pasta has cooked, drain and stir the pasta into the sauce. Whisk the eggs with a fork and stir through the pasta. Do not add any more heat to the pan or the egg will scramble.

Serve along with the roast sweet potatoes, a salad or soda garlic bread.

Hints & tips

Try adding a little goats cheese crumbled over the pasta before serving. Maybe even a little fresh chilli!

Don't mock until you try pasta and roast potatoes. A guilty pleasure!

To make 'Patatas Bravas' top potatoes with your favourite spicy pasta sauce - potatoes are especially good with pesto or bolognese sauces.

If using fresh poultry (organic if possible and not stored even for one day) saute small cubed pieces in place of the beans. When cooked, stir into the bechamel sauce. **Make sure the meat is fully cooked before serving.**

'Noodle Stir Fry'

Ingredients

For 2 or 4 people -

100g or 200g	Wide ribbon noodles - egg free or organic free range if possible
30ml or 60ml	Sesame oil
1 or 2	Leeks
1 or 2	Carrots
½ or 1	Red pepper
90g or 180g	Babycorn
1 or 2	Red onions
2 or 4 leaves	Cabbage
1 or 2	Fresh lemongrass
2 or 4 cloves	Fresh garlic
6 or 12 cms	Fresh ginger
200g or 400g	Butter beans
2 or 4 handfuls	Fresh coriander

Method

Boil the kettle and cook noodles according to packet instructions, usually for around 10 minutes. Once cooked, drain well and stir in ½ of the sesame oil to prevent sticking.

As the noodles cook, working quickly so the vegetables remain crisp, slice the leeks, carrots and pepper into fine matchsticks. Cut the babycorn in half lengthways and the onion and cabbage into thin slices.

Remove the outer layers of the lemongrass and hit several times with a rolling pin to bruise it. Prepare garlic and ginger by finely dicing. Then sprinkle with sea salt, and crush with the back of a knife.

Heat the remaining oil in a wok (or large frying pan.) Add the lemongrass and stir to coat in oil. Quickly stir the red onion into the wok.

Add the garlic and ginger and then the leeks to the pan. Cook for 2 minutes before stirring in the carrots, pepper, babycorn and cabbage.

Once the vegetables have begun to soften, add the noodles and butter beans. Turn the heat up to high and cook for another minute. Stir.

Tear the coriander into the wok, remove the lemongrass. Season well.

Hints & tips

Unlike Pad Thai, you can stir fry an almost endless mix of vegetables!

Try - bamboo shoots, waterchestnuts, beansprouts, pak choi, fresh chilli, broccoli, courgette, mangetout, spring onion, kaffir lime leaves.

Replace noodles with rice (see special fried rice) and beans with seeds.

If using fresh poultry (organic if possible and not stored even for one day) cut into thin slices and add to the wok before the vegetables. When cooked, add the lemongrass. **Make sure the meat is fully cooked before serving.**

'Mexican Tortilla Pizza'

Ingredients -

For 2 or 4 people -

125g or 250g	Brown Self Raising flour
15ml or 30ml	Rapeseed oil
90ml or 180ml	Warm filtered water
1 or 2	Red onion
15ml or 30ml	Rapeseed oil
½ or 1 whole	Red pepper
1 or 2 small	Chilli or jalapeno
200g or 400g	Cannelini beans - drained
2 or 4 sprigs	Fresh basil
120g or 240g	Homemade pea guacamole (recipe)

Method

Sieve the flour into a bowl with a pinch (or 2) of unrefined sea salt. In a second bowl, pour in the warm water and oil. Add the water and oil to the flour 15ml at a time and mix into the flour using a fork.

Generously flour your workspace and knead the dough for 4-5 mins until smooth and flexible. Divide the dough into 2 (or 4) balls. Cover with kitchen film and rest for 20 mins.

Meanwhile, roughly chop the red onion and gently fry in oil for 2-3 mins. Then chop the red pepper to the same size as the onion and stir into the pan. Continue to fry gently.

Cut the chilli very finely, remove the seeds. Stir into the pan, along with the beans. Tear basil into the pan. Season. Coat in oil to warm through. Cover and remove from the heat. Make guacamole - blitz if preferred.

Roll the dough into thin circles. Heat a large frying pan on the hob. Do not add oil. Dry fry each circle at medium temperature, turn once until the surface forms brown spots.

Preheat oven to 180°c. Spread each cooked tortilla with the guacamole and divide the spicy beans between them. Cook for 8 minutes until hot.

Serve 'pizzas' with crispy lettuce, homemade salsa or crumbled feta.

Hints & tips

Spread the 'pizza' base with refried beans or salsa instead of the pea guacamole. Alternatively, use 'Quesadillas' (see recipe) in place of the tortilla to make 'Pizzadillas.'

For variety, make tortilla wraps into taco cups by shaping in muffin tins - and filling once cool. Or slice tortillas into triangles and fry in hot oil for 2-3 mins until crispy. Season.

If using fresh poultry (organic if possible and not stored even for one day) cut into small pieces in place of the beans. Add to the pan at the same time as the onion. **Make sure the meat is fully cooked before serving.**

'Piri Piri Beans & Rice'

Ingredients

For 2 or 4 people -

125g or 250g	Brown rice
45ml or 90ml	Rapeseed oil
1 or 2	Red onion
½ or 1	Red pepper
2 or 4 cloves	Fresh garlic
6 or 12 cms	Fresh ginger
1 or 2 sprigs	Fresh rosemary
1 or 2 small	Fresh chilli
1 or 2 hard	Mango
100g or 200g	Chickpeas
100g or 200g	Cannelini beans
60g or 120g	Green beans
90g or 180g	Babycorn

Method

Lightly fry the rice on the hob with ¼ rapeseed oil. Cover the rice with 2 parts water and add a sprig of basil. Stir once, return to the boil then cover and simmer for 30 mins.

Meanwhile, preheat the oven to 250 °c. Peel and quarter the onion, roughly chop the red pepper and toss in ¼ oil. Roast for 10 minutes.

Prepare garlic and ginger by finely dicing. Then sprinkle with sea salt, and crush with the back of a knife. Put the garlic in the roasting tin for the last 2-3 mins roasting time. Finely chop rosemary and chilli (if using) and add to the tin for 1 minute.

Put all the ingredients from the roasting tin into a blender, cover and blend until smooth. Peel and cube the mango and add ½ to the blender and blitz for another minute.

Add the puree to a pan, along with the beans and green beans. Bring to the boil then simmer for 2 minutes. Season to taste.

When the rice is almost cooked, add the remaining oil to a small pan. Gently fry the ginger then stir through ½ the mango and babycorn. Continue to cook until the mango softens. Drain the rice and stir into the mango and babycorn pan.

Hints & tips

These beans are a spicy alternative to baked beans. Try with toasted soda bread, on pasta or jacket potatoes or even in a lasagne! Simply replace the mango with a little stock!

Be careful when cooking rice. Always wash the rice and add a few basil leaves to the water during cooking. Make sure that all other food preparation is done while the rice cooks.

If using fresh poultry (organic if possible and not stored even for one day) saute small cubed pieces and use in place of the beans. When cooked, stir into the piri piri mix. **Make sure the meat is fully cooked before serving.**

'Thai Green Curry'

Ingredients

For 2 or 4 people -

125g or 250g	Brown rice
30ml or 60ml	Rapeseed oil
1 or 2 litres	Filtered water
125g or 250g	Green split peas
1 or 2	Onion
2 or 4	Spring onions
1 or 2 cloves	Fresh garlic
3 or 6 cms	Fresh ginger
1 or 2 sticks	Fresh lemongrass
2 or 4 sprigs	Fresh curry leaves
250 or 500ml	Almond milk
2 or 4 handfuls	Fresh coriander

For extra kick, chopped fresh chilli.

Method

Boil kettle. Cover green split peas with the other ½ water, bring to the boil, then simmer for 20 minutes. Top the water up a little after 10 mins.

Meanwhile, lightly fry the rice on the hob with ½ rapeseed oil. Cover the rice with ½ the water and add a sprig of basil. Stir once, return to the boil then cover and simmer for 30 mins.

Then finely chop the onion and spring onion. Fry gently in ½ the oil for 2 minutes. Prepare garlic and ginger by finely dicing then sprinkle with sea salt, crush with the back of a knife. Add to the pan, stirring for a minute.

Remove the outer layers of the lemongrass and hit several times with a rolling pin to bruise it. Finely chop the curry leaves and add both to the pan. Stir and reduce the heat a little. Pour the almond milk into the pan.

Simmer for 20 minutes. Once the split peas are al dente, drain and add to the simmering pan. If needed, stir through a little extra split pea stock or freeze the liquid for future use.

After 20 minutes add torn coriander and season to taste. Remove whole lemongrass and discard.

Rest the sauce by allowing to cool for just 2 minutes - then serve over rice.

Hints & tips

I grow curry leaves in a pot at home - it's cheap to buy from garden centres. If you can find it, try also growing kafir lime leaves to add to dishes.

For a deep green colour - try roasting green pepper, blitz and stir through the sauce just before serving. Use for other sauces - including pestos. Always add basil to rice as it cooks!

If using fresh poultry (organic if possible and not stored even for one day) saute small cubed pieces and use only half the split peas. When cooked, stir into the sauce mix. **Make sure the meat is fully cooked before serving.**

'Leek & Swede Tart'

Ingredients

For 2 or 4 people -

2 or 4	Leeks
½ or 1 whole	Swede
15 or 30ml	Rapeseed oil
50g or 100g	Oats - ground
30g or 60g	Sesame seeds
100g or 200g	Brown flour
40g or 85g	Butter
40g or 85g	Fortified dairy-free spread*
30 or 60ml	Filtered water
1 or 2 cloves	Fresh garlic
150ml or 300ml	Almond milk
1 or 2 sprigs	Fresh rosemary
1 or 2	Organic egg yolk

Method

Preheat the oven to 200°c. Wash and chop the swede and leeks into small chunks. Toss in oil and season with sea salt and black pepper. Roast in the oven for 20 minutes.

Meanwhile, mix oats, sesame seeds, and 90% of flour in a bowl. Rub in the fats to make breadcrumbs. Add the water and mix to make a rough dough. Press the dough evenly into a greased pie or tart tin. Bake in the oven for 15 minutes until golden.

Prepare the garlic by finely dicing. Then sprinkle the garlic with sea salt, and crush with the back of a knife. Add to the leeks for a further minute.

Carefully take the tin from the oven and remove the swede to use later. Place the tin on a hot hob. Sprinkle with the remaining flour and stir in to cook for just a minute.

Gradually add the milk a little at a time and stir well each time. Finely chop and add the rosemary. Take the tin off the heat, season to taste.

Beat the egg yolk and stir well into the leeks. Pour the mix into the baked tart base and add the swede.

Push the swede slightly into the mix. Bake in the oven for 20 minutes until the filling is golden brown.

Hints & tips

This quiche-like topping could be used with several different fillings.

Try adding other roast vegetables such as carrots, sweet potato, parsnip, celery, courgette or peppers.

To make this an even more filling dish, stir through your choice of beans or seeds as you add the egg.

'Pea & Potato Curry'

Ingredients

For 2 or 4 people -

125g or 250g	Brown rice
45 or 90ml	Rapeseed oil
1 or 2 litres	Filtered water
2 or 4 medium	Sweet potato
125g or 250g	Red lentils
2 or 4 sprigs	Fresh curry leaves
1 or 2	Red onion
2 or 4 cloves	Fresh garlic
3 or 6 cms	Fresh ginger
100g or 200g	Green peas
30g or 60g	Sesame seeds
2 or 4 handfuls	Fresh coriander

For extra kick, chopped fresh chilli.

Method

Lightly fry the rice on the hob with 30 (or 60ml) rapeseed oil. Cover the rice with ½ the water and add a sprig of basil. Stir once, return to the boil then cover and simmer for 30 mins.

Wash and cut sweet potato into large chunks - toss in 15ml (or 30ml) oil and season with sea salt and pepper. Roast in a hot oven (250°c) for 15 minutes until they start to brown.

Boil kettle. Cover red lentils with the other ½ water, bring to the boil, then simmer for 20 minutes. Finely chop and add curry leaves to the pan.

Meanwhile, cut the onion into large chunks. Stir into potatoes. Put back in the oven for 5 mins. Prepare garlic and ginger by finely dicing. Then sprinkle with sea salt, and crush with the back of a knife. Add to the tin for a further minute.

Add green peas and sesame seeds to the oven tin. Shake to coat in oil. If using chilli, stir into the tin now.

Once the red lentils and potatoes are cooked, remove from the heat and stir vegetables into the pan. Tear coriander and stir into the curry. Season with sea salt and black pepper.

Rest the sauce by allowing to cool for just 2 minutes - then serve over rice.

Hints & tips

Serve this curry with homemade Chapati or poppadom (see recipes) and mango chutney (also see recipe.)

Try replacing the peas with cauliflower or broccoli - if you're feeling adventurous... Apple or mango!

For bombay potatoes - parboil and roast cubed sweet potatoes with chilli, garlic, sesame seeds and salt.

'Colcannon Potato Cakes'

Ingredients

For 2 or 4 people -

½ or 1	Swede
½ or 1	Cabbage
125g or 250g	Green beans
100ml or 200ml	Almond milk
25g or 50g	Butter
1 or 2	Red onion
½ or 1	Red pepper
45ml or 90ml	Rapeseed oil
1 or 2 cloves	Fresh garlic
1 or 2 sprigs	Fresh rosemary
1 or 2 small	Fresh chilli
200g or 400g	Haricot beans

Method

Boil kettle. Peel and chop the swede into chunks, put into a pan. Pour water over the swede, bring to the boil then simmer for 15 minutes.

Meanwhile, finely slice the cabbage and green beans. Place in a colander over the water as it boils. Cover with the lid of the pan. Once cooked, drain swede by pouring through the colander. Save the cooking liquor to use some as stock in the beans.

Bring the milk to the boil in the pan. Carefully pour all the vegetables into the milk. Reduce the heat to a simmer, roughly mash with a fork. Add butter and season well. Mould mash into patties. Put in fridge to cool.

Preheat the oven to 250°c. Add ½ oil to the tin and cook the patties for 20 minutes until light golden brown. As the patties cook prepare the beans; Peel and quarter the onion, roughly chop the red pepper and toss in ½ oil. Roast for 10 mins. Prepare garlic by finely dicing. Sprinkle with sea salt, and crush with the back of a knife. Chop and add herbs and chilli, then garlic to the tin for 2 minutes.

Put all the roasted ingredients into a blender - plus a dash of stock - cover and blend until smooth. Add the pepper sauce to a pan, with the beans. Stir and then simmer for 5 minutes.

Hints & tips

Serve with toasted homemade soda bread for an Irish-inspired breakfast. Traditionally served at Halloween, sometimes containing lucky charms.

Alternatively, serve alongside savoury crepes or use in place of bubble & squeak (see recipes.) Or try adding extra stock and milk, plus white beans to make a tasty soup.

'Bunny Chow'

Ingredients

For 2 or 4 people -

125g or 250g	Red lentils
½ or 1 whole	Swede
1 or 2 large	Carrot
2 or 4 small	Red onion
½ or 1	Red pepper
30ml or 60ml	Rapeseed oil
1 or 2 small	Fresh chilli
2 or 4 cloves	Fresh garlic
6 or 12cm	Fresh ginger
2 or 4 sprigs	Fresh curry leaves
½ to 1 whole	Cabbage
50g or 100g	Sweetcorn
50g or 100g	Green peas

1 or 2 whole soda bread - cooked in a loaf tin - do not mark with a cross.

Method

Boil a kettle of water. Cover red lentils with the water, bring to the boil, cover then simmer for 10 mins.

Meanwhile, cut the swede, carrot and 1 onion into small chunks. Add to the lentils and continue to simmer until all ingredients are cooked. Finely chop and stir in ½ the fresh chilli.

Turn off the heat as soon as the ingredients are cooked. Top up with a little water if needed.

As the ingredients cook, chop 1 onion and pepper. Gently fry in oil for 2-3 minutes until they begin to soften.

Prepare garlic and ginger by finely dicing. Then sprinkle with sea salt, and crush with the back of a knife. Finely chop the curry leaves and remaining chilli. Gently fry along with the onion and pepper for 2 minutes.

Shred the cabbage leaves and add to the lentils, along with the sweetcorn and green peas. Stir the gently fried herbs and spices into the lentil mix.

Return the lentil curry to the heat and simmer very gently for a few minutes until warmed through.

Cut the soda bread in half, scoop out the middle of the bread. Serve the curry inside the bread crust, using the middle to dip into the curry.

Hints & tips

The name 'Bunny Chow' is thought to come from a combination of the vegetable curry 'Bhunia' and 'Chow' meaning food. Traditionally used as a take-away meal using the bread in place of plates or bowls.

Fill the bread with many dishes - try thick soups, stews, bolognese, mexican or other curries (see recipes!)

If using fresh poultry (organic if possible and not stored even for one day) saute small cubed pieces and use as well as the lentils. When cooked, stir into the lentil mix. **Make sure the meat is fully cooked before serving.**

'Scone-Baked Pizza'

Ingredients

For 2 or 4 people -

1 or 2	Red onion
½ or 1 whole	Red pepper
1 or 2 medium	Carrots
1 or 2 sticks	Celery
15ml or 30ml	Rapeseed oil
1 or 2 cloves	Fresh garlic
50g or 100g	Sunflower seeds
150g or 300g	Wholegrain Self-Raising flour
20g or 40g	Butter
2 or 4 sprigs	Fresh basil
110 or 220ml	Almond milk
25g or 50g	Green peas
25g or 50g	Sweetcorn

Handful fresh basil to serve.

Method

Preheat oven to 220°c. Peel and quarter the onion, roughly chop the red pepper, carrots and celery and toss in oil. Roast for 10 mins.

Prepare garlic by finely dicing. Sprinkle with sea salt, and crush with the back of a knife.

After 10 minutes, separate the red pepper and add to a blender along with the garlic, sunflower seeds and a tiny dash of water. Cover and blend until smooth.

For the base - In a bowl, rub the flour with the butter to make breadcrumbs. Finely chop and stir in herbs. Add the milk and use a knife to mix together until a dough is formed.

Place on a floured surface and knead lightly until the dough is smooth. Roll out a rough circle to 1cm thickness.

Place on a baking tray. Spread the red pepper pesto along the base leaving a 1cm gap between the edge of the base and the sauce.

Arrange the part-roasted vegetables on top of the pesto, add the peas and sweetcorn. Tear and add ½ the basil. Drizzle with the roasted oil.

Bake for 15-20 mins until golden brown and sounds hollow when tapped. Top with remaining herbs.

Hints & tips

Serve with coleslaw (see recipe) - make the mayonnaise while the pizza base is in the oven.

Use this base for any of your favourite pizza toppings. For low histamine ideas - see the recipes in this book.

Serve with a fresh salad or roasted sweet potato wedges or swede chips.

If using fresh poultry (organic if possible and not stored even for one day) grill and slice or saute cubes before topping the pizza. Alternatively, adapt the 'Neatballs' recipe. **Make sure the meat is fully cooked before serving.**

'Green Bean Casserole'

Ingredients
For 2 or 4 people -

125g or 250g	Green beans
2 or 4 sticks	Celery
50 or 100g	Butter
125 or 250ml	Brown flour
250 or 500ml	Almond milk
250 or 500ml	Filtered water
2 or 4 sprigs	Fresh sage
1 or 2	Bay leaf
1 or 2	Red onion
15ml or 30ml	Rapeseed oil
1 or 2 cloves	Fresh garlic
50g or 100g	Sunflower seeds
50g or 100g	Homemade soda bread *or cornbread* crumbs (see recipe)

Method

Prepare the green beans by topping and tailing then cutting them in half. Cut the celery to a similar size.

To make the bechamel, melt butter and stir in the flour. Gradually add the milk and water. Finely chop then add the sage and bay leaf. Season to taste, simmer for 5 mins. Stir often.

Put a colander over the pan as it simmers. Add the green beans and celery, cover with the pan lid.

Meanwhile, finely slice the red onion and gently fry in oil. Prepare garlic by dicing. Then sprinkle with sea salt, and crush with the back of a knife. Add to the oil for a minute.

Just before removing from the heat, stir the sunflower seeds into the oil to coat. Lightly grease an oven tin and preheat the oven to 180°c.

Remove the bay leaf from the sauce. Put the green beans and celery into an oven tin, pour over the bechamel.

Sprinkle with breadcrumbs. Top with the fried onions, garlic and sunflower seeds. Drizzle with the remaining oil.

Bake in the oven for 20 minutes or until the seeds have lightly browned.

Serve as a side or with cornbread.

Hints & tips

Originally devised by the Campbells soup company in the 1950's, this casserole uses homemade bechamel - giving you the flexibility to use different herbs and seasonings to taste.

Often served at Thanksgiving and makes a tasty light dish at any time. Vary the green vegetables and serve with lentil loaf, schnitzels or kievs.

'Spicy Fajitas'

Ingredients

For 2 or 4 people -

100g or 200g	Brown rice
30ml or 60ml	Rapeseed oil
50g or 100g	Green peas
60g or 120g	Brown flour
1 or 2	Organic egg yolk
200 or 400ml	Almond milk
20g or 40g	Butter
1 or 2	Red onion
1 or 2	Carrots
1 or 2	Pepper - red, green, yellow or orange
1 or 2 sticks	Celery
2 or 4 cloves	Fresh garlic
1 or 2 small	Fresh chilli
200g or 400g	Butter beans

Method

Lightly fry the rice on the hob with ½ oil. Cover the rice with 2 parts water. Stir once, return to the boil then cover and simmer for 30 mins. After 25 mins, add the green peas.

Meanwhile, sift the flour (and a pinch of sea salt) into a bowl. Make a well in the centre of the flour and pour in the egg. Whisk the eggs and flour.

Gradually stir in the milk and keep whisking until all of the lumps have disappeared and the batter is cream-like. Melt a knob of butter (5g) in a small saucepan. Using a cup, pour in 70ml of batter mix and swirl around the pan to coat the base.

Cook for 2 mins or until the bottom side browns. Loosen and turn over. Cook the second side until brown. Repeat for each crepe - 2 per person. Remember to melt a knob of butter each time. Put in oven to keep warm.

Now work quickly so the vegetables remain crisp, slice the onion, carrots, peppers and celery into thin strips. Gently fry in a pan with 1 (or 2) tbsp of oil until they just begin to soften.

Prepare garlic by finely dicing. Sprinkle with sea salt, and crush with the back of a knife. Finely chop chilli and stir with the garlic into the pan for 2 mins. Turn heat up to high, add butter beans. Serve sizzling in the pan with crepes and rice as a side dish.

Hints & tips

For variety - in place of the rice - serve with shredded lettuce, pea guacamole and salsa (see recipes.)

Be careful when cooking rice. Always wash the rice and add a few basil leaves to the water during cooking.

Try making double the quantity of crepes and freezing the extra once cooked. Place a piece of kitchen film between each before freezing.

If using fresh poultry (organic if possible and not stored even for one day) saute small cubed pieces and use in place of the beans. When cooked, stir into the piri piri mix. **Make sure the meat is fully cooked before serving.**

'Toad in the Hole'

Ingredients

For 2 or 4 people -

125g or 250g	Green lentils
1 or 2 sprigs	Fresh rosemary
2 or 4 small	Red onion
25g or 50g	Butter
1 or 2 cloves	Fresh garlic
60ml or 120ml	Oats - ground
½ or 1	Yellow pepper
2 or 4 sticks	Celery
1 or 2	Carrots
45ml or 90ml	Rapeseed oil
125g or 250g	Brown flour
2 or 4	Organic egg yolk
300 or 600ml	Almond milk

Method

Boil kettle. Cover green lentils with 500ml (or 1 litre) water, bring to the boil then simmer for 15 mins. Finely chop the herbs and add to the lentils.

Finely dice 1 onion and fry gently in butter for 2 mins. Prepare garlic by finely dicing. Then sprinkle with sea salt, and crush with the back of a knife. Add to the oil for a min.

Preheat oven to 200°c. Drain and roughly mash the lentils. Stir in the onion and garlic - plus oats and herbs. Season and mould into sausages. Cook in oven for 20 mins, turning twice to brown each side. Freeze any leftover lentil 'stock' to make gravy.

As the sausages cook, quarter the remaining onion and roughly chop the pepper, celery and carrots. Toss vegetables in ¼ oil and season. Add the vegetables to the sausage tin and roast for 10 mins.

Remove sausages and vegetables from the tin. Pour remaining oil into the tin, put in the oven for 10 mins.

Meanwhile, sieve the flour into a bowl and whisk in the egg yolk and milk to make the batter. Take the tin from the oven and immediately pour in the batter. Carefully add the sausages and vegetables to the batter. Cook in the oven for 40 mins until the batter has browned. Do not open the oven until the batter has cooked!

Hints & tips

To make sure the batter starts cooking as soon as it hits the pan (and isn't soggy) the oil must be very hot. Eat straight away or it'll go flat!

For a family lunch, try serving with a 'puy' gravy, mashed or roasted sweet potatoes, parsnips or swede, steamed broccoli, cabbage and green beans or peas.

If using fresh poultry (organic if possible and not stored even for one day) saute finely cubed pieces and use only half the lentils. When cooked, stir into the lentil mix. **Make sure the meat is fully cooked before serving.**

'Calzone'

Ingredients

For 2 or 4 people -

Thin & crispy pizza dough (see 'Garlic Bread Pizza' recipe) - enough for 2 or 4 people.

65g or 130g	Puy lentils
1 or 2	Red onion
15ml or 30ml	Rapeseed oil
100g or 200g	Green beans
¼ or ½ whole	Cabbage
1 or 2 cloves	Fresh garlic
1 or 2 handfuls	Fresh parsley

Method

Boil a kettle of water. Cover puy lentils with water, bring to the boil then simmer for 30 minutes. After 10 mins, add more water to cover. Stir.

Meanwhile, prepare pizza dough (following the 'Garlic Bread Pizza' recipe in this book) until you get to the stage of rolling out the dough.

Refrigerate the dough ball. Slice the onion into strips. Heat the oil in a pan, add the onion and fry for 2 mins. Top and tail the green beans and cut in half. Cut the cabbage into thin strips. Stir into the pan with the onion. Continue to fry gently.

Prepare garlic by finely dicing. Sprinkle with sea salt, and crush with the back of a knife. Add to the vegetables in the pan for the last minute.

Drain the puy lentils and freeze the cooking liquor for gravies in future.

Roll the dough into 2 (or 4) circles and divide the filling between them - but only on one half on each circle. Season with sea salt, black pepper - tear and add herbs.

Preheat oven to 180°c. Lift up the empty side of the dough and press down hard over the filling, crimping the edges. Prick the top once with a knife. Bake in oven for 25 mins.

Hints & tips

Calzone 'toppings' can be the same as your favourite pizza - although they are usually filled with those vegetables that need using up. The calzone sauce is also served on the side - unlike a folded 'Stromboli' that has the sauce contained inside.

For the sauce, follow the 'Ketchup' recipe in this book, but do not sieve and only simmer for 2-3 minutes.

If using fresh poultry (organic if possible and not stored even for one day) saute finely cubed pieces and use only half the lentils. When cooked, stir into the lentil mix. **Make sure the meat is fully cooked before serving.**

'Lurkey Escalopes'

Ingredients

For 2 or 4 people -

10g or 20g	Butter
20g or 40g	Brown flour
60ml or 120ml	Almond milk
60ml or 120ml	Filtered water
1 or 2 handfuls	Fresh parsley
125g or 250g	Yellow split peas
1 or 2	Onion
15ml or 30ml	Rapeseed oil
1 or 2 cloves	Fresh garlic
60ml or 120ml	Oats - ground
2 or 4	Organic egg yolks
30g or 60g	Brown flour
50g or 100g	Homemade bread crumbs (see recipe)

Method

To make the bechamel, melt the butter and stir in the flour. Gradually add the milk and water. Finely chop and stir the herbs into the sauce. Simmer for 5 mins. Pour into ice cube trays and freeze for 1 hour.

After 30 mins - cover split peas with 500ml (or 1 litre) water, bring to the boil, cover then simmer for 20 mins.

Meanwhile, finely dice the onion and fry gently in oil for 2 mins. Prepare garlic by dicing. Then sprinkle with sea salt, and crush with the back of a knife. Add to the oil for a min.

Drain and mash the split peas. Stir in the onion and garlic - plus oats. Season and mould into patties. Slice in two and allow to cool. Take two of the patties, put 4 cubes of bechamel on each. Press the other two patties over the top and mould to seal. Don't worry if it crumbles a little.

Preheat oven to 200°c. Place the flour, egg and breadcrumbs onto 3 separate plates. Whisk the egg, season the flour with a pinch of sea salt and ground black pepper. Carefully dust each folded patty with flour, brush with the egg then coat with the breadcrumbs. Grease oven tray.

Drizzle with a little oil or butter. Cook in oven for 20 mins. Freeze left-over split pea 'stock' to make gravy.

Hints & tips

Also known as Schnitzles and really popular with kids - try making mini versions without bechamel (even cut into shapes if you dare!)

Vary the ingredients in the bechamel - try tiny pieces of broccoli, courgette, leeks, watercress or rocket. Or in place of the sauce - use slices of mozzarella or goats cheese!

If using fresh poultry (organic if possible and not stored even for one day) cut a pocket into a skinned breast and fill with the bechamel. Coat in breadcrumbs to seal. **Make sure the meat is fully cooked before serving.**

'Chilli Beans & Rice'

Ingredients

For 2 or 4 people -

2 or 4 large	*Carrots*
1 or 2 sticks	*Celery*
125 or 250ml	*Beetroot juice*
125 or 250ml	*Light 'stock'*
125g or 250g	Green lentils
125g or 250g	Brown rice
1 or 2	Red onion
30ml or 60ml	Rapeseed oil
1 or 2 cloves	Fresh garlic
1 or 2 medium	Fresh chilli
1 or 2	Red pepper
100g or 200g	Kidney beans
1 or 2 handfuls	Fresh basil

Method

To make the 'Faux Mato', finely dice the carrots and celery, cover with the beetroot juice and 'stock'. Bring to the boil and then simmer uncovered for 30 minutes.

Meanwhile, cover green lentils with water, bring to the boil and simmer for 15 mins. Top up water if needed. Once the lentils have cooked, carefully drain and retain the cooking liquor. Add and stir the liquor into the 'Faux Mato' as it simmers.

Lightly fry the rice on the hob with ½ rapeseed oil. Cover the rice with two parts water and add a sprig of basil. Stir once, bring to the boil then cover and simmer for 30 mins.

Dice the onion. Fry gently in ½ oil for 2 mins then prepare garlic by finely dicing then sprinkle with sea salt, crush with the back of a knife.

Finely chop the fresh chilli and roughly chop the red pepper. Stir with the garlic into the oil for 1 min.

Remove the 'Faux Mato' from the heat. Mash the mix carefully until you get a finer texture, similar to that of chopped, tinned tomatoes.

Stir 'Faux Mato' into the lentils along with vegetables and drained beans. Cover with 200ml (or 400ml) filtered water. Season, stir, bring to the boil. Simmer for 20 mins. Serve over rice.

Hints & tips

In place of the green lentils, try a mixture of chopped vegetables such as green beans, mixed peppers, leeks, baby corn and courgette.

Replace rice with swede 'chips' or jacket sweet potato. Alternatively, serve a 'Tex Mex' feast with nachos, pea guacamole, salsa, crumbled feta and cornbread (see recipes.)

If using fresh poultry (organic if possible and not stored even for one day) saute finely cubed pieces and use only half the lentils. When cooked, stir into the lentil mix. **Make sure the meat is fully cooked before serving.**

'Celebration Roast'

Ingredients

For 2 or 4 people -

2 or 4 medium	Sweet potato
15ml or 30ml	Rapeseed oil
1 or 2	Red onion
40g or 80g	Flaked almonds
1 or 2 cloves	Fresh garlic
3 or 6 cms	Fresh ginger
1 or 2 small	Fresh chilli
Plus -	
2 or 4	Parsnips
15ml or 30ml	Rapeseed oil
50g or 100g	Green peas
50g or 100g	Sweetcorn

Method

Boil kettle. Preheat oven to 220°c. Wash and peel the sweet potatoes. Take the first 1 (or 2), cut into rough chunks, cover with water, bring to the boil and simmer for 15 mins.

Meanwhile dice the remaining sweet potato, toss in rapeseed oil and season. Add to an oven proof tin and roast in the oven for 15 minutes.

As the sweet potatoes cook, dice the onion and stir into the roasting vegetables with ¾ of the flaked almonds. Return to the oven for 5 minutes.

Prepare garlic and ginger by finely dicing. Then sprinkle with sea salt, and crush with the back of a knife. Finely slice the chilli and stir with the garlic and ginger into the roasting pan and cook for 2-3 minutes.

Drain and mash the sweet potatoes.

Fold the roasted vegetables together into the mashed potato. Season. Grease a loaf tin and pack tightly with the mix. Cover and cook for 15 mins then remove cover and sprinkle with ¼ almonds, cook for 10 mins.

As the roast cooks, cut parsnips into wedges, toss in oil and season. Add to the oven tin, roast in the oven for 20 mins, turning. Lightly steam peas and sweetcorn by placing a colander over a pan of boiling water.

Hints & tips

This is a tasty and unusual roast that is ideal for when you're celebrating. Try as an alternative to Turkey dishes at Thanksgiving or Christmas.

If serving the roast parsnips separately to this spicy roast, you could try adding a little roast garlic, ginger or chilli to the pan. Or maybe brushed with a little agave nectar.

'Stew & Dumplings'

Ingredients

For 2 or 4 people -

1 or 2	Red onion
30ml or 60ml	Rapeseed oil
2 or 4	Carrots
2 or 4 sticks	Celery
¼ or ½	Swede
2 or 4 cloves	Fresh garlic
20ml or 40ml	Brown flour
½ or 1 litre	Dark puy 'stock'
100g or 200g	Green peas
200g or 400g	Butter beans
2 or 4 sprigs	Fresh sage
¼ or ½	Cabbage
125g or 250g	Self Raising brown flour
65g or 130g	Butter

Method

Keep the butter in the fridge until you need to use it. It must stay cold.

Working quickly so the vegetables remain crisp, roughly chop the onion and fry gently in the oil for 2 mins.

Cut the carrots, celery and swede into small chunks and stir into the oil. Continue to cook until the vegetables start to soften. Prepare garlic by dicing. Then sprinkle with sea salt, and crush with the back of a knife. Add to the oil for a minute.

Stir the plain flour through the vegetables and slowly stir the stock into the pan. Bring the stock to the boil, then cover and simmer for 20 mins.

After 20 mins, stir the peas, beans and ½ herbs into the stew. Cut the cabbage into slices and add to the pan. Season. As the stew simmers - Cut the butter into chunks. Rub the self raising flour with the butter using fingers to make breadcrumbs. Tear in the other ½ of the herbs, add a pinch of sea salt and black pepper.

Add 80ml (or 160ml) water to form a dough. Mould the dough into 'golf balls'. Press these balls into the stew so they are half under the liquid. Cover the pan and continue to simmer for 12 minutes until the dumplings have risen and are soft to touch.

Hints & tips

Instead serve the stew with a puff or shortcrust pastry lid, or serve with homemade soda bread and butter.

Replace sage with thyme, rosemary, marjoram or other robust herbs.

Other vegetables include - sweet potatoes, parsnips, turnips, leeks, sprouts, broccoli or cauliflower.

If using fresh poultry (organic if possible and not stored even for one day) saute small cubed pieces in place of the beans. When cooked, stir into the stew mix. **Make sure the meat is fully cooked before serving.**

'Filo Strudel'

Ingredients

For 2 or 4 people -

3 or 6 sheets	Filo pastry
1 or 2	Sweet potato
30ml or 60ml	Rapeseed oil
1 or 2	Red onion
250g or 500g	Brussels sprouts
1 or 2 whole	Green, red, orange or yellow pepper
¼ or ½ whole	Broccoli
50g or 100g	Sunflower seeds
1 or 2 handfuls	Fresh coriander

Method

Remove the filo pastry from the freezer - I usually defrost the pastry for 2 mins in the microwave and then allow to rest for 30 mins while I prepare the filling. However, always follow manufacturer's instructions.

Preheat the oven to 200°c. Dice the sweet potatoes and toss in rapeseed oil and season. Add to an oven proof tin and roast in the oven for 20 mins.

Meanwhile, quarter the onion and stir into the tin. Return the tin to the oven. Peel the sprouts and cut into quarters. Roughly chop the peppers into chunks. Add to the tin and put back in the oven.

Finally, cut the broccoli into florets and then in half again. Add to the oven tin for the final 5 minutes. Remove the tin from the oven and stir in the seeds to coat in oil.

Place a piece of kitchen film on your worktop as big as the filo sheets. Brush the first sheet with a little oil. Place the second sheet on top but 2cm higher, and oil. Place the third sheet on top (but 2cm higher again.)

Place the filling in the centre of the sheets. Add torn herbs. Roll the filo over one at a time. Tuck the ends under. Place on it's seam on a baking sheet - decorate with leftover pastry. Brush with oil and bake for 25 mins.

Hints & tips

In place of seeds, try 100g drained white beans or 50g cubed feta or 50g sliced goats cheese per person. Otherwise, for a creamy sauce, drizzle a little bechamel over the filling.

Dessert - use apple, pear, fig, mango or rhubarb pulp (see chutney or rhupple recipes.) If making sweet filo pastry - brush each layer with butter and sprinkle with glucose.

If using fresh poultry (organic if possible and not stored even for one day) cut into small pieces and toss in the seasoned oil. Roast in the oven with the sweet potatoes. **Make sure the meat is fully cooked before serving.**

'Savoury Mincemeat Pie'

Ingredients

For 2 or 4 people -

250g or 500g	Shortcrust pastry store-bought (or see recipe.)
100g or 200g	Puy lentils
1 or 2	Red onion
15ml or 30ml	Rapeseed oil
1 or 2	Apples
20g or 40g	Flaked almonds
1 or 2 cloves	Fresh garlic
3 or 6 cms	Fresh ginger
1 or 2 sprigs	Fresh mint
50ml or 100ml	Apple juice
15ml or 30ml	Almond milk

Method

Firstly, prepare the short crust pastry following the recipe in this book. Wrap in cling film and leave to rest in the fridge. Alternatively, use frozen pastry and defrost at room temperature instead. Allow 25 minutes.

While the pastry is in the fridge, boil a kettle of water. Cover puy lentils with water, bring to the boil then simmer for 30 minutes. After 10 minutes, add more water to cover. Stir.

Preheat oven to 250°c. While the lentils cook, wash and quarter the onion, toss in oil and season with sea salt and pepper. Add to an oven tin and cook for 3-4 mins.

Chop apple and add to the tin - along with the almonds. Prepare garlic and ginger by finely dicing, sprinkle with sea salt and crush with the back of a knife. Add to the tin for 2 mins.

Cut 2/3rds from the pastry dough, roll into a circle (see recipe) and place in pie tin. Drain the lentils. Mix together with the vegetables. Spread the mix on top of the pastry base.

Reduce the puy liquor and juice by ½, finely chop and add herbs, season and pour over the pie filling. Roll the ¼ pastry to the same thickness as the base. Press on top of the pie mix. Brush the top of the pie with milk. Bake at 200°c for 30 mins.

Hints & tips

Mincemeat pies always used to be savoury. Try this as a tasty meal in the run up to Xmas - before you have too many figgy puddings! Serve with roasted swede 'chips' and steamed green peas, carrots or sweetcorn.

For crumbly pastry - once the 'crumbs' are made put in the freezer for 15 mins. And use iced cold water.

If using fresh poultry (organic if possible and not stored even for one day) saute finely cubed pieces and use only half the lentils. When cooked, stir into the lentil mix. **Make sure the meat is fully cooked before serving.**

'Sage & Onion Loaf'

Ingredients

For 2 or 4 people -

150g or 300g	Green or yellow split peas
½ or 1 litre	Filtered water
1 or 2	Red onion
25g or 50g	Flaked almonds
15ml or 30ml	Rapeseed oil
1 or 2 cloves	Fresh garlic
2 or 4 sprigs	Fresh sage
150g or 300g	Plain flour
15ml or 30ml	Olive oil

Method

Boil kettle. Cover green split peas with the water, bring to the boil, then simmer for 20 minutes. Top the water up a little after 10 mins.

Meanwhile, preheat oven to 200°c. Finely chop the red onion and toss in the oil along with the almonds. Season with a pinch of unrefined sea salt and ground black pepper. Add to an oven tin and roast for 15 mins, shaking after 10 mins.

Prepare the garlic by dicing. Sprinkle with sea salt, and crush with the back of a knife. Tear the sage into small pieces and stir both into the tin, roast for a further minute.

After the 20 mins, drain all but 100ml (or 200ml) of liquor out of the split peas. Or add water to make up that amount. Roughly blitz the split peas with a hand blender. Season.

Sieve the flour into the split peas. Stir well to combine then form a dough with your hands. Generously flour your workspace and knead the dough for 5 mins. Roll out into a rectangle 1cm thick. Spread evenly with the roasted sage and onion mix.

Carefully and tightly roll the dough up and over the filling. Place the roll into a lightly greased loaf tin and bake in the oven for 30 minutes.

Hints & tips

Alternatively, make a savoury 'crust' for the loaf out of a combination of crushed seeds, roasted garlic and your choice of finely chopped herbs.

Other loaf flavourings to try include - puy lentil & mint, green lentil & basil, chickpea & coriander or cannelini bean & apple sauce stuffing.

'Giant Yorkshire Pudding'

Ingredients -

For 2 or 4 people -

2 or 4	Parsnips
2 or 4	Carrots
30 or 60ml	Rapeseed oil
125g or 250g	Brown flour
4 or 8	Organic egg yolk
300 or 600ml	Almond milk
125g or 250g	Green lentils
½ or 1 whole	Leek
1 or 2 sprigs	Fresh sage
¼ or ½ whole	Broccoli
1 or 2	Onion
10g or 20g	Butter
15 or 30ml	Brown plain flour

Method

Preheat oven to 220°c. Put a roasting tin - plus one yorkshire pudding tin per person in the oven to heat up. Cut the parsnips and carrots into chunky wedges. Toss in ½ oil, season with sea salt and black pepper.

Add vegetables to the roasting tin, roast for 15 mins. Then turn them over and cover with foil and put on the bottom shelf of the oven. Pour remaining oil into the pudding tins, put back in the oven for 5 mins.

Meanwhile, sieve the flour into a bowl and whisk in the egg yolk and milk to make the batter. Take the tin from the oven and immediately pour in the batter. Cook in the oven for 20 mins until brown. *Do not open the oven until batter has cooked!*

Boil kettle. Cover lentils with water, bring to boil, simmer for 15 minutes.

Finely chop the leek and sage and add to the pan as it simmers. Chop the broccoli and put in a colander over the lentils for 2-3 mins.

Drain the lentils. Bring the liquor - plus 100ml (or 200ml) water to the boil. Quarter the onion and add to the pan. Make a paste using the butter and flour, stir into the gravy to thicken. Season to taste. Once the pudding is ready, fill with the lentils, then vegetables and onion gravy.

Hints & tips

Giant yorkshire puddings are also good filled with some favourite meals such as casserole or stew (see recipes.) Do try more unusual fillings such as - cubed sweet potatoes (with a kick of finely chopped fresh chilli!)

Small sizes work well to accompany a main meal - try really small puddings with tiny sausages as party food.

If using fresh poultry (organic if possible and not stored even for one day) cut into small pieces and toss in the seasoned oil. Roast in the oven with the parsnips and carrots. **Make sure the meat is fully cooked before serving.**

‘Sausage Dumpling Casserole’

Ingredients -

For 2 or 4 people -

125g or 250g	Yellow split peas or red lentils
1 or 2	Red onion
2 or 4 sticks	Celery
15ml or 30ml	Rapeseed oil
60ml or 120ml	Oats - ground
1 or 2 large	Sweet potato
½ or 1 whole	Swede
2 or 4	Carrots
½ or 1 litre	Root vegetable stock
1 or 2	Leek
15ml or 30ml	Rapeseed oil
1 or 2 sprigs	Fresh thyme
1 or 2	Apples
1 or 2	Courgette

Method

Boil a kettle of water. Cover peas (or lentils) with the water, bring to the boil again then simmer for 20 mins.

Dice onion and celery finely. Gently fry the onion for 2-3 mins until soft.

Roughly chop the sweet potato, swede and carrots. Put into a large pan and cover with root vegetable ‘stock’ (see recipe.) Bring to the boil and then simmer for 15 minutes.

Preheat the oven to 200°c. Drain the peas (or lentils) and retain the water. Stir in the onion - plus oats. Season, mash and mould into balls. Put in oven tin and cook for 20 minutes, turning twice to brown each side.

While the dumpling balls cook and the vegetables simmer, roughly chop the leek and gently fry in the remaining oil. Stir to coat in oil.

Strip the thyme from its stems and add to the leeks. Roughly chop the apple, add to the pan and continue to gently fry for 2 mins. Season.

Chop the courgette into chunks and add to the simmering pan. After a min, also add the leeks and apples.

Cover the vegetable pan with a lid and continue to simmer for 10 minutes until the apples are soft. Serve hot, topped with the dumpling balls.

Hints & tips

Freeze any pea (or lentil) ‘stock’ to make light sauces and gravies. You may also need a little liquor when moulding the dumpling balls.

Try replacing the thyme with other robust herbs - if using bay leaf add it whole and remove before serving.
To make the casserole even more substantial try adding pearl barley at the same time as you add the stock.

If using fresh poultry (organic if possible and not stored even for one day) cut into small pieces, add to pan with the sweet potato. Alternatively adapt the ‘sausage’ recipe. **Make sure the meat is fully cooked before serving.**

‘Pasta Crumble’

Ingredients

For 2 or 4 people -

150g or 300g	Over-sized brown pasta shapes
2 or 4	Red onion
30ml or 60ml	Rapeseed oil
1 or 2 cloves	Fresh garlic
40g or 80g	Sesame seeds
1 or 2 sprigs	Fresh sage
½ or 1 whole	Broccoli
¼ or ½	Homemade soda bread (see recipe)
15ml or 30ml	Olive oil

Method

Boil a kettle. Cover pasta with water, bring to the boil then simmer for 20 minutes. Wash and cut broccoli into florets. Put in a colander over the pan of pasta as it boils for the last 2-3 minutes. Meanwhile -

Preheat the oven to 170°c. Finely chop the onion and add to an oven tin - stir in the rapeseed oil to coat.

Put the tin in the oven while you prepare the garlic by finely dicing. Then sprinkle with sea salt, and crush with the back of a knife.

Stir the garlic into the oven tin along with the sesame seeds. Cook for 5 mins before finely chopping and adding the herbs. Cover with foil and put back in the oven for 5 mins.

Once the broccoli begins to steam, blitz the soda bread into crumbs.

Stir breadcrumbs into the oven tin and stir to coat in oil. Remove the foil - cook for 4-5 mins until browns.

Once cooked, drain the pasta then put back in the pan. Stir through the olive oil and broccoli, and ½ to crumble - season to taste.

Serve the pasta into bowls and sprinkle with the remaining crumble mix.

Hints & tips

Replace the broccoli with cauliflower, carrots, sprouts, parsnip, sweet potato, leek, courgette or peppers!

And although the ‘sage and onion crumble’ combination is a classic, experiment with other fresh herbs.

Use the roasted crumble mix as a rub around or on top of your Sunday loaf.

'Sweet Potato Gumbo'

Ingredients -

For 2 or 4 people -

2 or 4 large	*Carrots*
1 or 2 sticks	*Celery*
125 or 250ml	*Beetroot juice*
½ or 1 litre	*Light 'stock'*
1 or 2	Red onion
1 or 2	Pepper
30ml or 60ml	Rapeseed oil
1 or 2 cloves	Fresh garlic
1 or 2 small	Fresh chilli
1 or 2 sprigs	Fresh thyme
1 or 2 large	Sweet potato
¼ or ½ whole	Red cabbage
100g or 200g	Red rice
125g or 250g	Red lentil

Method

To make the 'Faux Mato', finely dice the carrots and celery, cover with the beetroot juice and 125ml (or 250ml) 'stock'. Bring to the boil then simmer uncovered for 30 minutes.

Roughly chop the red onion and peppers. Gently fry in ½ oil for 3-4 minutes until they begin to soften. Prepare garlic by finely dicing, sprinkle with sea salt and crush with the back of a knife. Cut chilli into very small chunks, remove the seeds.

Add garlic and chilli to the pan then strip the thyme from its' stems. Add herbs to the pan. Roughly chop the sweet potato and cabbage. Also add to the pan - stirring to coat in oil.

Fry the rice on the hob with ½ oil. Cover rice with two parts water. Add a sprig of basil. Stir once, bring to the boil, cover, simmer for 20 mins.

After its 30 minutes is up, remove the 'Faux Mato' from the heat. Mash the mix carefully so not to splash until you get a finer texture, similar to that of chopped, tinned tomatoes.

Add the 'Faux Mato' and remaining stock to the onion pan. Add to the pan with the red lentils. Stir and bring the sauce to the boil. Reduce heat to a simmer for 15 mins until the sweet potato is soft. Season.

Hints & tips

In place of the red rice, serve 'Sweet Potato Gumbo' with whole grain and wild rice or cornbread (see recipe.)

Try replacing the thyme with other robust herbs - if using bay leaf add it whole and remove before serving.

Try serving this Gumbo recipe in place of traditional stews and casseroles. Tastes great with dumplings.

If using fresh poultry (organic if possible and not stored even for one day) cut into small pieces and gently fry in the oil with the onion and peppers. **Make sure the meat is fully cooked before serving.**

‘Ravioli’

Ingredients -

For 2 or 4 people -

3 or 6	Organic egg yolks
125g or 250g	Pasta flour
15ml or 30ml	Olive oil
15ml or 30ml	Rapeseed oil
60ml or 120ml	Filtered water
100g or 200g	Puy lentils
1 or 2 small	Onion
15ml or 30ml	Rapeseed oil
1 or 2 cloves	Fresh garlic
1 or 2 sprigs	Fresh basil
50g or 100g	Oats - ground

Serve with - ‘Simple Pasta Sauce.’

Method

Beat 2 (or 4) egg yolks together in a small ramekin. In a large bowl, combine the flour, egg yolks, oil, water and a pinch (or 2) of sea salt.

Mix together and, when it starts to form a dough, knead on a lightly floured surface for 5-6 mins until the dough is smooth and flexible. Wrap in kitchen film and place in the fridge for 20 mins. Meanwhile -

Boil a kettle of water. Cover lentils with the water, bring to the boil then simmer uncovered for 20 mins.

Dice onion very finely and gently fry in oil for 2 mins. Prepare garlic by finely dicing, sprinkle with sea salt and crush with back of a knife. Add to pan, with the torn basil, to warm.

Drain the lentils. Mash into the onion pan. Add the ground oats, dash of water, stir well to combine. Season.

Using a pasta maker (or a rolling pin and floured board) roll pasta out in two strips around 2mm thick. On one strip put tsps of filling 5cm apart.

Beat the remaining egg, brush between each tsp of filling. Put the 2nd strip on top - press down firmly around the filling. Cut into 5cm squares with a sharp knife or cutter.

Boil a pan of water, cook each ravioli square for 5-6 mins until soft.

Hints & tips

Use the ‘Simple Pasta Sauce’ (see recipe) to pour over the ‘Ravioli’.

‘Ravioli’ can be made large or small and the pasta flavoured with many herbs. Other fillings could include: ‘Spanakopita’ feta - or soda breadcrumbs mixed with added crushed almonds or seeds. Even mini diced vegetables and fruits! (See recipes.)

If using fresh poultry (organic if possible and not stored even for one day) saute finely cubed pieces and use only half the lentils. When cooked, stir into the lentil mix. **Make sure the meat is fully cooked before serving.**

'Tagliatelle'

Ingredients -

For 2 or 4 people -

2 or 4	Organic egg yolks
125g or 250g	Pasta flour
15ml or 30ml	Olive oil
15ml or 30ml	Rapeseed oil
60ml or 120ml	Filtered water
2 or 4 sprigs	Fresh thyme
1 or 2	Red onion
15ml or 30ml	Rapeseed oil
40g or 80g	Sunflower seeds
1 or 2	Courgette
1 or 2 cloves	Fresh garlic
1 or 2 handfuls	Fresh basil
15ml or 30ml	Olive oil

Method

Beat 2 (or 4) egg yolks together in a small ramekin. In a large bowl, combine the flour, egg yolks, oil, water and a pinch (or 2) of sea salt.

Mix together with the herbs and when it starts to form a dough, knead on a lightly floured surface for 5-6 mins until the dough is smooth and flexible. Wrap in kitchen film and place in the fridge for 20 mins.

Meanwhile, preheat oven to 180°c. Quarter the red onion and toss in oil. Season with unrefined sea salt and ground black pepper. Pour into an oven tin and roast for 15 mins.

After 5 mins, stir the seeds into the tin, coating in oil. After another 5 mins, cut the courgette into 1cm circles, add to the tin in the oven. Prepare garlic by finely dicing, sprinkle with sea salt and crush with the back of a knife. Add to the tin.

Remove the tin from the oven before the garlic is allowed to burn. Tear the basil into the pan to warm.

Using a pasta maker (or a rolling pan and floured board) roll the pasta out in large strips around 2mm thick. Cut each strip into thin ribbons with the machine or by rolling and using a sharp knife. Boil a pan of water and cook the pasta for 5-6 mins until soft. Drain the pasta and stir into the sauce and olive oil. Serve hot.

Hints & tips

Add this quick and easy sauce to many of your favourite pasta shapes - or even as a warm dressing to a green salad. Just add croutons!

Vary the herbs - such as sage, lemon thyme. Make sure they're in very small pieces without any hard stems.

Smaller seeds need less cooking time - add at the same time as the garlic.

If using fresh poultry (organic if possible and not stored even for one day) cut into small cubes and toss in the seasoned oil. Roast in the oven with the onion. **Make sure the meat is fully cooked before serving.**

'Risotto Rosso'

Ingredients -

For 2 or 4 people -

125g or 250g	Red rice
30ml or 60ml	Rapeseed oil
60ml or 125ml	Beetroot juice
250ml or 500ml	Medium 'stock'
1 or 2	Red onion
2 or 4	Carrots or celery stick
125g or 250g	Kidney beans
50g or 100g	Green peas
1 or 2 cloves	Fresh garlic
1 or 2 small	Fresh chilli
¼ or ½ whole	Broccoli
1 or 2 sprigs	Fresh basil
15ml or 30ml	Agave nectar

Method

Lightly fry the rice in a large pan on the hob with ½ the rapeseed oil.

Combine the beetroot juice and 'stock' together in a jug. Add this liquor to the rice a little at a time - enough to cover but do not allow to dry out - until almost all of the liquid has been absorbed. Meanwhile...

Roughly chop the red onion. Gently fry in ½ oil for 2-3 minutes until it begins to soften. Finely chop the carrots or celery, stir into the onions.

Drain the beans and also add to the vegetable pan - along with the peas - stirring to coat well in oil.

Prepare garlic by finely dicing, sprinkle with sea salt and crush with the back of a knife. Cut chilli into very small chunks, remove the seeds.

Add the garlic and chilli to the pan. Cut the broccoli into small florets and stalks. Tear the basil and stir both into the pan - and allow to warm through.

Once the rice is cooked, pour the vegetables and beans into the large pan. Add the agave nectar and mix together well. Season to taste.

Return the pan to the heat and simmer gently, covered, for 5 minutes.

Hints & tips

Be careful when cooking rice. Always wash the rice and add a few basil leaves to the water during cooking.

Other options - red, yellow or orange pepper, red cabbage, sweet potato - almost any low histamine vegetable!

Also experiment with fresh herbs, lightly toasted organic seeds, crumbled feta or melted goats cheese.

If using fresh poultry (organic if possible and not stored even for one day) cut into small pieces in place of the beans. Add to the pan at the same time as the onion. **Make sure the meat is fully cooked before serving.**

'Croquettes'

Ingredients -

For 2 or 4 people -

125g or 250g	Red lentils
1 or 2	Red onion
15ml or 30ml	Rapeseed oil
½ or 1 whole	Red pepper
2 or 4	Spring onion
1 or 2 cloves	Fresh garlic
60ml or 120ml	Oats - ground
1 or 2	Organic egg yolk
50g or 100g	Homemade bread crumbs (see recipe)

<u>Other options -</u> Goats cheese with sweet potato, parsnip or swede. Vary the fresh herbs and the 'crumb' mix - add ground oats and sunflower seeds.

Method

Boil a kettle of water. Cover red lentils with the water, bring to the boil again then simmer for 20 mins.

Dice onion finely. Gently heat oil in a pan and cook the onion, stirring, for two minutes. Slice the red pepper to the same size as the onion and the spring onion into thin rings. Add both to the pan. Stir well to coat in oil.

Prepare garlic by finely dicing then sprinkle with sea salt, crush with the back of a knife. Add the garlic to the pan for a further minute until soft.

Preheat the oven to 220°c. Drain the red lentils and retain liquor. Stir in the onion and vegetables - plus oats.

Season. Use your hands to mould mix into 2 patties per person. Whisk the egg yolk in a small ramekin and pour the breadcrumbs onto a side plate.

Brush the patties with egg yolk and then dip to coat in the breadcrumbs. Grease an oven tray and add patties. Cook in the oven for 15 minutes, turning once to brown each side.

Freeze any red lentil 'stock' to make light sauces and gravies in future.

Serve with 'Hassleback' sweet potatoes and steamed organic green peas.

Hints & tips

Serve croquettes as part of a light lunch, or a starter with a selection of dips and chutneys (see recipes) - simply add a fresh salad garnish.

Root vegetable croquettes make a great side order to accompany a traditional family Sunday lunch.

Also try stuffing jalepeno peppers with goats cheese before coating in egg yolk and rolling in breadcrumbs.

If using fresh poultry (organic if possible and not stored even for one day) saute finely cubed pieces and use only half the lentils. When cooked, stir into the lentil mix. **Make sure the meat is fully cooked before serving.**

'Chickpea Salad'

Ingredients -

For 2 or 4 people -

1 or 2	Red onion
15ml or 30ml	Rapeseed oil
½ or 1 whole	Red pepper
1 or 2 cloves	Fresh garlic
200g or 400g	Chickpeas - drained
2 or 4 heads	Little gem
¼ or ½ whole	Cauliflower
50g or 100g	Sugar snap peas or mangetout
2 or 4	Spring onion
15ml or 30ml	Olive oil
50ml or 100ml	Apple juice
1 or 2 hard	Pears

Method

Roughly chop the onion and fry gently in oil for 2-3 mins until it starts to soften. Cut the pepper to a similar size to the onion and add to the pan, stir to coat in oil and continue to fry.

Meanwhile, prepare garlic by finely dicing, sprinkle with sea salt, crush with the back of a knife. Add garlic to the pan for a minute until soft.

Stir in the chickpeas and warm through. Remove from the heat and cover pan with a lid as you prepare the fresh salad base.

Working quickly so the ingredients remain fresh, wash and then rinse in cold water. Shred the lettuce in thick strips and divide between serving plates. Cut the cauliflower into small florets (including the stalks) and scatter on top of the lettuce along with whole sugar snap peas.

Finely slice the spring onions and add to a small jar. Pour in the olive oil and juice, season with unrefined sea salt and ground black pepper. Cover and shake the jar to mix. Set aside.

Cut the pear into thin wedges and place on top of the salad plates. Drizzle the salad with the dressing from the jar. Finally, pile the chickpea mix in the centre of the plate.

Serve quickly with a bowl of chunky celeriac chips, sprinkle with sea salt.

Hints & tips

Exchange traditional salad leaves for rocket or watercress and add a handful of fresh herbs. Try basil, parsley, mint, coriander or a little tarragon.

Alternatively, serve with sweet potato wedges, flatbread or pitta (see recipes) and crumble with feta cheese. Even use the warm chickpea mix as a baked sweet potato filling!

If using fresh poultry (organic if possible and not stored even for one day) grill and serve either sliced on the salad or cubed and mixed with homemade mayo and sweetcorn. **Make sure the meat is fully cooked before serving.**

'Cauliflower Grill & Chips'

Ingredients -

For 2 or 4 people -

125g or 250g	Red lentils
½ or 1 large	Celeriac
1 or 2	Red onion
30ml or 60ml	Rapeseed oil
½ or 1 whole	Cauliflower
1 or 2	Carrots
50g or 100g	Green peas
2 or 4	Spring onions
60ml or 120ml	Oats - ground
1 or 2	Organic egg yolk
50g or 100g	Homemade bread crumbs (see recipe)

Method

Boil a kettle of water. Cover red lentils with the water, bring to the boil again then simmer for 20 mins.

Preheat the oven to 220°c. Peel and slice the celeriac into thick chip shapes. Toss in ½ oil and season with a pinch of sea salt and black pepper. Add to an oven tin and roast for 25 mins, turning after 15 mins.

Dice onion finely. Chop the cauliflower and carrot to the same size as the peas and cut spring onion into thin rings. Add all vegetables to the pan. Stir to coat in oil. Cook for 5 mins until they just start to soften.

Meanwhile, drain the red lentils and retain liquor. Stir in the onion and vegetables - plus oats. Season. Use your hands to mould mix into 2 patties per person. Freeze lentil 'stock' to make light sauces and gravies.

Whisk the egg yolk in a small ramekin and pour the breadcrumbs onto a side plate. Brush the patties with egg and then dip to coat in breadcrumbs. Grease an oven tray and add patties. Cook in the oven for 15 mins.

To make a 'crunchy' chip - add finely chopped herbs to any leftover breadcrumbs. Dip the part cooked celeriac chips in egg yolk and then into the breadcrumbs. Return to the oven for the final 10 minutes.

Hints & tips

Alternatively, serve with buttered celeriac mash and homemade baked beans (see recipe.) Or rub whole sweet potatoes with oil and sea salt, bake in a hot oven until soft.

Make chip shop-style fritters - boil and mash sweet potatoes, swede, celeriac or parsnip. Season. Mould into patties, coat in breadcrumbs. Cook in hot oven for 15 mins.

If using fresh poultry (organic if possible and not stored even for one day) saute finely cubed pieces and use only half the lentils. When cooked, stir into the lentil mix. **Make sure the meat is fully cooked before serving.**

'Hotpot'

Ingredients -

For 2 or 4 people -

2 or 4	Carrots
¼ or ½	Cabbage
½ or 1 litre	Root vegetable stock
1 or 2	Bay leaf
1 or 2	Onion
15ml or 30ml	Rapeseed oil
1 or 2 cloves	Fresh garlic
1 or 2	Leek
1 or 2 sprigs	Fresh thyme
200g or 400g	Butter beans
¼ or ½	Broccoli
1 or 2 small	Sweet potato
½ or 1 small	Swede
20g or 40g	Butter

Method

Cut the carrots and cabbage into small pieces. Put in a pan and cover with the root vegetable 'stock'. Add the bay leaf, bring to the boil and simmer for 10 mins (only) to parboil.

Meanwhile, roughly chop the onion and fry gently in the oil for 2-3 mins until it begins to soften. Prepare garlic by finely dicing, sprinkle with sea salt, crush with the back of a knife.

Cut the leek into 1cm rings, stir with the garlic into the onion pan. Strip the thyme off its stems and stir to coat in oil. Drain beans and combine with ingredients in the oiled pan.

Preheat the oven to 180°c. Stir the ingredients in the oiled pan into the pan containing the carrots and cabbage. Cut broccoli into small pieces. Add these to the pan, season, cover and remove from the heat.

Using a mandolin or vegetable peeler, cut the sweet potato and swede into thin slices. Melt the butter.

Grease an oven proof tin and add the vegetables and bean mix from the pan. Top with a layer of alternating sweet potato and swede slices. Brush each layer with the melted butter.

Season. Cook in the lower part of your oven for 30 minutes or until the sweet potato is golden and crispy.

Hints & tips

As an alternative, try topping with slices of parsnip or beetroot. The crispy layers can be used with different pie fillings - even your favourite stew or casserole (see recipes.)

Serve with hunks of homemade soda bread or topped with melted goats cheese to make the dish even more filling. A great winter warmer!

If using fresh poultry (organic if possible and not stored even for one day) cut into small pieces in place of the beans. Add to the pan at the same time as the onion. **Make sure the meat is fully cooked before serving.**

'Polenta'

Ingredients -

For 2 or 4 people -

1 or 2	Sweet potato
1 or 2	Carrot
30ml or 60ml	Rapeseed oil
1 or 2	Red onion
1 or 2	Pepper
¼ or ½	Broccoli
60ml or 120ml	Apple juice
1 or 2 cloves	Fresh garlic
1 or 2 sprigs	Fresh lemon thyme
200g or 400g	Kidney beans
100g or 200g	Polenta flour
250 or 500ml	Root vegetable stock
10g or 20g	Butter

Method

Preheat oven to 200°c. Wash and cut the sweet potato and carrots into chunks, toss in the oil. Season with unrefined sea salt and ground black pepper. Pour into an ovenproof tin and roast for 25 minutes.

After 10 minutes, quarter the red onion and stir into the tin. After another 2-3 minutes, cut the pepper into 2cm pieces and add to the tin. Coat in oil. Return to the oven.

5 minutes before the potatoes are ready, chop the broccoli into small florets. Add to the tin with the juice.

Prepare garlic by finely dicing, sprinkle with sea salt and crush with the back of a knife. Add to the tin.

Remove the tin from the oven before the garlic is allowed to burn. Tear the thyme into the pan to warm.

Drain and stir the beans into the tin. Cover with kitchen foil and put in the bottom of the oven (switched off.)

In a saucepan, pour in the polenta, root vegetable stock and a good pinch of unrefined sea salt and ground black pepper. Cook at a medium temperature - stirring all the time until it starts to thicken. Stir in the butter and serve before it thickens too much. Pour the roast vegetables and beans over while still hot.

Hints & tips

For a tangy flavour, beat feta or ricotta cheese into the polenta at the same time as you add the butter.

Or, melt goats cheese over the roast vegetables once you add the beans.

Use the polenta in place of mashed potato with many dishes - including 'Bangers & Mash', with 'Toad in the Hole', pies or lasagne (see recipes.)

If using fresh poultry (organic if possible and not stored even for one day) cut into small cubes and toss in the seasoned oil. Roast in the oven with the sweet potatoes. **Make sure the meat is fully cooked before serving.**

‘Paella-cooked Rice’

Ingredients -

For 2 or 4 people -

1 or 2	Red onion
30ml or 60ml	Rapeseed oil
2 or 4	Spring onion
½ or 1	Red pepper
50g or 100g	Flaked almonds
2 or 4 cloves	Fresh garlic
½ or 1 small	Fresh chilli
125g or 250g	Rice - mix of red, brown and wild
½ or 1 litre	Root vegetable stock
2 or 4 whole	Bay leaf
¼ or ½ whole	Red cabbage
50g or 100g	Mangetout or sugar snap peas
50g or 100g	Green peas

Method

Roughly chop the red onion. Heat the oil in a large frying or Paella pan and gently fry the onion for 2-3 mins until it softens. Cut the spring onion into ½ cm rings and add to the pan.

Cut the pepper to the same size as the onion and stir into the pan - along with the almond flakes. Prepare garlic by finely dicing then sprinkle with sea salt, crush with the back of a knife. Finely chop the chilli removing the seeds. Stir both into the pan, be careful they don't burn.

Add the mix of rice and a sprig of basil to the pan. Stir to coat in oil. Pour the ‘stock’ into the pan with the bay leaf (remove before serving) and bring to the boil. Reduce heat and simmer, covered, for 15 mins.

As the rice simmers, shred the cabbage. Cut the mangetout or sugar snap peas in half diagonally.

Remove the lid and add the remaining vegetables on top of the rice. Continue to simmer part-covered but do not stir, for 15 mins until almost all of the liquor has been absorbed.

Stir the vegetables into the rice. Season to taste with unrefined sea salt and ground black pepper. Fully cover the rice and stand for a few mins to absorb the flavours before serving. Enjoy with salad or home-made flatbread (see recipe.)

Hints & tips

Try a variety of vegetables - courgette, cauliflower, broccoli, celery, leek, sweetcorn, carrot, beetroot, sweet potato, parsnip - even swede.

Also vary the protein - exchange almonds for 100g of white beans or 50g sunflower/pumpkin seeds per person. Crumble feta on at the end. If you can't get a variety of rice, simple brown or red rice is as delicious!

If using fresh poultry (organic if possible and not stored even for one day) cut into small pieces in place of the almonds. Add to the pan at the same time as the onion. **Make sure the meat is fully cooked before serving.**

'Sweet & Sour Sauce'

Ingredients -

For 2 or 4 people -

200g or 400g	Butter beans
60ml or 120ml	Oats - ground
2 or 4	Spring onions
15ml or 30ml	Sesame oil
2 or 4	Red, yellow or orange peppers
2 or 4 cloves	Fresh garlic
3 or 6 cms	Fresh ginger
1 or 2 small	Fresh chilli
45ml or 90ml	Agave nectar
45ml or 90ml	Apple juice
30ml or 60ml	Beetroot juice
150 or 300ml	Light 'stock'

Method

Preheat the oven to 220°c. Drain the butter beans and put in a bowl. Add the ground oats and a pinch of sea salt and ground black pepper. Mash together and form into small balls.

Put the balls on a greased oven tin and cook in the oven for 15 mins, turning once, until lightly browned.

Finely chop the spring onions and add to a pan or wok and fry in the oil while you prepare the pepper. Cut peppers into small chunks, add to pan. Continue to fry for 2-3 mins.

Prepare garlic and ginger by finely dicing, sprinkle with sea salt, crush with the back of a knife. Finely chop chilli, removing seeds. Stir into the pan or wok for a min. Don't let burn!

Stir in the agave, then the apple and beetroot juices. Pour in the stock.

Bring the sauce to the boil and continue to boil for 5-6 mins to reduce. Remove from the heat and season.

Stir in the cooked butter bean balls to coat evenly in the sauce. Or simply spoon the sauce over. Sprinkle with organic sesame seeds and torn fresh coriander before serving.

Try this sauce as part of a meal with 'Spring Rolls', 'Sweet Chilli Dipping Sauce', rice or noodles.

Hints & tips

Without the addition of agave, apple juice and beetroot juice this would be similar to a 'Sichuan-style Sauce.'

Other vegetable options include - beansprouts, waterchestnuts, pak choi, baby corn, broccoli, cabbage, peas, carrots, mangetout, sugar snap peas, courgette or red onion.

Try toasted sunflower seeds on top!

If using fresh poultry (organic if possible and not stored even for one day) saute finely cubed pieces and use only half the beans. When cooked, stir into the bean mix. **Make sure the meat is fully cooked before serving.**

'Gram Flour Pizza'

Ingredients -

For 2 or 4 people -

160g or 320g	Gram flour
250ml or 500ml	Filtered water
1 or 2 sprigs	Fresh basil
1 or 2	Onion
1 or 2	Green pepper
15ml or 30ml	Rapeseed oil
1 or 2 cloves	Fresh garlic
2 or 4	Spring onions
¼ or ½	Cauliflower
50g or 100g	Sugar snap peas or mangetout
30ml or 60ml	Rapeseed oil (for frying)

Method

To make the pizza base, sieve the flour and a good pinch of sea salt into a bowl. Gradually add the water into the bowl, stirring all the time, until smooth. Tear in the fresh basil. Cover and set aside.

Preheat the oven to 220°c. Peel and quarter the onion, chop the green pepper and toss in oil. Roast for 10 mins. Prepare garlic by finely dicing. Sprinkle with sea salt, and crush with the back of a knife. Add to the tin.

Once the garlic is ready, add roasted ingredients to a blender along with a tiny dash of water. Cover and blend until smooth. Put to one side.

Cut the cauliflower into small florets (including the stalks,) slice the spring onion into ½ cm pieces. Add the cauliflower, spring onion and whole peas to the oven tin. Stir to coat in the seasoned oil. Cook for 10 mins until they just soften.

Heat a medium frying pan (or smaller for a doughy base) and brush generously with rapeseed oil. Pour ½ (or ¼) of the batter into the pan and cook at a low temperature until the bottom is brown and the top has set.

Repeat until each base has cooked. Spread the pepper pesto evenly between each and top with the vegetables. Return to oven for 10 mins.

Hints & tips

In place of all gram flour (chickpea), try replacing with half-and-half lentil flour, rice flour or ground oats! Follow the packet instructions.

Other topping ideas - organic courgette, fine green beans, broccoli and roasted herbs such as thyme or finely chopped rosemary. Also crumble with feta cheese before serving.

If using fresh poultry (organic if possible and not stored even for one day) grill and slice or saute cubes before topping the pizza. Alternatively, adapt the 'Neatballs' recipe. **Make sure the meat is fully cooked before serving.**

'Panzanella Salad'

Ingredients -

For 2 or 4 people -

½ or 1 whole	Homemade soda bread (see recipe)
30ml or 60ml	Rapeseed oil
1 or 2 cloves	Fresh garlic
1 or 2	Red onion
1 or 2	Carrots
100g or 200g	Kidney beans
¼ or ½ whole	Broccoli
½ or 1 whole	Red pepper
30ml or 60ml	Olive oil
1 or 2 handfuls	Fresh basil
1 or 2 head	Romaine lettuce
Optional -	
¼ or ½	Cucumber

Method

Firstly, prepare the soda bread following the recipe in this book. Leave the oven on to keep warm. Once bread is cool, tear into 2cm pieces. Cut the garlic clove(s) in half and rub on the soda bread pieces - plus onto the inside of your salad serving bowl.

Toss the bread pieces in the rapeseed oil and season with unrefined sea salt and ground black pepper. Put into a greased oven tin and return to the oven for 10 mins, shaking after 5 mins so they brown evenly but still stay a little soft inside.

While the croutons cook, roughly chop the red onion and carrots and gently fry using the remaining seasoned oil for 2-3 mins until they just start to soften. Remove from heat.

Drain beans, chop broccoli and peppers into small pieces. Stir into pan.

Pour the olive oil and tear the basil into the pan. Season and stir well.

Wash and cut the salad leaves into bite sized pieces. Toss all ingredients together in the garlicky bowl.

Once the croutons are ready allow to cool before using so they don't wilt the leaves. Serve before the croutons start to soften.

Top with chopped cucumber if using.

Hints & tips

Alternatively, soak the bread pieces in a seasoned root vegetable stock. To turn bread into crunchy croutons for soup and salads, keep in the oven for an extra 2-3 mins until crispy.

For a more filling meal, add crumbled goats cheese or fresh buffalo mozzarella. Other leaves you could try include - rocket or watercress. Serve with a large dollop of pesto.

If using fresh poultry (organic if possible and not stored even for one day) saute small pieces in place of the beans. Once cooked, add the onion and carrots to the pan. **Make sure the meat is fully cooked before serving.**

‘Chimichangas’

Ingredients -

For 2 or 4 people -

2 or 4	Red onion
15ml or 30ml	Rapeseed oil
2 or 4	Orange, red, yellow or green peppers
1 or 2 cloves	Fresh garlic
1 or 2 small	Fresh chilli
200g or 400g	Beans - mix of kidney & cannelini
45ml or 90ml	Beetroot juice
2 or 4 sheets	Filo pastry - de frosted (approx. 24cm by 50cm)
30ml or 60ml	Olive oil

Serve with Organic red rice.

Method

Roughly chop the red onion and gently fry in the rapeseed oil for 2-3 mins until they just start to soften.

Cut peppers to the same size as the onion and add to the pan. Continue to fry gently for a further 2 mins.

Prepare garlic by finely dicing, sprinkle with sea salt, crush with the back of a knife. Finely chop chilli, removing seeds. Stir into pan for 1 min.

Drain and stir the beans into the pan. Add the beetroot juice and boil for two minutes to reduce slightly. Season to taste. Grease an oven tray.

Preheat the oven to 200°c. Cut the filo sheets in half width-ways. Brush half of the pieces with ½ olive oil, lay the remaining pieces on top. You should end up with one layer of oiled filo pastry per person.

Pile 100ml of filling in the centre of each sheet. You may have some filling leftover to serve as a side-order.

Fold side ends into the centre. Then fold the bottom end up and over the filling, brushing the top open edge with oil. Roll up and over the oiled edge. Place ‘Chimichanga’ on its seam on the tray. Brush with ½ oil.

Repeat with remaining sheets and bake in oven for 15 mins until golden.

Hints & tips

In place of the filo pastry, try using wholewheat flatbread tortillas (remember to steam them first!)

‘Bolognese’ makes an alternative filling. And if you bake in the oven drizzled in bechamel or ‘Faux Mato’ sauce, the Chimichangas would be better known as ‘Enchiladas’!

Crumbled feta on top or inside: yum!

If using fresh poultry (organic if possible and not stored even for one day) cut into small pieces in place of the beans. Add to the pan at the same time as the onion. **Make sure the meat is fully cooked before serving.**

'Stuffed Crust'

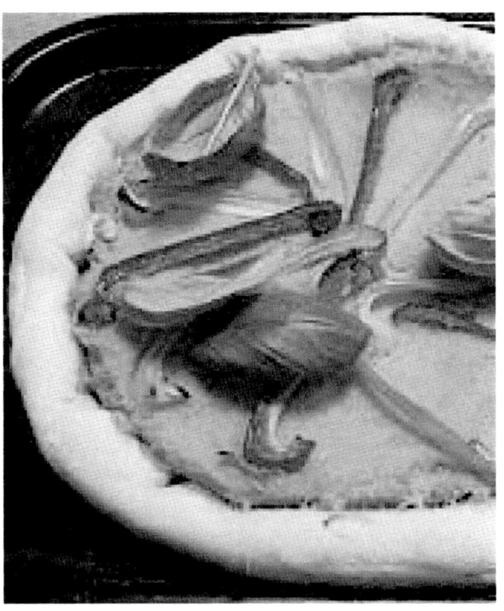

Ingredients -

For 2 or 4 people -

1 or 2 large	Sweet potato
20g or 40g	Butter
300g or 600g	Plain flour
45ml or 90ml	Rapeseed oil
5ml or 10ml	Unrefined sea salt
220ml or 440ml	Filtered water
60g or 120g	Spread-able fresh goats cheese
2 or 4	Organic yellow and red peppers

Optional - Add a little finely chopped fresh chilli or crushed fresh garlic to the mashed potato topping.

Method

Boil kettle. Peel and dice the sweet potato, add to a pan and cover with water. Bring to the boil for 10 mins until soft. Retain and freeze any cooking liquor for future stocks. Put the potato back in the pan for 2 mins on a low heat to 'dry out' the water.

Mash the potato until smooth. Put in a bowl with a good pinch of seasoning. Melt the butter and stir into the potato. Allow to cool. Meanwhile -

Put the flour, oil and sea salt into a mixing bowl and stir together by hand. If using a food processor, mix slowly together - adding just enough water until a dough is formed.

Flour your work surface and place the dough on top. Gently knead the dough for 2-3 mins until flexible. Dust a rolling pin with flour. Divide the dough into 2 (or 4) and roll out thinly to the size of 2-3 mm thick.

Put the dough into a cold frying pan. Scatter the fresh goats cheese 2 cms all around the edge of the dough. Roll the edge up tightly up and over the cheese. Preheat oven to 180 °c.

Put the frying pan on the hob and turn the heat to high. Dry-fry each pizza base on the 'un-stuffed' side for 2-3 mins until light brown. Lift the pizza base onto an oven tray.

Top with the mashed potato. Slice the peppers and arrange on top. Bake in the oven for 30 mins until crispy.

Hints & tips

For another option in place of the goats cheese - spread quark or finely crumbled feta into the stuffed crust.

Top with a selection of vegetables - try sliced courgette, red onion or leeks. And vary the pizza topping - mashed parsnip or a mixture of swede and carrots also works nicely.

If using fresh poultry (organic if possible and not stored even for one day) grill and slice or saute cubes before topping the pizza. Alternatively, adapt the 'Neatballs' recipe. **Make sure the meat is fully cooked before serving.**

'Korma'

Ingredients -

For 2 or 4 people -

100g or 200g	Brown rice
30ml or 60ml	Rapeseed oil
25g or 50g	Wild rice
1 or 2	Onions
1 or 2	Pepper
50g or 100g	Mangetout
50g or 100g	Babycorn
50g or 100g	Flaked almonds
2 or 4 cloves	Fresh garlic
3 or 6 cms	Fresh ginger
2 or 4 sprigs	Fresh curry leaves
1 or 2 small	Fresh chilli
30ml or 60ml	Tahini - light
100 or 200ml	Double cream
200 or 400ml	Almond milk

Method

Lightly fry the brown rice on the hob with ½ rapeseed oil. Cover the rice with two parts water and add a sprig of basil. Stir once, return to the boil then cover and simmer for 30 mins. After 15 mins, stir in the wild rice.

Meanwhile, roughly chop the onion and gently fry in ½ oil in a large pan for 2-3 mins. Cut the pepper into pieces the same size as the onion.

Cut both the mangetout and baby-corn into thirds and add all vegetables - plus the flaked almonds to the pan. Stir and continue to fry gently for another 2-3 mins.

Prepare garlic and ginger by finely dicing, sprinkle with sea salt, crush with the back of a knife. Finely chop the curry leaves and chilli, removing seeds. Stir all spices into the pan for a min. Don't let them burn!

Spoon the tahini into the vegetables and mix well to combine. Pour in the cream and almond milk and increase the heat slightly but do not allow to boil - or the cream may separate.

Season to taste with unrefined sea salt and ground black pepper. Partly cover the korma pan with a lid and continue to simmer until the rice is ready and the vegetables are 'al dente'. Serve while still hot.

Hints & tips

Also serve with homemade poppadom, samosa and raita (see recipes.)

To make this meal more substantial, add cubed fresh organic paneer (curd cheese) or parboiled root vegetables.

Try roasting the almonds with seasoning before adding to the pan - or add sunflower or pumpkin seeds.

If using fresh poultry (organic if possible and not stored even for one day) cut into small pieces in place of the almonds. Add to the pan at the same time as the onion. **Make sure the meat is fully cooked before serving.**

'Breakfast Pizza'

Ingredients -

For 2 or 4 people -

<u>For the pizza dough -</u>

250g or 500g	Plain flour
2 or 4	Organic egg yolks
300 or 600ml	Almond milk

<u>Optional -</u>

1 or 2 handful	Fresh basil

<u>Top with -</u>

250g or 500g	Homemade 'Faux Mato' baked beans
200g or 400g	Homemade 'Sausages' (see recipes.)

Method

Start by preparing the homemade 'Sausages' (see recipe) until you reach the part where you have added herbs. Form several 'mini sausages', place on an oven tray, refrigerate.

Preheat oven to 220°c and lightly grease 1 (or 2) medium baking tins. Sieve the flour into a mixing bowl and add a pinch (or 2) of unrefined sea salt and ground black pepper.

Beat the egg yolks in a small ramekin then add the milk. Stir well to combine. Pour the liquid straight into the mixing bowl and stir together to make a batter. Add herbs if using.

Once smooth, pour the batter into the prepared tin(s.) Make sure the batter is evenly spread in the tin. Put batter in the oven for 20 mins until the dough begins to firm. After 5 mins, add the sausages for 15 mins.

Once the sausages are in the oven, prepare homemade 'Baked Beans.'

Take the tin and tray from the oven and top the dough with 'Faux Mato' baked beans. Spread out to cover the base as though using a pizza puree. Arrange the homemade 'mini sausages' on top and drizzle with olive oil.

Return to the oven for another 10 mins until the dough becomes crispy and golden brown. Serve hot.

Hints & tips

You'll probably make far too many mini sausages - if so, simply serve them alongside the breakfast pizza!

If you really like eggs, as this pizza cooks, make a batch of scrambled eggs (see recipe.) And of course, serve with homemade ketchup.

Try other low-histamine toppings!

If using fresh poultry (organic if possible and not stored even for one day) saute finely cubed pieces and use only half the lentils. When cooked, stir into the lentil mix. **Make sure the meat is fully cooked before serving.**

What About Meat & Fish?

I didn't set out to deliberately write a vegetarian cookbook. However few animal products are sufficiently low in histamine. For instance, as they decay fish and seafood quickly acquire high levels of the bacteria that produce histamine: I find that it is often recommended that you eat fish within 30 minutes of it being killed and gutted.

The only animal products that might have low enough histamine levels are poultry, which don't need to be hung to become tender enough to eat. Nonetheless, the poultry must be fresh and eaten on the same day it's purchased.

Neither frozen, or previously frozen - its difficult to determine for sure how many times a product has been frozen and defrosted.

As these histamine levels are so hard to determine the decision to eat poultry must be yours, and you *must* take responsibility for its freshness. Please choose organic where possible.

If another reason to avoid meat and fish were needed, animal proteins often contain more histidine than non-meat proteins. Histidine is the amino acid that converts into histamine within the body.

Meat is considered as a great source of protein, yet we may need to eat less protein than people generally think. There's protein in many other foods you may not immediately think of including pulses, grains and vegetables. When eating plant-derived proteins however, it's important to include a variety in your daily diet to ensure that you receive a 'complete protein.'

The good news though, is that we think all the recipes in this book are delicious even without meat or fish. I've served them to former meat-lovers, and their verdict is that they're just as good without. But if you absolutely *must* have your poultry-fix, several recipes can be easily adapted.

Occasionally, people on a meat-free diet might have trouble getting enough vitamin B_{12}, as this is most commonly obtained from animal products. In fact, having too much B_{12} can store histamine within our bodies, so it should also be consumed with care. I personally use a fortified non-hydrogenated dairy-free spread* for my daily B_{12} requirements, and I ask my doctor to monitor my B_{12} levels with a blood test at my regular check-ups.

* Please see 'Resources' page for details.

Side Dishes

'Mayo & 'Slaw'

Ingredients
For 2 or 4 people -

1 or 2	Organic egg yolk
5ml or 10ml	Apple juice
120 or 240ml	Rapeseed oil
Or -	
120 or 240ml	Olive oil
To combine to make coleslaw -	
200g or 400g	Cabbage
1 or 2 medium	Carrot
½ or 1 small	Onion

For variety - use red or green cabbage, or red onions (remember that white onions can be strong!) Some people prefer to add a little glucose to sweeten or more oil to thin.

Method

When making mayonnaise (mayo) it is important to add the oil very slowly while you whisk very quickly. Ask a friend to help pour the oil and place the bowl on a damp tea towel to stop it from moving around too much.

Interestingly, it is the egg yolk that binds the ingredients together and thickens the mayo. If, after you've added the oil, the mixture hasn't thickened enough try adding another egg yolk and another portion of oil.

To make the mayo - Whisk together the egg yolk and apple juice in a bowl. Continue to whisk as you add a thin steady stream of oil very slowly. If the mayo seems to be too thick, whisk in 5ml of water at a time until you get to the thickness you require.

Season to taste with sea salt and ground black pepper. Even garlic!

To make the coleslaw - Place the mayo in a bowl. If using added ingredients such as glucose, herbs or garlic, whisk them into the mayo now.

Wash and carefully grate the cabbage, carrots and onion. If using a food processor, always follow the manufacturer's instructions.

Stir the vegetables into the mayo, coat evenly. Refrigerate or serve immediately. **Take care with raw egg.**

Hints & tips

Homemade mayonnaise has a milder taste than many store-bought varieties. You can of course, add ingredients such as fresh herbs and spices, or other vegetables for variety.

Use this mayonnaise in sandwich fillings, stirred through pasta salads, or even as a dip for swede chips! Always be careful to refrigerate straight away and eat as soon as possible.

'Ketchup'

Ingredients

For 2 or 4 people -

1 or 2	Red pepper
1 or 2	Red onion
1 or 2	Carrot
1 or 2 sticks	Celery
15ml or 30ml	Rapeseed oil
2 or 4 cloves	Fresh garlic
3 or 6 cms	Fresh ginger
½ or 1 small	Fresh chilli
1 or 2 handfuls	Fresh parsley
125ml or 250ml	Light 'stock' (see recipe)

Method

Preheat oven to 220°c. Peel and quarter the onion, roughly chop the red pepper, carrots and celery - toss in oil. Season with a pinch of sea salt and ground black pepper. Roast in the hot oven for 20 minutes.

Meanwhile, prepare garlic and ginger by finely dicing. Sprinkle with sea salt, and crush with the back of a knife. Finely chop the chilli. Add garlic, ginger and chilli to the vegetables in the pan for the last 2-3 minutes.

Put all the roasted ingredients into a blender - plus the herbs and ½ of the stock - cover and blend until smooth.

Sieve the pepper sauce into a pan, with the remaining stock. Season to taste with sea salt and ground black pepper. Stir and then simmer for 10 minutes until the sauce thickens and reduces by ½.

Depending on the dish you intend to serve the ketchup with, either serve while still warm or allow to cool in the fridge. This ketchup does not contain vinegar or sugar so will not keep for more than a day or two.

If you do plan to serve the ketchup from the fridge, pour into a sterilised jar and seal with a tight lid. See instructions on to do this in the 'Hints & tips' section for 'Tea-time Jam.'

Hints & tips

Ketchup is a traditional name for sauce. It doesn't have to be tomato! Vary the colour of the ketchup with different coloured peppers - and experiment with fresh herbs!

Use this Ketchup as a condiment served with your favourite meals - or do not sieve and only simmer for 2-3 mins to serve with pasta or as soup.

'Red Lentil Dhal'

Ingredients

For 2 or 4 people -

125g or 250g	Red lentils
½ or 1 litre	Light 'stock' (defrosted)
2 or 4 sprigs	Fresh curry leaves
1 or 2	Red onion
15ml or 30ml	Rapeseed oil
1 or 2 cloves	Fresh garlic
3 or 6 cms	Fresh ginger

Experiment with different lentils; green, brown - even puy. Perhaps also add a little chopped fresh chilli to the lentils as they cook.

Method

Place red lentils in a pan and cover with the stock, bring to the boil and then simmer for 20 minutes.

As the stock simmers, finely chop curry leaves and add to the lentils.

Then dice onion finely. Heat oil in a pan and cook the onion, stirring, for two minutes.

Prepare garlic and ginger by finely dicing then sprinkle with sea salt, and crush with the back of a knife.

Add the garlic and ginger to the onion for a further minute. Stir well.

Once the lentils have cooked and most (but not all) of the stock has absorbed, stir through the onions, garlic and ginger. If required, add a little more hot stock or water.

Continue to heat lentils through for 2-3 minutes. Be careful to keep stirring so that the lentils do not stick to the bottom.

Serve this dhal as a side order with your favourite low histamine curry (for more ideas, see recipes in this book) along with chapatti, poppadoms and rice.

Hints & tips

Alternatively, for a warming supper, add extra hot stock to thin the dhal to a soup consistency.

Or for sandwich fillings, use half quantities of stock, garlic and ginger. Blitz' until smooth with a hand blender. Serve with homemade soda bread or pitta and salad vegetables.

‘Fresh Salsa Dips’

Ingredients

For 2 or 4 people -
10ml or 20ml Apple juice
10ml or 20ml Oils (see method)
Plus -
25g or 50g Mango
½ or 1 small Red onion
25g or 50g Sweetcorn
Or -
25g or 50g Mangetout
2 or 4 Spring onions
1.5 or 3 cms Fresh ginger
Or -
2 or 4 handfuls Fresh parsley
2 or 4 handfuls Fresh mint
2 or 4 handfuls Fresh basil

Method

For the fruity mango salsa -

Mix together the base of apple juice and *rapeseed* oil into a small glass jar. Peel and finely dice the mango and red onion, drain the sweetcorn.

Add to a small jar with the juice and oil. Season with sea salt and black pepper. Shake well.

For the mangetout salsa -

Mix together the base of apple juice and *sesame* oil into a small glass jar. Finely slice the mangetout and spring onions.

Prepare the ginger by finely dicing. Sprinkle with a little glucose and crush with the back of a knife. Add to a small jar with the juice and oil. Season with sea salt and black pepper. Shake well.

For the herb salsa -

Mix together the base of apple juice and *olive* oil into a small glass jar.

Prepare the herbs by finely chopping and crush together in a pestle and mortar with a little sea salt.

Add to a small jar with the juice and oil. Season with sea salt and black pepper. Shake well.

Hints & tips

See the ‘Burger in a Bun’ recipe for another fresh salsa recipe - with red apple, spring onion and coriander.

The herb salsa is my version of a ‘Salsa Verde’ - other herbs you could try include chervil and rosemary.

For the other two salsa, add fresh coriander and/or crushed garlic.

'Garlic Bread Pizza'

Ingredients

For 2 or 4 people -

300g or 600g	Brown flour
45ml or 90ml	Rapeseed oil
5ml or 10ml	Unrefined sea salt
225 or 450ml	Filtered water
2 or 4	Red onion
50g or 100g	Butter
2 or 4 cloves	Fresh garlic
1 or 2 sprigs	Fresh rosemary
2 or 4 sprigs	Fresh basil to serve

Method

Preheat the oven to 180°c. Put the flour, oil and sea salt into a food processor (if using) and mix slowly together - adding filtered water until a dough is formed. Otherwise, mix by hand in a bowl with a fork.

Flour your work surface and place the dough on top. Gently knead the dough for 2-3 mins until flexible. Dust a rolling pin with flour. Divide the dough into 2 (or 4) and roll out thinly to the size of your frying pan.

Put the frying pan on the hob and turn the heat to high. Fry the rolled pizza bases on each side (without oil) until light brown.

Slice the onion into strips. Heat the butter in a pan - add the onion once the butter has melted. Fry for 2 mins until they only just begin to soften.

Finely chop the rosemary and stir with the onion into the pan for 2 mins. Prepare garlic by finely dicing. Sprinkle with sea salt, and crush with the back of a knife. Add to the pan.

Put the pizza base onto an oven tray, brush with the garlic butter and arrange the red onion and rosemary on top. Bake in the oven for 10 minutes.

Season with sea salt and ground black pepper. Add torn basil and serve.

Hints & tips

Replace the butter with olive oil - but do not heat too high.

Experiment with toppings - you can use this garlic sauce on many of your favourite pizzas. Do try a mixture of the red pepper pesto (see recipe) and this garlic butter - teamed with fresh buffalo mozzarella and torn basil leaves. Simple but tasty.

'Sweet Potato Cakes'

Ingredients

For 2 or 4 people -

2 or 4 medium	Sweet potato
25g or 50g	Brown flour
25g or 50g	Butter
15ml or 30ml	Olive oil
Plus -	
125g or 250g	Brussels sprouts
1 or 2	Red onion
Or -	
2 or 4	Spring onions
½ or 1 small	Fresh chilli
Or -	
40g or 80g	Flaked almonds
10g or 20g	Glucose powder

Method

For all sweet potato cakes -

Peel and grate the potatoes. Using either a clean tea towel (with no noticeable detergent odours) or your hands, squeeze out as much liquid as possible. Place the potato in a bowl.

Melt butter and stir into the bowl. Sieve the brown flour and stir also.

Preheat the oven to 220°c.

Plus for the brussels sprouts -

Finely slice the onion, peel sprouts and slice thinly. Stir into the potato mix. Season.

Plus for the spring onions -

Finely slice the spring onion, finely chop the chilli. Add ½ of olive oil. Stir into the potato mix. Season.

Plus for the almonds -

Crush the almond into small pieces (or buy ready ground.) Stir into the potato mix along with the glucose.

For all sweet potato cakes -

Divide mix into 2 (or 4) and grease a ramekin. Press the mix tightly into the bottom and then tip upside down out on a baking sheet. Cover and cook in the oven for 15 minutes.

Hints & tips

An unusual way to cook brussels sprouts - or other greens - serve them with a traditional family meal. Accompany the spring onion and chilli potato cakes with the dipping sauce on the 'Dips' recipe page. Or stack the rosti with pate between.

Almond sweet potato cakes can be served with apple sauce (see recipe.)

‘Cornbread’

Ingredients

For 2 or 4 people -

180g or 360g	Self Raising brown flour
120g or 240g	Cornmeal (ground polenta)
15ml or 30ml	Glucose (optional)
5ml or 10ml	Unrefined sea salt
15ml or 30ml	Rapeseed oil
1 or 2	Organic egg yolk
330 or 660ml	Almond milk
50g or 100g	Butter
1 or 2 sprigs	Fresh sage
100g or 200g	Sweetcorn

An extra sprinkle (or 2) of cornmeal.

Method

Sift the flour into a bowl. Add the cornmeal (ground polenta), glucose (if using; almond milk is often sweet) and a pinch of sea salt. Stir well to combine. Preheat oven to 200°c.

Grease a small (or medium) oven tin with the oil. Sprinkle the tin with a thin layer of extra cornmeal to add a crunchy texture when cooked!

Put the greased tin into the oven while you prepare the remaining ingredients. The cornmeal will brown.

Stir in the egg yolk with a fork until well mixed. Slowly add the almond milk, stirring all the time to form a creamy yet still-a-bit-lumpy batter.

Melt the butter in a small pan on the hob and stir into the cornmeal mix. Finely chop the sage and fold into the mix along with the sweetcorn.

Carefully pour the cornmeal mixture into the hot oven tin. Bake for 15 - 20 minutes (uncovered) until the top is springy to the touch.

Test the cornbread is ready by pricking with a cocktail stick - it should come out clean. If not, return to the oven for a couple more minutes.

When ready, allow to cool before slicing into wedges. Serve as a side.

Hints & tips

Options are plentiful - add chopped fresh chilli (especially jalapeno), mixed colour peppers - plus different herbs, garlic, small cubes of feta, red onion and broccoli, leek, peas...!

For sweet cornbread - replace salt with double quantities of glucose, add chopped apples, pears or fig.

Cornbread can top cottage pies, go in stuffing or dumplings (see recipes.)

'Sage & Onion Stuffing'

Ingredients

For 2 or 4 people -

1 or 2	Onion
15ml or 30ml	Rapeseed oil
1 or 2 cloves	Fresh garlic
1 or 2 sticks	Celery
1 or 2 handfuls	Fresh sage
50g or 100g	Homemade bread crumbs (see recipe)
1 or 2	Organic egg yolks

Try replacing half of the bread-crumbs with ground oats.

Method

Finely chop the onion and celery and gently fry in oil for 2 minutes.

Prepare the garlic by dicing. Then sprinkle with sea salt, and crush with the back of a knife. Add to the onions and celery for a minute.

Tear the sage into small pieces and stir into the onion and garlic.

Remove from the heat and stir in the breadcrumbs and season to taste with sea salt and ground black pepper.

Beat the egg with a fork and add to the breadcrumb mix. Press together with wet hands to mould into shape.

Try making small stuffing balls or spread out evenly into a greased small oven tin (1 inch thick) to serve cut into slices. If serving roasted in the oven, add a dash of 'stock' first.

Preheat the oven to 180°c. Place onto a greased oven tin and roast for 20 minutes or until brown and crispy.

Serve stuffing balls alongside meals such as Escalopes, Lentil Loaf or Sausages (see recipes.)

Alternatively, try using to stuff kievs or burgers (see recipes.) If so, follow the individual recipe cooking times.

Hints & tips

Serve this savoury side order at Sunday lunch, Thanksgiving or Christmas! This recipe makes 2 stuffing balls per person. But they're so delicious, you may want to make double!

Other flavour options include - chopped apple, leeks, crushed seeds or almonds and herbs such as basil, rosemary, thyme or parsley.

'Potato Salad'

Ingredients

For 2 or 4 people -

50g or 100g	Sunflower seeds
5ml or 10ml	Olive oil
1 or 2 sprigs	Fresh curry leaves
1 or 2 large	Sweet potato
1 or 2	Red onion
2 or 4 sticks	Celery
1 or 2	Organic egg yolk
5ml or 10ml	Apple juice
120 or 240ml	Rapeseed oil
1 or 2	Apple

Method

Preheat the oven to 175°c and place a small ovenproof tin in to heat up.

Mix the seeds in a bowl with the olive oil. Season with a little sea salt and ground black pepper. Spread out in a tin and then into the oven for 15 mins. After 10 mins, shake the seeds and add finely chopped herbs.

Meanwhile, wash and peel the sweet potatoes. Roughly cut into chunks and put into a pan on the hob. Cover with filtered water, bring to the boil for 10 mins. To take the sharp taste away from the onion and celery, finely dice them both. Add to a colander and place over the pan of sweet potatoes as it boils.

Once the seeds, potatoes and vegetables are ready, drain and allow to cool as you make the mayonnaise.

To make the mayo - Whisk together the egg yolk and apple juice in a bowl. Continue to whisk as you add a thin steady stream of oil very slowly. If the mayo seems to be too thick, whisk in a tsp of water at a time until you get to the thickness you require.

Finely chop the apple - stir with the potatoes, vegetables and most of the seeds into the mayo. Place in a dish and sprinkle with remaining seeds.

Hints & tips

For advice on making mayo see the 'Mayo & Slaw' recipe in the book. Remember to eat straight away.

You can make a more simple potato salad and not include all the options here. Alternatively, vary the ingredients to your tastes - try chopped peppers or mango and experiment with fresh herbs and different seeds.

'Sides - Leeks I'

Ingredients

For 2 or 4 people -

<u>For the filo leeks -</u>

2 or 4	Leeks
15ml or 30ml	Rapeseed oil
1 or 2 sheets	Organic filo pastry (defrosted)
10g or 20g	Sesame seeds
1 or 2 handfuls	Fresh tarragon
5ml or 10ml	Agave nectar

<u>For the buttered leeks -</u>

2 or 4	Leeks
25g or 50g	Butter
1 or 2 sprigs	Fresh thyme
40g or 80g	Flaked almonds

Method

For the filo leeks -

Preheat oven to 200°c. Wash, top and tail leeks but don't peel. Add to an oven tin and coat with oil, place into the oven for 15 mins. Cool.

Place a piece of kitchen film on your worktop as big as the filo sheets. Cut the filo sheets into 8 (or 16) and brush with a little oil. Sprinkle the fresh tarragon and seeds as a layer on top of each sheet. Season.

Carefully peel the outer layer from each leek. Cut into 4 strips. Lay each strip at the corner of each filo sheet. Roll the filo and the leek together tightly on a diagonal (cigar-shaped.)

Place each filo leek its seam on a baking sheet. Brush with agave and sprinkle with remaining seeds. Bake in the oven for 15 mins until golden.

For the buttered leeks -

Wash, peel, top and tail leeks and cut into ½ cm rings. Melt the butter in a small pan on the hob. Stir the leeks into the butter and reduce the heat to medium-low. Season.

Finely chop the herbs and add with the almonds into the pan. Cover the pan with a lid and simmer for 5 mins or until the leeks have softened.

Hints & tips

A handy snack, the 'filo leeks' make easy party food if cut into smaller lengths. Or to make them more dainty, use baby leeks and leave out the sesame seeds altogether.

Try the 'buttered' method for many vegetable dishes, including - sprouts, cabbage, cauliflower, broccoli, carrots, courgette or spring greens.

'Sides - Leeks II'

Ingredients

For 2 or 4 people -

<u>For the baked leeks -</u>

1 or 2 large	Leeks
15ml or 30ml	Rapeseed oil
1 or 2 large	Sweet potato
10g or 20g	Butter
20ml or 40ml	Almond milk
40g or 80g	Flaked almonds

<u>For the braised leeks -</u>

2 or 4 small	Leeks
15ml or 30ml	Rapeseed oil
50ml or 100ml	Light 'stock'
10g or 20g	Butter
25ml or 50ml	Double cream

Method

For the baked leeks -

Preheat oven to 200°c. Wash, top and tail leeks but don't peel. Add to an oven tin and coat with oil, place into the oven for 15 mins. Cool.

Boil the kettle. Wash and cube sweet potatoes, cover with water, bring to the boil and simmer for 15 mins.

Drain the sweet potatoes. Mash with butter and almond milk. Season.

When cool, carefully peel the outer layer from each leek. Cut in the centre and then again lengthways to create four equal sized pieces.

Place back in the oven tin on the cut edge. Spread the mash potato over the leeks and sprinkle with almonds.

Bake in the oven for 15 minutes.

For the braised leeks -

Wash and peel the leeks, top and tail and then cut into thin 5cm strips. Heat the rapeseed oil in a pan and gently fry the leeks for 2 minutes. Pour over the 'stock' - cover and simmer for 5 minutes.

Reduce the heat to lowest setting. Stir in the butter and cream. Cook gently until the butter is melted. Be careful that you do not allow to boil.

Hints & tips

Baking, sauteeing or roasting leeks retains and intensifies their flavour.

Mix fresh goats cheese into the sweet potato mash. Or try different mashed root vegetables such as parsnip or swede (or a mixture of both.)

Alternatively, place the baked leeks into a pie case, top with mash potato and cook for 20 minutes.

'Dips'

Ingredients

For 2 or 4 people -

Dipping sauce -	
3 or 6 cms	Fresh ginger
1 or 2 small	Fresh chilli
15ml or 30ml	Agave nectar
60ml or 120ml	Apple juice
2 or 4 sprigs	Fresh coriander
10g or 20g	Sesame seeds
Creamy dip -	
1 or 2	Red onion
15ml or 30ml	Olive oil
1 or 2 sprigs	Fresh thyme
100g or 200g	Cannelini beans (drained)
50ml or 100ml	Double cream

Method

For the dipping sauce -

Prepare ginger by finely dicing. Then sprinkle with sea salt, and crush with the back of a knife.

Finely chop the fresh chilli and put with the ginger into a small bowl. Stir in the agave syrup and slowly add the apple juice - mixing well.

Chop the fresh coriander and add to the bowl, along with the sesame seeds. Mix everything together, season and serve in a small dipping dish.

For the creamy dip -

Roughly chop the red onion and fry very gently in the olive oil for 2 minutes. Finely chop the fresh thyme and stir into the onions for 2-3 mins.

Stir the cannelini beans into the pan. Take the pan off the heat. Blitz to a smooth paste using a hand blender. Stir in the cream and season to taste.

For both -

Serve the dipping sauce with the 'Tempura' vegetables (see recipe.) Spread the creamy dip over grilled crostini (mini bruschetta) or use to dip crudités (crunchy raw vegetables sticks), nachos or swede 'chips' in.

Hints & tips

Experiment with different herbs and beans in this creamy dip. Also try blitzing in other ingredients - such as peppers, feta cheese or garlic.

Another popular dip is 'Hummus' - there are so many variations that there's a recipe page dedicated to it.

Also see the pea guacamole recipe.

'Sides - Sunday Lunch I'

Ingredients

For 2 or 4 people -

<u>Swede & carrot mash -</u>

½ or 1 whole	Swede
2 or 4	Carrots
30ml or 60ml	Rapeseed oil
10g or 20g	Butter

<u>Red cabbage & apple -</u>

½ or 1 whole	Red cabbage
15ml or 30ml	Rapeseed oil
1 or 2	Red apple
125 or 250ml	Apple juice
10g or 20g	Glucose powder

Method

For the swede & carrot mash -

Preheat oven to 200°c. Meanwhile, peel and cut swede in small chunks.

Put the swede in a pan on the hob and cover with filtered water. Bring to the boil then simmer for 5 mins. As the water simmers, cut the carrot to the same size as the swede.

Drain the vegetables, toss in oil and season with a pinch of sea salt. Add to an oven tin and roast for 20 mins. Roughly crush the roast chunks in a bowl with the butter - so that you can still see the different colours.

For the red cabbage & apple -

Wash and slice the cabbage into thin strips, and then in half again. Heat the rapeseed oil in a pan on the hob and stir in the red cabbage.

Cover the pan and reduce the heat to a simmer. Meanwhile, finely slice the apple (no need to peel.) Add to the pan and stir to coat in the oil.

Pour the apple juice into the pan along with the glucose. Stir until the glucose dissolves then simmer part-covered until the juice has absorbed.

Season to taste with unrefined sea salt and black pepper. Serve hot.

Hints & tips

If you prefer the cabbage and apple with more 'bite' - add sliced red onion along with the cabbage and replace the glucose with fresh ginger.

Try the swede and carrot mash with an Irish-inspired meal - fill home-made crepes with the 'Mince & Potato Pie' filling. Also try serving with 'Colcannon Potato Cakes'.

'Sides - Sunday Lunch II'

Ingredients
For 2 or 4 people -

Brussels sprouts gratin -

15ml or 30ml	Rapeseed oil
250g or 500g	Brussels sprouts
20g or 40g	Flake almonds
180 or 360ml	Almond milk
¼ or ½ half	Homemade soda bread 'crumbs'

Bread sauce -

1 or 2	White onion
125ml or 250ml	Almond milk
2 or 4	Fresh bay leaves
¼ or ½ whole	Homemade soda bread 'crumbs'
10g or 20g	Butter

Method

For the brussels sprouts gratin -

Heat the oil in a pan on the hob. Peel the sprouts and cut into quarters. Fry gently for 2-3 mins.

Meanwhile, add the almond flakes to the pan and continue to fry until the brussels sprouts are almost soft.

Pour in the almond milk, bring to the boil for 3-4 mins until sauce has reduced by ½. Preheat oven to 200°c.

Season to taste with sea salt and black pepper. Pour into a greased oven dish and top with breadcrumbs. Bake for 15 mins until golden brown.

For the bread sauce -

Peel and quarter the onion. Add to a saucepan on the hob and cover with the almond milk. Add the bay leaves. Heat the almond milk until it almost boils - then remove from the heat. Cover pan with a lid and let infuse for 45 mins. Then remove the bay leaves and the onion from the pan.

Return the pan to the heat and warm through gently. Add the breadcrumbs to the milk and stir to combine. Keep the temperature low and cook for 5 -7 mins, stirring, until the sauce thickens. At the last moment, stir the butter into the pan. Season.

Hints & tips

To turn the gratin into a more filling dish - add goats cheese to the mixture before pouring in an oven dish. Also try adding fresh chopped thyme.

Rather than throw away the onion (used to flavour the almond milk in the bread sauce,) try roasting in an oven tin with rapeseed oil. The roast onion can then be added to your homemade 'puy' gravy (see recipe.)

'Creamy Bean Mash'

Ingredients -

For 2 or 4 people -

200g or 400g	White beans
<u>With Garlic & Thyme -</u>	
1 or 2	Onion
15ml or 30ml	Olive oil
1 or 2 cloves	Fresh garlic
1 or 2 sprigs	Fresh thyme
<u>Or Creamy Bay leaf -</u>	
1 or 2	Onion
50ml or 100ml	Almond milk
2 or 4 leaves	Fresh bay leaf
<u>Plus for added 'bite' -</u>	
1 or 2 small	Fresh chilli
50g or 100g	Fresh feta cheese

Method

For the Garlic & Thyme mash - Finely chop the onion and add to a saucepan, gently fry with the olive oil for 2-3 minutes until soft.

While the onions cook, prepare garlic by finely dicing, sprinkle with sea salt and crush with the back of a knife. Add to the pan with the thyme (stripped from the stem) for 2 mins.

Drain and add the beans, stir well to coat in oil and herbs. Warm through on the heat - then remove and crush to your preferred texture. Season.

For the Creamy Bay Leaf mash - Peel and quarter the onion. Add to a saucepan on the hob and cover with the almond milk. Add the bay leaves.

Heat the almond milk until it almost boils - then remove from the heat. Cover pan with a lid and let infuse for 45 mins. Then remove the bay leaves and the onion from the pan. Season.

Drain and add the beans, warm through on the heat - then remove and crush to your preferred texture.

For added bite - Finely chop the fresh chilli and add to the pan at the same time as adding the onion. Crumble the feta cheese and stir into the mash just before serving.

Hints & tips

Use in place of mashed potato - such as in 'Bangers & Mash' or to top pies. Also make a great dip (adjust almond milk) - serve with chips and crisps.

Or when making canapes, the mash works well with soda bread bruschetta (thinly sliced as crostini.) Alternatively, try rolling courgette ribbons with the creamy bean filling.

'Pakora & Mango Chutney'

Ingredients

For 2 or 4 people -

1 or 2 cloves	Fresh garlic
1.5 or 3 cms	Fresh ginger
1 or 2 small	Fresh chilli
15ml or 30ml	Rapeseed oil
½ or 1 whole	Mango
10g or 20g	Glucose powder
100ml or 200ml	Apple juice
1 or 2	Red onion
½ or 1 whole	Broccoli
100g or 200g	Gram flour
100ml or 200ml	Filtered water (from the fridge)
Approx. 500ml	Rapeseed oil

Method

Prepare garlic and ginger by finely dicing. Then sprinkle with sea salt, and crush with the back of a knife. Finely slice ½ chilli and add with the garlic and ginger into a pan and fry gently in the oil for 2-3 minutes.

Meanwhile, peel and chop the mango into small chunks. Stir into the hot pan along with the glucose and apple juice. Bring to the boil, simmer un-covered, for 20 mins until thickens.

As the chutney simmers, slice the onion and place in a colander over the simmering pan. Cover with the pan lid, cut the broccoli into small florets and also steam for 3-4 mins.

Make the batter by sieving the flour and a pinch of unrefined sea salt into a bowl. Finely chop the remaining chilli and add to the bowl, stirring well to combine. Slowly pour the water into the flour while whisking.

Heat the oil into a small pan. Drip a small amount of batter into the oil - if the batter quickly rises to the top, it's ready to use. **Be careful when cooking with hot oil.**

Coat broccoli florets in the batter and carefully lower into the oil. The onions should be dipped and lowered in spoonfuls. Fry in small batches for 5-6 mins until light and crispy. Don't let any stick to the bottom. Remove with slotted spoon, and drain well.

Hints & tips

Pakora is a general name for fried snacks - the onion filling is commonly known as 'bhaji'. In place of the broccoli try - cauliflower, cubed sweet potato, paneer cheese - even brussels sprouts on Boxing Day!

I buy gram flour in huge bags from the Asian section of my local super-market. If you don't need that much, health food stores sell small packs.

If using fresh poultry (organic if possible and not stored even for one day) grill and slice or saute cubes before dipping spoonfuls into the batter. **Make sure the meat is fully cooked before serving.**

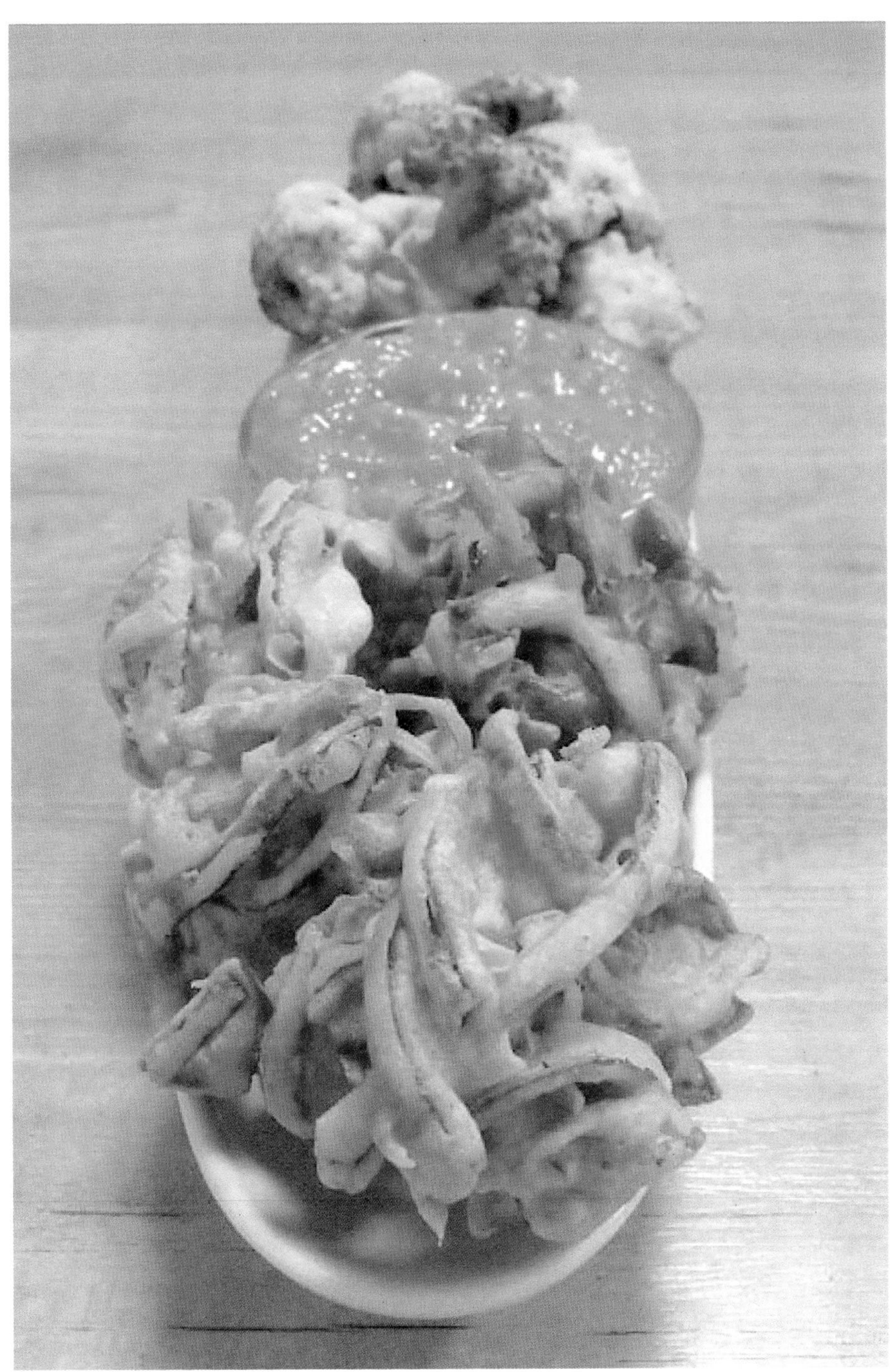

'Sweet Potato Farls'

Ingredients -

For 2 or 4 people -

<u>For the sweet potato farls -</u>

400 or 800g	Sweet potato
120g or 240g	Brown flour
30g or 60g	Butter

<u>For the red onion chutney -</u>

1 or 2 medium	Red onion
½ or 1 whole	Red pepper
15ml or 30ml	Olive oil
¼ or ½ small	Fresh chilli
15ml or 30ml	Beetroot juice
25g or 50g	Glucose powder

Method

Boil kettle. Peel and dice the sweet potato, add to a pan and cover with water. Bring to the boil for 10 mins until soft. Retain and freeze any cooking liquor for future stocks. Put the potato back in the pan for 2 mins on a low heat to 'dry out' the water.

Mash the potatoes until very smooth. Put in a bowl with a good pinch of unrefined sea salt and ground black pepper. Melt the butter and stir into the potato.

Add the flour to the bowl and mix quickly but until well combined. Bring together with your hands to make a dough. Knead lightly for 1-2 mins on a well-floured surface before dividing into 2 (or 4) balls. Press each ball out to approx. ½ cm thick.

Using a sharp knife cut into quarters. Cover with kitchen film until frying.

Gently heat a little rapeseed oil in a small frying pan. Once at a medium temperature, fry the farls in batches for 2-3 mins each side.

For the red onion chutney - Dice the red onion and pepper, gently fry on a low heat with the olive oil. Finely chop chilli, remove the seeds and add to the pan. Continue to fry until onions soften and brown.

Add the juice, glucose and simmer for 4-5 mins - stirring occasionally. Season to taste. Serve hot or cold.

Hints & tips

Sweet potato farls are the ultimate low histamine 'bread' - requiring no baking powder or self raising flour!

Serve with a cooked breakfast, or with your favourite low histamine 'Sandwich' filling - including home-made pate or hummus (see recipes.)

If using fresh poultry (organic if possible and not stored even for one day) grill and slice or saute small cubes and mix with homemade mayo and sweetcorn. **Make sure the meat is fully cooked before serving.**

'Sides - Sweet Potatoes I'

Ingredients -

For 2 or 4 people -

<u>Hassleback Sweet Potatoes -</u>

2 or 4 medium	Sweet potato
30ml or 60ml	Rapeseed oil
1 or 2 pinches	Unrefined sea salt

<u>Sweet Potato Chips & Wedges -</u>

2 or 4 medium	Sweet potato
30ml or 60ml	Rapeseed oil
½ or 1 pinch	Ground black pepper
1 or 2 cloves	Fresh garlic
1 or 2 small	Fresh chilli

Method

Hassleback Sweet Potatoes -

Wash the sweet potatoes (no need to peel if organic.) Chop off the ends.

Cut each sweet potato into thirds. Then with a sharp knife, carefully make several straight cuts into each piece to around ½ of the way down.

Preheat oven to 220°c. Add the oil and sea salt to a large bowl and toss each potato piece in the oil to coat well. Rub the salt into each piece.

Place the potato pieces cut side up on a baking tin. Brush with any leftover oil and sea salt. Cook in the oven for 30 minutes until the skin is crisp.

Sweet Potato Chips & Wedges -

Wash the sweet potatoes (no need to peel if organic.) Chop off the ends.

Cut the potatoes into chunky wedges or thinner rectangular chip shapes. Add the oil and pepper to a large bowl. Prepare garlic by finely dicing then sprinkle with sea salt, crush with the back of a knife. Finely slice the chilli and stir both into the bowl.

Toss the potato shapes to coat in the oil. Put in a single layer on a large baking tray. Cover with the remaining seasoning. Cook in oven for 25 mins, turn once to brown each side.

Hints & tips

Alternatively, interchange the seasonings between the 'Hassleback' potatoes and 'Chip & Wedges.'

Serve the 'Chips & Wedges' with homemade mayonnaise and ketchup.

However, my favourite way to roast delicious thick chips is to use peeled swede, tossed in oil and sea salt. Even better than regular potato!

'Sides - Sweet Potatoes II'

Ingredients -

For 2 or 4 people -
Boulangere Sweet Potato -
2 or 4 medium Sweet potato
1 or 2 Onion
200ml or 400ml Root vegetable stock
Dauphinoise Sweet Potato -
2 or 4 medium Sweet potato
1 or 2 cloves Fresh garlic
150 or 300ml Double cream
Lyonnaise Sweet Potato -
2 or 4 medium Sweet potato
1 or 2 Onion
40g or 80g Butter
2 or 4 sprigs Fresh herbs (see 'hints & tips')

Method

Carefully slice the potatoes thinly using a sharp knife or mandolin. There's no need to peel if organic. Preheat oven to 170 °c. Grease oven dishes - or 1 ramekin per person.

Boulangere Sweet Potato - Start with one layer of potato. Finely slice the onion. Season with a pinch of sea salt and ground black pepper. Add a thin layer of onion. Repeat with alternating layers of potato and onion - finishing with a potato topping.

Pour in the stock, cover tin with foil. Bake covered for 30 mins then uncover for 15 more mins until soft.

Dauphinoise Sweet Potato - Prepare garlic by finely dicing, sprinkle with sea salt and crush with the back of a knife. Toss the potatoes and garlic together in a bowl. Season with a pinch of sea salt and ground black pepper. Mix in the double cream. Layer the potato mix, pressing down to flatten. Use all the double cream. Bake for 40 mins until brown on top.

Lyonnaise Sweet Potato - Finely slice the onion. Melt the butter. Gently fry onions for 2-3 mins until soft. Remove from the heat, tear in the herbs and mix in the potatoes to coat in butter. Season. Layer the potato mix, pressing down to flatten. Drizzle with the remaining butter. Bake for 40 mins until brown on top.

Hints & tips

Alternatively, try using parsnip, swede or beetroot in place of the sweet potato. Even a mix of several!

Also use these sliced root vegetables as toppings to your favourite pies, stews or casseroles.

Try other fresh herbs - thyme, basil, sage and rosemary work well.

'Chappati & Poppadom'

Ingredients -

For 2 or 4 people -

For the chapatti -

100g or 200g	Chapatti flour
1 or 2 pinch	Unrefined sea salt
70ml or 140ml	Warm filtered water
1 or 2 pinch	Ground black pepper

For the poppadom -

100g or 200g	Gram flour
1 or 2 pinch	Unrefined sea salt
1 or 2 pinch	Ground black pepper
1 or 2 cloves	Fresh garlic
50ml or 100ml	Filtered water
250ml or 500ml	Rapeseed oil

Optional -

1 or 2 small	Fresh chilli

Method

For the chapatti - Sieve the chapatti flour into a bowl, add the sea salt and warm water. Stir together and using your hands, bring into a dough.

Lightly flour your workspace and knead the dough for 4-5 mins until smooth. Divide into 2 pieces per person. Roll into thin circles.

Dust one side of each circle with the ground black pepper and press into the dough gently with your hands.

Heat a large frying pan on the hob. Do not add oil. Dry fry each circle at medium temperature, turn once until the surface forms brown spots.

For the poppadom - Sieve the gram flour into a bowl, add the sea salt and ground black pepper. Prepare garlic by finely dicing, sprinkle with sea salt and crush with the back of a knife. Add to the bowl.

Add ¾ of the water, stir together and using your hands, bring into a dough. The dough should not be too wet, but add more water if it still feels dry.

Lightly flour your workspace and knead the dough for 4-5 mins until smooth and flexible. Divide into 3 pieces per person. Roll in thin circles.

Heat the oil in a small saucepan on a medium heat. Carefully put each circle in the oil until golden brown.

Hints & tips

Serve the 'Chappati & Poppadom' along with your favourite curry, raita and chutneys (see recipes.)

Alternatively, stack the 'Chappati & Poppadom' with layers of sliced 'Aloo Tikka', organic peppers, lettuce and 'Raita' (see recipes.)

Also delicious with your favourite pizza or lunchtime sandwich fillings.

'Salsa & Guacamole'

Ingredients -
For 2 or 4 people -
For the salsa -

1 or 2 small	Red onion
10ml or 20ml	Apple juice
½ or 1 whole	Red pepper
¼ or ½ whole	Cucumber
40g or 80g	Green beans
½ or 1 small	Fresh chilli
10ml or 20ml	Olive oil

For the pea guacamole -

1 or 2 cloves	Fresh garlic
½ or 1 small	Fresh chilli
2 or 4	Spring onion
100g or 200g	Green peas
10ml or 20ml	Apple juice
2 or 4 sprigs	Fresh basil

Method

Prepare these 'Salsa & Guacamole' recipes a few mins before serving.

For the salsa -

Finely chop the red onion, add to a bowl and stir to coat into the apple juice. Chop the red pepper, cucumber and green beans to the same size as the onion. Also stir into the bowl.

Cut the chilli very finely and remove the seeds. Stir in the bowl along with the olive oil. Season to taste.

For the pea guacamole -

Prepare garlic by finely dicing, sprinkle with sea salt and crush with the back of a knife. If preferred, gently fry in 15ml oil for a minute to soften.

Cut the chilli very finely, remove the seeds. Stir in a bowl with the garlic.

Finely chop the spring onion and add to the bowl. Pour in the peas and mash the mix roughly with a fork.

Pour in the apple juice and tear with the basil into the bowl. Stir together to mix well. Season to taste.

Also try the salsa recipe featured in the 'Burger in a Bun' recipe.

Hints & tips

Serve these dips with mexican-inspired dishes (see recipes.)

Alternatively, make your own 'Blinis': Put 75g (or 150g) self raising brown flour and 1 (or 2) egg yolks in a bowl. Season with unrefined sea salt and ground black pepper.

Gradually beat in 50 (or 100ml) almond milk to make a thick batter. Heat 10g (or 20g) butter in a frying pan. Gently fry in small batches for 1-2 mins on each side until golden.

'Sides - Green Beans'

Ingredients -

For 2 or 4 people -

For the herby green beans -

125g or 250g	Green beans
2 or 4	Spring onions
¼ or ½ whole	Cabbage
25g or 50g	Butter
2 or 4 sprigs	Fresh basil

For the green beans and almonds -

125g or 250g	Green beans
50g or 100g	Green peas
2 or 4	Shallots
30g or 60g	Flaked almonds
15ml or 30ml	Rapeseed oil

Method

When preparing vegetables for a meal, where possible steam (rather than boil) to retain their valuable vitamins. If you're already cooking lentils or pasta in hot water, simply place a colander on top of the pan, add your vegetables and then cover with the pan lid to create steam.

For the herby green beans - Slice the green beans on a diagonal angle approx. 1 cm long. Also cut the spring onions diagonally but much thinner. Thinly shred the cabbage and in half again lengthways.

Lightly steam the vegetables in a colander over a pan of hot water until they just start to soften.

Meanwhile, gently heat the butter in a pan on the hob. Tear the herbs into the pan, coat in oil and remove from the heat. Stir the steamed vegetables into the pan, season to taste.

For the green beans and almonds - Top, tail and halve the green beans. Add to a colander over hot water with the peas. Lightly steam until they just start to soften.

Meanwhile, slice the shallots and gently fry with the almonds in the oil. Add the steamed vegetables to the pan and stir well to coat in oil.

Season to taste with unrefined sea salt and ground black pepper.

Hints & tips

Replace green beans with mange tout or sugar snap peas. For an Asian-style twist,add fresh ginger, garlic and bruised lemongrass.

Vary the fresh herbs in the herb butter. Use in place of the garlic butter in kievs or garlic bread (see recipes.)

To make the dishes more filling, add crumbled feta or melt goats cheese.

'Creamy Dips'

Ingredients -
For 2 or 4 people -

75ml or 150ml Double cream
<u>Plus -</u>
<u>For the Horseradish sauce -</u>
15ml or 30ml Fresh horseradish
5ml or 10ml Glucose powder
<u>For the Thousand Island dressing -</u>
½ or 1 small Red onion
¼ or ½ Red pepper
3 or 6 cms Cucumber
2.5ml or 5ml Beetroot Juice
<u>For the Ranch dressing -</u>
½ or 1 small White onion
1 or 2 cloves Fresh garlic
1 or 2 sprigs Fresh parsley

Method

For all dressings, firstly -

In a cold bowl lightly whip the cream and glucose with a whisk. Don't over-whip as it becomes grainy.

For the Horseradish sauce -

Peel and finely grate the horseradish root and stir into cream. Finely grind the glucose in a pestle and mortar until the texture of icing sugar.

For the Thousand Island dressing -

Finely chop the red onion and lightly steam in a colander over a pan of boiling water for 2 mins. Cool.

Meanwhile, cut the pepper and cucumber to the same size as the onion. Stir all ingredients with the beetroot juice into the cream.

For the Ranch dressing -

Finely chop the red onion and lightly steam in a colander over a pan of boiling water for 2 mins. Cool.

Meanwhile, prepare garlic by finely dicing. Then sprinkle with sea salt, crush with the back of a knife.

Finely chop the parsley and stir all ingredients into the cream.

Season all of the dressings to taste with unrefined sea salt and ground black pepper. Serve immediately.

Hints & tips

In place of the whipped double cream, try adding the ingredients to the homemade mayo (see recipe.)

Finely chopped fresh chilli and hard-boiled egg yolk can also be added to the Thousand Island dressing.

Goodbye Ready-Meals, Hello Kitchen!

We live in an age when ready-meals are rife. Not only have they had an impact on the amount of histamine we consume, they've also influenced the way many of us think about cooking and eating a family meal.

Perhaps these days some people don't really know how to cook a meal from scratch, or at least they haven't done so in a very long time. We're encouraged to spend money on beautiful kitchens with all mod cons - then what do we do? Pierce the film on a plastic tray and zap it in the microwave!

If you don't regard yourself a natural cook, don't worry: You'll be making fabulous meals in no time. The recipes in this book aren't intended to be complicated fine dining. Throughout the book you'll find a basic repertoire of techniques that you can apply to different meals again and again, such as thickening sauces with a paste of flour and butter (called a Beurre manié,) or freezing 'stock' using the cooking liquor from meals and a variety of vegetables.

I hope that these recipes will inspire you to perfect a couple of dozen favourites that you can rotate for everyday use, and then every now and again get adventurous with something more challenging. Crucially, be patient. Allow yourself some time to learn. You may even find that you really enjoy practicing your new skills.

If this already sounds a bit too daunting, imagine how impressed your guests will be when you invite them over for dinner, or how intrigued your work colleagues will be when you enjoy yet another mouth-watering homemade lunch.

To lighten your load, each ingredient used had to be readily purchased from many major supermarkets or high-street health food chains. Likewise, if a recipe couldn't fit on one page and be explained clearly enough then it just didn't make it into the book.

I know that there are days when you just don't have the time to cook from scratch (that's why ready meals became so ubiquitous after all!) To prepare for those days, I often make large or double quantities and freeze the extra portions (but not poultry.)

Experiment with taking frozen meals to work and defrost them in the fridge in time for lunch. *Don't eat any leftovers older than this though.*

Desserts

'Quick Rhubarb Chutney'

Ingredients

For 2 or 4 people -

2 or 4 stalks	Rhubarb
2 or 4	Carrots
1 or 2	Red onion
1 or 2	Apple
3 or 6 cms	Fresh ginger
250 or 500ml	Apple juice
1 or 2 sprigs	Fresh mint

Try replacing the rhubarb with the same quantity of sweet potato, pear, mango, fig or peaches. Or simply use the 'Faux Mato Bruschetta' topping - with less seasoning - it's quite sweet!

Method

Preheat the oven to 220°c.

Do not take vegetables and fruit out of the fridge too early. Work quickly so that they remain crisp.

Cut the rhubarb into 1 cm widths and dice the carrots, onion and apple.

Prepare ginger by finely dicing. Then sprinkle with sea salt, and crush with the back of a knife. Chop herbs.

Place everything together in a loaf tin. Pour over the apple juice and cover with foil. Roast in the oven for 30 mins, stirring at 10 and 20 mins.

When the carrot is soft, carefully drain the mixture from the cooking liquor. Be sure to save the liquid.

Over a low heat, mash the fruit and vegetables roughly with a fork.

Drizzle a little of the cooking liquor into the roughly mashed pulp. Stir over a low heat, until the desired consistency is achieved.

Season to taste (a little black pepper works well) and serve with home-made soda bread, oatcakes or crisp-breads and salad.

Eat straight away or freeze - it does not contain vinegar or added sugar.

Hints & tips

Any leftover cooking liquor can be used as a fruit punch, or frozen for future use as tasty ice cubes or to be reused as part of a fruit sauce.

If using sweet potato, try making a savoury side order. Replace the ginger with crushed garlic and stir through some butter in place of the drizzled liquor.

'Fruit tarts'

Ingredients

For 2 or 4 people -

250g or 500g	Puff pastry - store bought (or see recipe.)
2 or 4 stalks	Rhubarb
½ or 1 litre	Apple juice
60ml or 120ml	Brown flour
15ml or 30ml	Almond milk

A sprig of mint to serve.

Method

Firstly, prepare the puff pastry following the recipe in this book.

Wrap in cling film and leave to rest in the fridge. Allow 25 minutes. Alternatively, use frozen pastry and defrost at room temperature instead.

Preheat the oven to 220˚c. Cut the rhubarb into thirds and place in a loaf tin. Pour over the apple juice and cover with foil. Roast in the oven for 10-15 minutes, until tender.

When the rhubarb is soft, remove carefully from the cooking liquor and allow to cool.

On a floured surface, roll out the puff pastry to a thickness of ½ cm. Cut into 2 (or 4) squares. Cut the sides of each square with a sharp knife 1 cm away from the edge - do not join the cuts at two diagonal corners.

Lift one pastry corner and fold over to the opposite edge. Repeat with the other side. Brush with milk.

Place the squares on a baking tray and arrange the cooled rhubarb equally between them. Be careful to put rhubarb within the 1 cm border.

Drizzle with a little of the cooking liquor and put in the oven for 15 mins - until the pastry is risen and brown.

Hints & tips

Alternative fruits include - apple, pear, fig, mango and peaches. Sprinkle the top with crushed almonds or a variety of seeds. In place of the fruit sauce, try serving with home-made ice cream (see recipe.)

For a savoury starter, top with fresh goats cheese and place under the grill until starting to turn brown.

'Pear Crumble Pie'

Ingredients

For 2 or 4 people -

250g or 500g	Shortcrust pastry (see recipe)
2 or 4 hard	Pears (dessert if available)
250ml or 500ml	Apple juice
1 or 2 inch	Fresh ginger
60g or 120g	Brown flour
60ml or 120ml	Oats - ground
60g or 120g	Almonds
50g or 100g	Glucose powder
50g or 100g	Butter
50g or 100g	Fortified dairy-free spread*

Method

Firstly, prepare the short crust pastry following the recipe in this book - replacing the sea salt with 10g (or 20g) glucose.

Wrap in cling film and leave to rest in the fridge. Alternatively, use frozen pastry and defrost at room temperature instead. Allow 25 minutes.

While the pastry is in the fridge, wash but do not peel the pears. Score the skin from top to bottom as if quartering but do not cut too deeply.

Place the pears on their sides in a pan and pour the juice over. Finely dice the ginger, sprinkle with glucose, crush with the back of a knife. Add to the pan.

Bring juice to the boil and simmer to poach the pears for 15 mins. Turn over half way through cooking time.

Mix together flour, oats, almonds, sweeteners and fats together. Combine to make a 'flapjack-like' dough.

Remove and chop pears into small chunks. Continue to cook the juice.

Roll the pastry (see recipe) into a large circle. Place in the bottom of a round pie tin. Put the pears in the centre and spoon over a little of the juice. Sprinkle the crumble over the top. Bake for 25 mins at 220°c.

Hints & tips

This pie is made even more tempting by the second pastry layer underneath. However, you can miss this step and simply top with crumble.

Also try apple, rhubarb, or mango.

For savoury crumble to top pasta or pies, replace sweeteners with fresh herbs, seeds, sea salt and pepper.

'Refrigerator Fudge'

Ingredients -

Makes 1 or 2 bars -

60g or 120g	Butter
60g or 120g	Glucose powder
110 or 220g	Double cream - whipped
5ml or 10ml	Tahini - light

Method

Gently melt the butter in a large pan on the hob. Remove from the heat and place on a steady surface. Add the glucose to the butter and stir well to combine. Allow to cool.

Whip the double cream with a whisk in a cool bowl until thick - but do not over-whip and let become grainy.

Once cool, beat into the butter and glucose until smooth by hand - or with an electric mixer on low if you have one. Stir in the light tahini.

If using additional flavour (see 'Hints & tips' box for ideas) fold them into the mix once smooth.

Generously line 1 or 2 small loaf tins with greaseproof or edible rice paper, allowing enough to wrap up the sides. Spoon the mix into the tin and smooth the top with a spatula.

Cover the loaf tin with kitchen film and place in a very cold fridge for 2 hours until firm when pressed.

Once firm, pull the edges of the greaseproof paper to remove from the tin. Cut into servings with a sharp knife dipped in freshly boiled water to make the fudge easier to cut.

Serve as soon as the fudge has firmed - to freeze, cut into pieces and wrap first in greaseproof and then in foil.

Hints & tips

Try adding finely chopped mint leaves, crushed ginger, sesame seeds or carob powder to the fudge mix. Experiment with a mix of half and half - make two smaller batches and press one on top of the other just before the fudge mixture firms.

For complete indulgence, top with 'Carob Frosting' (see recipe.)

'Sweet Potato Pie'

Ingredients

For 2 or 4 people -

250g or 500g	Shortcrust pastry Store bought or (see recipe)
15ml or 30ml	Rapeseed oil
2 or 4 large	Sweet potato
25g or 50g	Butter
3 or 6 cms	Fresh ginger
45ml or 90ml	Glucose powder
30ml or 60ml	Brown flour
1 or 2 large	Organic egg yolks

In the US, sweet potatoes are interchanged in this famous pie with pumpkins. Unfortunately, pumpkins are a HIT no-no but you can of course munch on the dried or roasted seeds!

Method

Firstly, prepare the short crust pastry following the recipe in this book.

Wrap in cling film and leave to rest in the fridge. Alternatively, use frozen pastry and defrost at room temperature instead. Allow 25 minutes.

While the pastry is in the fridge, wash and cube the sweet potato. Add to an oven proof tin and roast in the oven at 220°c for 10 minutes.

Prepare ginger by finely dicing. Sprinkle with a little glucose, and crush with the back of a knife.

Melt the butter in a pan and stir in the ginger. Remove from the heat.

Mash the sweet potato. Whisk the egg and add almost all of it to the potato - along with butter, ginger, flour and two thirds of the glucose.

Sprinkle the pastry with the remaining glucose and roll (see recipe) into a circle. Place in the bottom of a round pie tin with the edges slightly overlapping. Spoon the sweet potato mix in the centre and smooth the top with the back of a spoon.

Press the edge of the pastry up to the top of the tin and brush with the leftover egg. Bake the pie for 25 minutes until golden brown.

Hints & tips

Sweet Potato Pie usually also includes vanilla, nutmeg and cinnamon (all well-known HIT no-nos.)

However this pie tastes delicious by roasting the sweet potatoes instead of boiling, adding ginger and glucose.

Serve with almond milk ice cream and sprinkle with crushed almonds.

'Pear Tart Tatin'

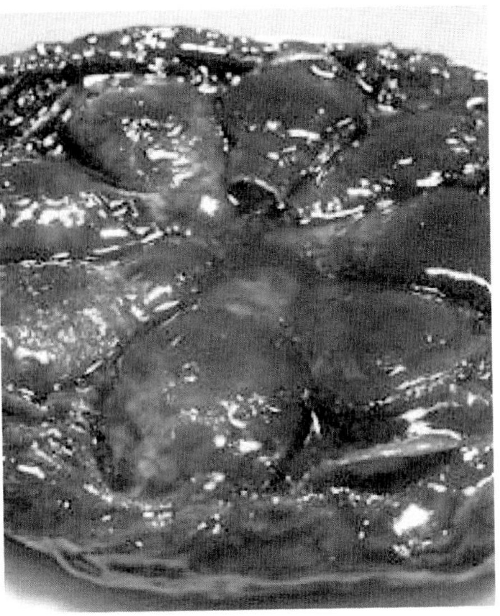

Ingredients

For 2 or 4 people -

250g or 500g	Puff pastry - store bought or (see recipe)
50g or 100g	Butter
50g or 100g	Glucose powder
100 or 200ml	Apple juice
2 or 4 hard	Pears (dessert if available)

You need a 15cm (or 30cm) frying pan or skillet, with an ovenproof handle. And good oven gloves!

Method

Firstly, prepare the puff pastry following the recipe in this book.

Wrap in cling film and leave to rest in the fridge. Alternatively, use frozen pastry and defrost at room temperature instead. Allow 25 minutes.

Melt the butter in the saucepan on the hob then reduce the heat to low. Pour in the glucose and apple juice. Stir regularly until the glucose begins to dissolve.

Turn up the heat to medium and cook the caramel mixture for 8 -10 minutes until the sauce starts to thicken.

As the caramel cooks, wash and quarter the pears, removing the cores with a knife. Prick the pear skin.

Carefully place the pears into the caramel. Turn occasionally to coat.

Keep turning the pears on the hot hob for 20 minutes to allow the pears to get a golden brown colour. Preheat the oven to 220°c.

A few minutes before the pears are ready, roll out the pastry into a circle big enough to cover the pears in the saucepan (either 15 or 30 cms.)

Put the pastry over the fruit and tuck in the edges, bake for 20 mins. Cool slightly then turn out onto a plate.

Hints & tips

Remember that glucose caramelises to a deep brown by itself - so make sure to use fruit juice as well - also try (unfermented) pear or mango.

Alternative fruits include - apple, mango, rhubarb or fig. And for a savoury twist, try - sweet potato, caramelised onion and a little goats cheese just before adding the pastry.

'Tea-Time Scones & Jam'

Ingredients

For 2 or 4 people -

2 or 4	Apples
4 or 8	Apricots
130 or 260ml	Apple juice
200g or 400g	Glucose powder

Try replacing apricot with - mango, pear, rhubarb, fig or fresh ginger.

10g or 20g	Glucose powder
150g or 300g	Whole grain self-raising flour
20g or 40g	Butter
110 or 220ml	Almond milk

Try adding - 25g (or 50g) finely chopped soft fruit or (for savoury) fresh herbs before adding the milk.

Method

Always sterilise the jars before using (see 'Hints & tips' box below.)

Chop the apples, remove cores but do not peel. Place in a saucepan and add the juice and filtered water to cover. Cover the pan and begin to simmer.

Meanwhile, peel and chop the apricot and add to the pan. Continue to simmer until the apples are soft. Once soft, sieve the soft fruit. Freeze the pulp to use in a future pie recipe.

Add the sieved juice and glucose into the saucepan and heat gently and stir until the glucose has dissolved. Bring to the boil and then boil very rapidly for 10 minutes.

Skim off any scum from the top with a metal spoon. Carefully ladle into warm jars and cover with a tight lid. Jam will thicken as it cools.

For the scones - Preheat oven to 220°c. Combine glucose with flour in a bowl and rub the butter to make breadcrumbs. Add the milk and use a knife to mix together until a dough is formed. Place on a floured surface and knead lightly until the dough is smooth. Roll to 2½ cm thickness and cut into 4 (or 8) squares.

Place on a baking tray 1cm apart. Bake for 15 mins until golden brown and sounds hollow when tapped.

Hints & tips

Make small batches of jam and eat them within days. Keep refrigerated.

To sterilise jars, make sure they have a tight fitting lid. Wash well in hot soapy water and rinse very carefully. Dry them in the oven at 150°c and fill with jam while still warm. When full, screw on lid, then briefly tip the jar upside down - let the jam touch the lid. Store right way up.

'Baked Apple Rice Pudding'

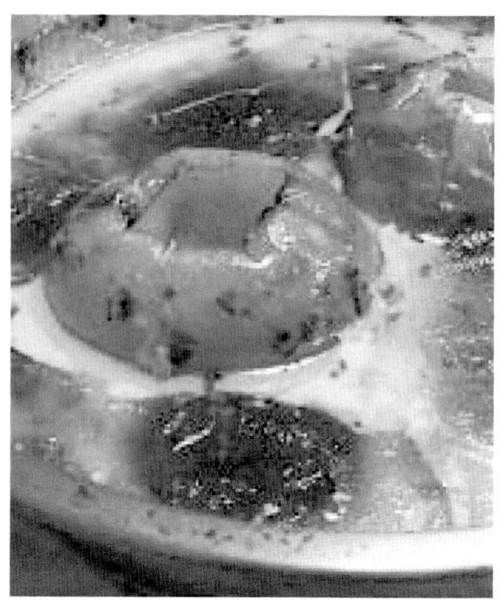

Ingredients

For 2 or 4 people -

65g or 125g	Pudding rice
¼ or ½ litre	Almond milk
1 or 2 sprigs	Fresh basil
2 or 4	Apples (dessert if available)
250ml or 500ml	Apple juice
25g or 50g	Butter

This creamy dessert can also benefit from a little sweetener - try adding 5ml or 10ml glucose to the milk.

Method

Be careful when cooking rice. Always wash the rice and add a few basil leaves to the liquid during cooking. Finely chop the basil so that you don't need to remove before serving.

Put the rice into a pan and add ½ of the almond milk and all the basil. Bring the milk to the boil then cover and simmer for 30 minutes.

While the rice simmers, wash and core the apples. Score the skin from top to bottom as though quartering the fruit but do not cut too deeply.

Place the apples in a small pan and cover up to the half-way mark with juice. Bring to the boil and then simmer to poach for 10 mins. Turn over half way through the cooking time.

After 20 mins, stir the remaining milk through the rice and add the butter.

Preheat the oven to 180°c. Drain and place the apples in a greased oven-proof dish. Spoon the rice pudding evenly in and around the apples. Put in the oven, uncovered, for 30 mins.

Meanwhile, reduce the leftover apple juice by continuing to simmer on the hob. When the rice has cooked, remove carefully from the oven and drizzle with the apple dressing, pour especially inside the apples cores.

Hints & tips

Sprinkle with ground almonds or grated apple to serve.

Alternatively, replace the apple with very hard pears. Pears are low in histamine as long as they aren't ripe.

If pudding rice isn't available, brown rice can work nicely as well and adds a slightly nutty flavour.

'American Muffins'

Ingredients

For 2 or 4 people -

40g or 80g	Glucose powder
125g or 250g	Whole grain self-raising flour
40g or 80g	Butter
1 or 2	Egg yolks
125 or 250ml	Almond milk
1 or 2	Rhubarb
3 or 6 cms	Fresh ginger
<u>Optional -</u>	
1 or 2 handfuls	Almonds
10g or 20g	Glucose powder

Method

Preheat the oven to 200°c. If using a muffin tin, grease with rapeseed oil - otherwise, use paper muffin cases.

Grind the glucose in a pestle and mortar until it resembles caster sugar. In a bowl, sieve together the glucose and self-raising flour.

Melt the butter over a low heat and allow to cool. Whisk the egg yolk and almond milk into the cooled butter.

Pour the egg mixture into the flour and stir quickly together. Don't try to make the mixture smooth - it should still be a little lumpy.

Peel and chop the rhubarb into small chunks. Roll in a little flour. Prepare the ginger by finely dicing and crush with the back of a knife. Fold the fruit and ginger into the muffin mixture.

Spoon the muffin mixture evenly between the cases (approximately 2-3 large muffins per person.)

If using, crush the almonds using a food processor. Stir together with the glucose and sprinkle on top of each muffin before baking.

Place muffins in the oven and bake for 20-25 minutes or until golden brown. Cool slightly before eating.

Hints & tips

In place of the rhubarb, try adding - almond, apple, carrot, carob, fig, mango or pear. Oats instead of flour.

Try reducing the glucose to 10g (or 20g), take out the ginger and add finely chopped fresh herbs, crushed seeds, chilli or garlic!

Not to be confused with English 'split' muffins - they contain yeast!

'Cupid's Cupcakes'

Ingredients

Makes 4 or 8 cupcakes -

40g or 80g	Glucose powder
1 or 2	Organic egg yolk
40ml or 80ml	Rapeseed oil (plus extra for greasing)
90ml or 180ml	Rhupple juice (see recipe)
80g or 160g	Brown rice flour (or white instead)
5ml or 10ml	Bicarbonate of soda

For the icing -

120 or 240g	Glucose powder
20ml or 40ml	Rhupple juice (see recipe)

Optional - Use apple, pear or mango juice - or fresh ginger syrup instead.

Method

Preheat the oven to 200°c. If only using a cupcake tin, grease lightly with rapeseed oil - otherwise, use paper cake cases (2 per person.)

Grind the glucose in a pestle and mortar until it resembles caster sugar, put into a large bowl. Also add egg yolk, rapeseed oil, rhupple juice and water. Beat gently to combine.

In a separate bowl, sieve together the rice flour and baking powder.

In one go, pour all of the flour mix into the larger bowl, and fold into the wet ingredients until no lumps remain. Work quickly and carefully.

Spoon cupcake mixture evenly between paper cases or directly into the tin. Gently tap the tin onto your workspace to smooth the batter mix.

Place tin into the oven and bake for 12-15 minutes - or until lightly browned and a toothpick comes out almost clean. Cool before icing.

When the cupcakes are cool, sieve the icing sugar into a small bowl. Add the rhupple juice and stir until smooth. Drizzle the icing evenly on top of each cupcake.

Allow the icing to set before eating.

Hints & tips

I originally designed this recipe for a friend's wedding - my friend had the condition HIT but was also fructose, dairy and gluten intolerant. She was planning an 'Alice in Wonderland' tea party for her guests and also wanted something delicious for herself!

I've adapted some of the original ingredients to make it even more flexible for most HIT diets. Enjoy!

'Almond Baklava'

Ingredients

Makes a medium or large tray -

75g or 150g	Almonds
7.5 or 15ml	Rapeseed oil
75g or 150g	Sesame seeds
6 or 12 sheets	Filo pastry
30g or 60g	Butter
20g or 40g	Rapeseed oil
For the syrup -	
75ml or 150ml	Filtered water
75ml or 150ml	Apple juice
150g or 300g	Glucose powder
60ml or 120ml	Agave nectar

Method

Remove the filo pastry from the freezer - I usually defrost the pastry for 2 mins in the microwave and then allow to rest for 30 mins while I prepare the filling. However, always follow manufacturer's instructions.

Preheat the oven to 170°c. Toss the almond in 7.5 (or 15ml) of oil. Place in an oven tin and roast for 10 mins. Add the sesame seeds, shake the tin to coat in oil. Roast for a further 2-3 mins. Put the almonds and seeds into a food processor - coarsely grind.

Melt the butter gently on the hob then mix together with the oil. Cool. Lightly grease an ovenproof dish. Carefully unfold the filo pastry, if making the smaller quantity, cut each sheet in half. Cover filo with a piece of kitchen film to keep moist.

Put the first filo sheet into the tin. Brush the first filo sheet with the butter and oil. Repeat with the next 3 sheets, sprinkle with ½ almonds and seeds. Drizzle with oil. Top with 4 more filo sheets then a layer of almonds and seeds. Finally add the last 4 filo sheets, oil top layer also.

Cut filo into small diamonds down to the base. Bake in oven for 35 mins. Simmer all syrup ingredients in a pan for 15 mins. Spoon ½ the syrup over the cooked baklava, leave for a few minutes to absorb then spoon over the rest. Cool before serving.

Hints & tips

Scatter a few sesame seeds over the top of the baklava once covered in syrup. In place of the seeds, try adding finely chopped fresh ginger.

Ideal for serving at Christmas time - or even to give as gifts. Or try serving after a meal with a fresh peppermint tea (see recipe.)

'Gingerbread - Lebkuchen'

Ingredients

Makes 12 or 24 biscuits -

30g or 60g	Butter
15 or 30ml	Apple juice
20g or 40g	Glucose powder
65 or 130ml	Agave nectar
1½ or 3 inch	Fresh ginger
140g or 280g	Wholegrain Self Raising flour
50g or 100g	Flaked almonds (ground)
1 or 2 pinch	Ground black pepper
1 or 2	Organic egg yolk

Method

Melt butter gently in a small saucepan. Stir in the apple juice and allow to simmer. Continue to stir while adding the glucose slowly. Once dissolved, remove the pan from the heat and stir in the agave nectar.

Prepare ginger by finely dicing. Then sprinkle with glucose, and crush with the back of a knife. Add to the pan.

Sieve the flour into a second bowl along with the ground almonds and black pepper. Mix to combine.

Beat egg yolk in a small ramekin. Stir egg yolk into the cooled butter, juice, glucose, agave and ginger. Preheat the oven to 180°c.

Make a well in the centre of the flour mixture and pour in the contents of the pan. Stir well to combine, then bring together to make a stiff dough.

Cover the dough with film and rest it for a few minutes. Generously dust your workspace with a combination of flour and ground glucose.

Either roll the dough out to ½ cm thick and cut into shape using a cutter of your choice or roll into golf-ball size balls. Lightly grease a baking tray with oil or baking paper. Place the biscuit dough on top - spaced around 2 cm apart. Bake for 15-17 mins, cool on a wire rack.

Hints & tips

Try coating in melted carob sauce (see recipe,) or a warmed homemade jam glaze (see recipe) - or simply with ground glucose as 'icing sugar'!

Lebkuchen is a traditional German Xmas biscuit, like a soft gingerbread. Try making shaped biscuits - such as gingerbread men, love hearts or 'Hansel and Gretal' inspired houses!

'Filo Tarts'

Ingredients

For 2 or 4 people -

1 or 2 sheets	Filo pastry
40g or 80g	Flaked almonds
1 or 2	Apple
125ml or 250ml	Apple juice
4 or 8	Fresh figs
1.5 or 3 cm	Fresh ginger
15ml or 30ml	Agave nectar
15ml or 30ml	Rapeseed oil
15g or 30g	Glucose powder

Method

Remove the filo pastry from the freezer - I usually defrost the pastry for 2 mins in the microwave and then allow to rest for 30 mins while I prepare the topping. However, always follow manufacturer's instructions.

Preheat the oven to 175°c. Place the almonds in an oven proof tin and roast for 10 mins. Allow to cool. Meanwhile, finely chop the apple and put in a small pan with the apple juice and gently simmer for 5 mins.

As the apples simmer, cut the figs into small pieces (peel bruised or rough parts) and add to the pan. Simmer, uncovered. Prepare ginger by finely dicing, sprinkle with glucose, crush with the back of a knife. Stir into the pan with the almonds.

Once almost all juice has absorbed, remove from heat, stir in agave.

Place a piece of kitchen film on your worktop as big as the filo sheets. Cut each filo sheet into 6 (or 12) squares. Brush each square with a little oil and sprinkle with glucose.

Grease ramekins, layer 3 squares for each ramekin to make rough star shapes. Spoon the fruit evenly between the filo stars. Bake in the oven for 10 mins or until light brown. Serve dusted with ground glucose and remove from ramekin once cool.

Hints & tips

Ideal as Xmas 'Mince tarts', but also good at other times of the year too!

Replace fig with other fruit including rhubarb, mango, apple and pear.

Instead of the star-shaped tarts, put the filling straight into greased ramekins and scrunch the buttered filo for 'pie' lids. Or, make the filo stars and bake in greased shallow muffin trays.

'Apple Pie'

Ingredients

Makes medium or large pie -

250g or 500g	Shortcrust pastry Store-bought or (see recipe)
3 or 6 large	Apples (cooking - if possible)
50g or 100g	Glucose powder
100 or 200ml	Apple juice
½ or 1 inch	Fresh ginger

Method

Firstly, prepare the short crust pastry following the recipe in this book. Wrap in cling film and leave to rest in the fridge. Alternatively, use frozen pastry and defrost at room temperature instead. Allow 25 minutes.

While the pastry is in the fridge, wash the apples, no need to peel. Cut 1 (or 2) of the apples into small cubes, place in a pan on the hob with ½ the glucose and ½ apple juice.

Prepare ginger by finely dicing. Then sprinkle with glucose, and crush with the back of a knife. Add to the pan.

Simmer, uncovered, for 10 mins until you get a soft apple sauce texture. Meanwhile, cut 2 (or 4) apples into thin slices, add to a second pan with the remaining glucose and juice. Over the pan, simmer for 7 mins.

Preheat the oven to 170°c. Cut ¼ from the pastry dough and roll into a circle (see recipe) and place in a pie tin. Spread the apple sauce layer across the bottom. Layer with the apple slices - retain the juice.

Roll the ¼ pastry to the same thickness as the base. Cut into 2 cm strips and place across the top of the sliced apples. Brush the top and edge of the pie with the apple 'stock'. Bake for 25 minutes.

Hints & tips

Roll 10g (or 20g) glucose into the pastry to make it sweeter. If you prefer crumbly pastry, once the 'crumbs' are made, freeze for 15 mins. And add ice cold water to mix.

Use the apple sauce to go with Sunday lunch or in kiev recipes. Or try puff pastry 'strudels' for Xmas-treats and mini pies for parties!

'Stollen'

Ingredients

For 1 or 2 large loaves -

200g or 400g	Wholegrain Self Raising flour
100g or 200g	Glucose powder
75g or 150g	Flaked almonds (ground)
75g or 150g	Butter
4 or 8	Fresh figs
2 or 4	Apples (dessert if available)
120 or 240ml	Apple juice
3 or 6cms	Fresh ginger
2 or 4	Organic egg yolks
100g or 200g	Marzipan (or see recipe.)

Method

In a large bowl, sieve the flour, glucose, almonds and a pinch of unrefined sea salt. Chop 60g (or 120g) of the butter into chunks, add to bowl.

Rub butter and flour together with your fingers to make breadcrumbs. Pour 'crumbs' into a food bag and place in the freezer for 15 mins.

Meanwhile, wash and cut the figs into small pieces (peel any bruised or rough parts) and add to a small bowl. Pour over the apple juice and stir.

Chop apples into small chunks but do not peel. Stir into the juice and fig mixture. Cover with kitchen film. Prepare ginger by very finely dicing, then sprinkle with glucose, crush with the back of a knife. Add to the bowl. Put covered bowl in the fridge.

Preheat oven to 180°c. Beat egg yolks with a fork into the 'crumbs'. Stir in the cooled fruit mixture and bring together with your hands to make a sticky dough. Generously dust your workspace with flour and gently knead the dough 3-4 times.

Dust a rolling pin and carefully roll the dough to 25 x 20 cm. Shape marzipan into a 3cm wide sausage and lay in the bottom ½ of the dough. Lift over the top ½, press to seal.

Place on greased baking tray. Melt remaining butter and brush over the dough. Bake for for 45-50 mins.

Hints & tips

For the traditional appearance of Stollen, dust with ground glucose.

Usually Stollen is a yeasty dough - the self raising flour gives a similar but lighter texture. Delicate to handle but results in a delicious way to use homemade marzipan! Marzipan freezes well in sealed containers.

'Almond Marzipan'

Ingredients

Makes 250g or 500g -

3 or 6 cms	Fresh ginger
60ml or 120ml	Apple juice
225g or 450g	Glucose powder
200g or 400g	Flaked almonds (ground)
2 or 4	Organic egg yolks
40g or 80g	Homemade apricot jam (see recipe.)

Take care with raw egg. Use the marzipan quickly after preparing.

Method

Prepare ginger by very finely dicing, then sprinkle with glucose and crush with the back of a knife.

Warm ½ the apple juice in a small pan on the hob and stir in the fresh ginger. Continue to simmer gently until the ginger has softened.

Grind the glucose in a pestle and mortar until the texture is fine - like that of caster or icing sugar.

Pour the glucose into a larger bowl and sieve the ground almonds on top. Stir well to mix thoroughly. Beat the egg yolks with a fork in a small ramekin. Pour ½ apple juice and ginger into the ramekin and mix.

Make a well in the centre of the ground almonds and glucose. Pour the egg mix into the bowl, stir. As the marzipan forms, press together.

Generously dust your workspace with ground glucose and gently knead the almond dough until smooth.

Roll the dough with a dusted rolling pin to the size required. Cover with kitchen film as you prepare the jam.

Warm the jam in a saucepan until it starts to simmer then remove from the heat. Brush the jam over the surface of the cake you wish to cover. Press the marzipan firmly on top.

Hints & tips

Use to cover Fruit Cakes, to fill Stollen, (see recipes) - or to create marzipan shapes and stars to decorate.

When applying marzipan, smooth any lumps with your hands - if very lumpy use a hot knife to spread them out. When covering a whole cake, you may find it easier to cut the top and sides separately. Lay the cake on its side, and roll, then lay on its top.

'Festive Figgy Pudding'

Ingredients - Makes 1 or 2 puddings -

40g or 80g	Flaked almonds
1 or 2	Apple
125 or 250ml	Apple juice
4 or 8	Fresh figs
1.5 or 3 cm	Fresh ginger
15 or 30ml	Agave nectar
125g or 250g	Wholegrain Self Raising flour
100g or 200g	Glucose powder
60ml or 120ml	Carob powder
2 or 4	Organic egg yolks
60ml or 120ml	Rapeseed oil
250g or 500g	Marzipan
60g or 120g	Butter
60g or 120g	Carob powder
120 or 240ml	Agave nectar

Method

Preheat the oven to 175°c. Place the almonds in an oven proof tin and roast for 10 mins. Allow to cool. Meanwhile, finely chop the apple and put in a small pan with the apple juice and gently simmer for 5 mins.

As the apples simmer, cut the figs into small pieces (peel bruised or rough parts) and add to the pan. Simmer, uncovered. Prepare ginger by finely dicing, sprinkle with glucose, crush with back of a knife. Stir into the pan along with the almonds.

Once almost all juice has absorbed, remove from heat stir in agave.

Sieve the flour, glucose and carob powder together into a large bowl. In a smaller bowl, whisk together the egg yolks and oil. Slowly stir in the eggs and oil to the flour mix. When combined, stir in the fig mixture.

Grease a loaf tin and spoon pudding mixture inside. Put in the oven and cook for 45 mins until springy on top.

Remove from the tin. Cut the marzipan to fit each side. Cover pudding with marzipan, using jam to seal.

Melt the butter. Remove from the heat, add the carob powder, stir in the agave. Spread the carob frosting generously over the marzipan and put in the fridge to set before cutting.

Hints & tips

More a cake than a pudding, 'Figgy Pudding' can be baked or steamed. Although if steaming, leave out the marzipan and carob toppings.

If steaming, put the pudding mixture into a covered metal bowl, which is then placed in a large saucepan of simmering water for 3 hours. Make sure the water doesn't boil dry.

'Yule Log'

Ingredients -
Makes 1 or 2 rolls -

4 or 8	Organic egg yolks
135g or 270g	Glucose powder
60ml or 120ml	Filtered water
30 or 60ml	Carob powder
125g or 250g	Wholegrain Self Raising flour
225 or 450ml	Double cream or 'Carob Mousse' (see recipe.)
10g or 20g	Butter
Optional -	
240 or 480g	Homemade carob frosting (see recipe for ingredients and method.)

Method

Line a swiss roll tin (or a medium sized shallow oven tin) with greaseproof paper. Preheat oven to 180°c.

In a large mixing bowl, whisk the egg yolks and the ground glucose - less 10g (or 20g) - together until light and airy. If using an electric mixer, keep the speed low. Gradually add the water, whisking into the egg mix.

Once mixed, stir in the carob powder. Then sieve the flour into the bowl a little at a time, folding into the mix. Try to get as much air in as possible to produce a lighter texture.

Pour the mix into the tin - bake in oven for 13 mins until the edges shrink from the sides. While the cake cooks, in a cold bowl, lightly whip the cream with a whisk. Don't let it become grainy. If making 'Carob Mousse' don't put into fridge yet.

Lay another piece of greaseproof on your workspace - as big as the first. Gently melt the butter in a small pan and brush over the top side of the greaseproof. Dust 10g (or 20g) of glucose evenly over the buttered paper.

Gently tip the cooked cake onto this greaseproof and remove the first piece of paper. Cover with a piece of kitchen film for 20 mins as it cools. When cool, spread with cream. Roll tightly away from you. Add frosting!

Hints & tips

Feel free to leave out the carob frosting (or simply frost with less.) For parties, make smaller individual 'Swiss Rolls' by baking a thinner cake layer, rolling width-ways and cut with a sharp knife into small pieces.

Try making a nutty light tahini flavoured swiss roll, filled with whipped double cream and homemade jam.

‘Panforte’

Ingredients -

For 2 or 4 people -

2 or 4	Peaches or apples
4 or 8	Fresh figs
125g or 250g	Almonds
3 or 6 cms	Fresh ginger
75g or 150g	Brown flour
45ml or 90ml	Carob powder
1 or 2 pinch	Ground black pepper
150g or 300g	Glucose powder
60ml or 120ml	Agave nectar
25ml or 50ml	Apple juice
50g or 100g	Butter

Method

Preheat oven to 180°c. Generously line a cake tin with greaseproof (also brush with oil on the top side) or edible rice paper, allowing enough to wrap over the top of the cake later.

Finely chop the peach or apple and figs (no need to peel unless bruised or rough parts) stir with the almonds in an oven proof tin and roast for 15 mins. Shake regularly so not to burn.

Prepare ginger by finely dicing, then sprinkle with glucose, crush with the back of a knife. Stir into the tin to warm through. Allow to cool.

Meanwhile, sieve the flour and carob powder into a large bowl plus a pinch of ground black pepper. Stir in the toasted fruit, almonds and ginger.

Heat the glucose, agave, juice and butter in a pan on the hob until glucose dissolves. Stir well to combine.

Continue to boil the sugar liquid for 4 minutes ONLY - without stirring.

Make a well in the centre of the dry ingredients. Pour the simmered liquid inside, stirring quickly to mix. Spoon mixture into the cake tin while it’s still warm and pliable. Be careful to fold the excess paper over the top.

Bake in the oven for 30 mins. Remove greaseproof paper while warm. Allow to cool before cutting into slices.

Hints & tips

Originally called ‘Panpepato’ - peppered bread. This cake can be served at Christmas and times of celebration. Panforte is also served after a meal as a dessert with mint tea - many people enjoy it at breakfast.

Try adding a carob frosting (see recipe) or sprinkled with ground glucose. Enjoy whole figs roasted for 10 mins and drizzled with sticky apple sauce.

'Biscuit Creams'

Ingredients -

For 2 or 4 people -

<u>For the biscuits -</u>

65g or 130g	Butter
15g or 30g	Glucose powder
65g or 130g	Wholegrain Self Raising flour
15g or 30g	Almonds - finely ground

<u>For the creamed filling -</u>

15g or 30g	Butter
20g or 40g	Glucose powder
10g or 20g	Almonds - finely ground

Method

Take butter from fridge a few mins before using. Cube butter, add to a large bowl. Pour in glucose and beat together with a fork - or electric hand mixer - until light and fluffy.

Sieve the flour into a second bowl, and mix in the finely ground almonds. Slowly add the dry ingredients to the butter and glucose, stirring until well combined.

Preheat oven to 180°c and lightly grease 1 (or 2) large baking trays.

Roll the biscuit mix into small cherry-sized balls - you'll make 20 (or 40!) in total. Place the balls onto the greased trays and press to 2-3mm flat with your fingertips.

Bake for 8 mins until just starting to brown. Using a fish slice, lift the biscuits off the tray and leave to cool completely on a wire rack.

As the biscuits cool, beat - or cream - the butter until soft. Then beat the finely ground glucose and almonds together with the butter.

Spread the butter cream evenly between half of the biscuits. Carefully press the second halves on top.

Store in an airtight container, also in the fridge if possible, and eat within a day or two. Remember that these biscuits do not contain preservatives!

Hints & tips

For a 'chocolate cream' biscuit, add carob powder to both the biscuit and the filling mix. Or try adding roughly ground oats for a chunky texture.

The biscuits themselves are delicious even without the filling. For a more wholewheat biscuit, replace the ground almonds with wholewheat flour. For occasional indulgence, top with carob frosting (see recipe.)

'Brandy Snap Thins'

Ingredients -

For 2 or 4 people -

50g or 100g	Butter
50g or 100g	Agave nectar
30ml or 60ml	Apple juice
50g or 100g	Glucose powder
50g or 100g	Brown flour
3 or 6 cms	Fresh ginger

Optional -
40g or 80g Sesame seeds
Or -
40g or 80g Quinoa grains

Method

Preheat the oven to 180°c. Lightly grease a large baking sheet or tin.

Gently melt the butter in a pan. Add the agave, apple juice and glucose - stirring until melted. Bring to a rolling boil for 1 minute without stirring.

Meanwhile, prepare ginger by finely dicing. Sprinkle with glucose, and crush with the back of a knife. Remove the pan from the heat, stir in the flour and ginger. Cool slightly.

If using sesame seeds or quinoa grains, prepare the thins up to a rolling boil. When you add the flour and ginger also stir in the added ingredients. Mix well to combine.

Using a 15ml spoon, drop the syrup mixture onto the baking sheet - leave large gaps between each as they will all spread out as they cook.

Bake in the oven for 8 mins until browning at the edges. Take the tray from the oven - make sure to leave the thins to cool for 3-4 mins before you touch them.

Using a fish slice, lift the thins off the tray and leave to cool completely on a wire rack. So quick to make, serve alongside a warm drink for 'elevenses' or at supper-time.

Hints & tips

Unlike traditional Brandy Snaps that use sugar and golden syrup, these thins do not harden completely and may not roll into tubes. However, the flavour is almost identical!

Alternatively, serve as a dessert with freshly whipped double cream and a selection of fruits (see fruit salad recipe for low histamine fruit ideas.)

To make the thins extra special, top with a carob frosting (see recipe.)

'Carrot Cake'

Ingredients -

Makes 1 or 2 loaf cakes -

100g or 200g	Glucose powder
100 or 200ml	Rapeseed oil
2 or 4	Organic egg yolks
7.5 or 15ml	Agave nectar
100g or 200g	Wholegrain Self Raising flour
1.5 or 3 cms	Fresh ginger
100g or 200g	Carrots
65g or 130g	Butter
65g or 130g	Mascarpone cheese (uncultured)
30g or 60g	Glucose powder

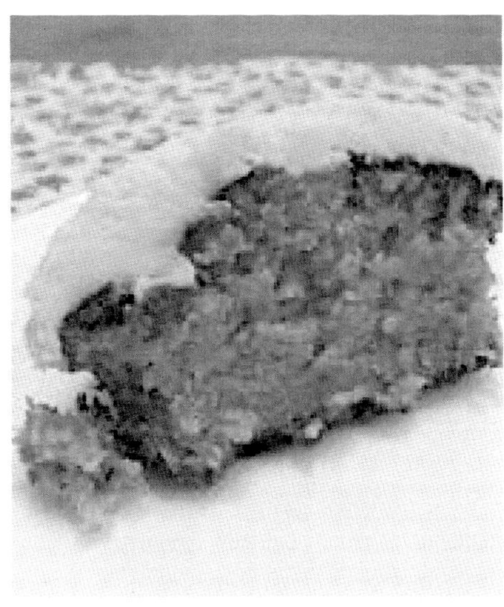

Method

Finely grind the glucose in a pestle and mortar until the texture of caster sugar - you may find it easier to do this in batches. Preheat the oven to 190°c and line 1 (or 2) small loaf tins with greaseproof paper.

Pour the oil and the ground glucose into a mixing bowl. Beat the eggs in a small ramekin and add to the bowl. Using a hot spoon, also add the agave nectar to the ingredients. Mix well with the spoon to combine.

Sieve the flour into the bowl and mix together to form a smooth batter. Prepare the ginger by finely dicing, sprinkle with a little glucose, crush with back of a knife. Add to bowl.

Wash and grate the carrots straight into the bowl. No need to peel unless the carrots are not organic. Mix the ginger and carrot into the batter.

Pour the batter into the prepared tin(s) and smooth the top with the back of a warm spoon. Bake in the oven for 35 mins or until a skewer or cocktail stick comes out clean.

Allow the cake to cool once cooked. Meanwhile, take the butter from the fridge a few mins before you want to use it to allow it to soften slightly.

Finely grind the remaining glucose in a pestle and mortar until the texture of icing sugar. Cut the butter into cubes and add to the clean mixing bowl. Beat the butter together with the mascarpone and ground glucose.

Spread the buttercream on top of the cooled cake. Refrigerate to set.

Hints & tips

Try replacing the mascarpone cheese with quark. Also try using grated beetroot in place of the carrot.

'Syrup Sponge & Custard'

Ingredients -
For 2 or 4 people -
<u>For the sponge -</u>

65g or 125g	Butter
65g or 125g	Glucose powder
1 or 2	Organic egg yolks
30ml or 60ml	Agave nectar
3 or 6 cms	Fresh ginger
65g or 125g	Wholegrain Self Raising flour
100ml or 200ml	Almond milk

<u>For the custard -</u>

1.5 or 3 cms	Fresh ginger
2 or 4	Organic egg yolks
100 or 200ml	Almond milk
100 or 200ml	Double cream
15g or 30g	Glucose powder

Method

For the sponge - Take the butter from the fridge a few mins before you want to use it to allow it to soften slightly. Cut into cubes and add to a mixing bowl.

Grind the glucose in a pestle and mortar until fine - cream together with the butter. Beat the egg in a small ramekin and stir in ½ the agave. Add the egg mix to the butter-cream and stir well to combine.

Prepare ginger by finely dicing, sprinkle with glucose, crush with the back of a knife. Stir into the bowl. Slowly add the flour to the mix, stirring all the time until smooth.

Grease a microwave safe bowl. Pour the sponge mix into the greased bowl but leave a 5 cm gap at the top. Cover with kitchen film. Microwave on full power for 4 ½ mins to set.

Serve turned upside down on a serving plate with the remaining golden syrup warmed and poured over.

For the custard - Prepare ginger by finely dicing, sprinkle with glucose, crush with the back of a knife. Add to a saucepan along with the milk and cream and bring to a gentle simmer. Allow to cool.

Beat egg and glucose in a large bowl. Slowly strain the cream into the egg - whisking all of the time. Pour liquid back into the saucepan. Return to a gentle heat until the custard thickens and coats the back of a spoon.

Hints & tips

Alternative flavourings include: carob, fudge - even try fresh mango!

I'm not usually a big microwave fan - aside from some defrosting - but microwaving this sponge saves you 3 hours steaming time on the hob.

'Panna Cotta Cheesecake'

Ingredients -

For 2 or 4 people -

<u>For the Panna Cotta -</u>

110 or 220ml	Almond milk
110 or 220ml	Double cream
15g or 30g	Glucose powder
1.5 or 3 cms	Fresh ginger
15ml or 30ml	Agar flakes

<u>For the 'Cheesecake' base -</u>

75g or 150g	Homemade flapjacks (see recipe.)
25g or 50g	Butter

Method

Pour the almond milk and cream into a saucepan on the hob. Add the glucose and prepare ginger by finely dicing, sprinkle with a little glucose, crush with the back of a knife. Stir both into the pan and simmer gently. Stir until all the glucose dissolves.

Allow to cool and infuse. Meanwhile, melt the butter in a second pan. Crush the flapjacks and stir into the pan, coating well with butter.

Grease one ramekin per person. Divide the flapjack base evenly between them and press down firmly.

Once the liquid has cooled, sprinkle with agar flakes. Bring to a simmer without stirring - then stir well to combine. Continue for 4 mins - stirring only occasionally. Once the liquid has simmered, pour on top of the biscuit base.

Cover the ramekins with film and put in a cold fridge until the topping sets.

For variety, use crumbled 'biscuit creams'. Alternatively, add a layer of apples, pear or rhubarb roasted in apple juice. Drizzle with carob sauce or a reduced 'Rhupple' coulis with a ¼ tsp beetroot juice (see recipes.)

Hints & tips

In place of 'Panna Cotta' try making 'Creme Brulee' instead - Bring 250ml (or 500ml) cream with crushed fresh ginger to the boil. Simmer for 5 mins while beating 50g (or 100g) glucose and 3 (or 6) egg yolks in a bowl.

Bring the cream back to the boil and pour over the egg, whisking all the time until it thickens. Strain and divide between greased ramekins - leaving a 5 cm gap at the top. Put ramekins into an oven tin and surround with boiling water. Bake in the oven at 140°c for 30 mins.

'Profiteroles'

Ingredients -

For 2 or 4 people -

For the choux pastry -

100 or 200ml	Filtered water
2.5 or 5 ml	Glucose powder
40g or 80g	Butter
60g or 120g	Flour
2 or 4 medium	Organic egg yolks

For the filling -

300 or 600ml	Double cream
7.5 or 15ml	Glucose powder

For the sauce -

30g or 60g	Carob powder
40ml or 80ml	Almond milk
60g or 120g	Agave nectar

Method

In a large pan - add the water, glucose and butter. Gently melt the butter, stirring to dissolve the glucose. Once dissolved, turn the heat to high and add a pinch of unrefined sea salt and sieve all of the flour to the pan. Remove from the heat.

Beat the mix very quickly until the paste is smooth and lump-free. Keep stirring and allow the heat of the pan to cook the paste a little. Once it starts to move away from the sides as you stir, add the paste to another bowl, cover with film and cool.

Once cool, preheat the oven to 200°c and grease 1 (or 2) baking trays. Beat the egg yolks into the paste one at a time - stirring quickly until the eggs are well combined.

Spoon out 5ml of the mixture - use hot water to dip the tsp in. Repeat. Finally dip your finger in the hot water and rub on top of each 'Profiterole.' Bake in the oven for 25 mins until turns crispy outside. Remove from oven, make a small hole in the base of each then return to the oven - upside down - for 3-4 mins.

Lightly whip the cream and glucose - but do not over-whip so it becomes grainy. When the pastries are cool, pipe the cream into the holes on the base. Serve with hot carob sauce.

Hints & tips

To make the carob sauce - heat the carob powder and milk in a pan, stirring until boiling. As soon as it boils, remove from the heat. Continue to stir to keep the sauce smooth. Add the agave and stir well to combine.

Alternatively, fill the choux pastry with - or even drizzle with - melted homemade jam (see recipe.)

'Dessert Pizza'

Ingredients -

Makes 1 or 2 pizzas -

75g or 150g	'OO' type flour - pasta flour
2.5 or 5ml	Glucose powder
45ml or 90ml	Rapeseed oil or olive oil
45ml or 90ml	Filtered water - cold
<u>For the topping -</u>	
30g or 60g	Carob powder
40ml or 80ml	Almond milk
60g or 120g	Agave nectar
20g or 40g	Sesame seeds
1 or 2 hard	Pears
10g or 20g	Butter

Method

Put a small cup of filtered water in the fridge to chill before you start.

Add the flour and glucose in a mixing bowl and pour in the oil. Stir well to combine then add the water. Mould with your hands into a soft dough. Dust with a little extra flour and wrap in kitchen film. Put in a cold fridge for 30 mins to allow it to rest.

To make the carob sauce - heat the carob powder and milk in a pan, stirring until boiling. As soon as it boils, remove from the heat. Continue to stir to keep the sauce smooth. Add the agave and stir well to combine.

After 30 mins, preheat the oven to 200°c and lightly flour 1 (or 2) baking trays. Put the dough on the flour, press to flatten - then gently roll with a floured rolling pin to make a rough circle around 3 mm thick.

Spoon the carob sauce in the centre of the base - leaving 2 cm around the edge. Scatter the sesame seeds over the sauce then take the hard pear from the fridge and finely slice. Arrange on top of the sauce and seeds.

Pull the sides of the base up and press over the edge of the topping. Melt the butter and brush over the edges and the pears. Bake in the oven for 30 mins until the edges turn light brown and crispy.

Hints & tips

Different dessert pizza toppings include - flaked almonds, sliced apples, rhubarb or mango and melted - homemade jam sauce (see recipe.)

Alternatively, make a savoury olive oil pizza - use a pinch of unrefined sea salt in place of the glucose. Top with many of your favourite low histamine pizza toppings (see recipes.)

'Carob Frosted Shortbread'

Ingredients -

Makes 1 or 2 bars -

<u>For the shortbread -</u>

110g or 220g	Butter
60g or 120g	Glucose powder
7.5 or 15ml	Tahini - light
80g or 160g	Wholegrain Self Raising flour

<u>For the carob frosting -</u>

35g or 70g	Butter
35g or 70g	Carob powder
60ml or 120ml	Agave nectar

<u>Optional -</u>

20g or 40g	Flaked almond, pumpkin or sunflower seeds.

Method

Take the butter from the fridge a few mins before you want to use it to allow it to soften slightly. Cut into cubes and add to a mixing bowl.

Grind the glucose in a pestle and mortar until finer - cream together with the butter. Once creamed, stir through the light tahini, mixing well. Sieve and slowly add the flour to the buttercream. Stirring all the time to keep smooth as the dough thickens.

Preheat the oven to 180°c and line 1 or 2 small loaf tins with kitchen foil. Lightly grease the top side of the foil with a little rapeseed oil.

Tip the shortbread dough into the tin(s) and press down firmly with the back of a hot spoon to flatten. Bake in the oven for 20 mins until lightly brown at the edges. Then wrap the foil over the top and bake for 5 mins.

Once the shortbread has cooled, melt the butter in a pan. Remove pan from the heat, add the carob powder and agave. Stirring well to combine.

Spread the frosting evenly over the shortbread and put in the fridge to set. If using the flaked almonds or seeds, scatter and press into the frosting before refrigerating.

Cut into servings with a sharp knife dipped first in freshly boiled water.

Hints & tips

If you like a nutty taste to shortbread add ground almonds in place of ¼ self raising wholemeal flour.

Alternatively, to make a carob-biscuit cake - simply make the shortbread biscuits, cool and break into pieces, combine with the carob frosting. Smooth back into the greased tin and place in the fridge to harden.

'Carob Swirl Tart'

Ingredients -

For 2 or 4 people -

1 or 2 bars	Homemade short bread (see recipe.)
35g or 70g	Butter
35g or 70g	Carob powder
60ml or 120ml	Agave nectar
100ml or 200ml	Double cream
3ml or 60ml	Glucose powder
2.5 or 5ml	Tahini - light

Method

Grease 1 individual tart tin per person. Turn the shortbread into crumbs by placing inside a food bag and hitting carefully with a rolling pin.

Preheat the oven to 180°c. Divide the 'crumbs between the tart tins. Press them firmly and evenly around the base and sides. Cover with foil and place the shortbread cases in the oven for 10 mins until crisp and browned. Then remove the foil and bake for a further 3-4 mins.

To make the carob sauce - melt the butter in a pan. Remove pan from the heat, add the carob powder and agave. Stirring well to combine.

To make the cream sauce - In a cold bowl, lightly whip the cream and glucose with a whisk - but do not over-whip so that it becomes grainy. Once thick, stir in the light tahini.

Once the shortbread cases are cooked and cooled, fill with the carob sauce. Drop spoons of the cream sauce on top of carob sauce.

Use a fork or a skewer to make the marbled effect between the sauces. Return to the fridge to cool for 30 mins until the carob sauce hardens.

Sprinkle the tarts with ground glucose or organic almonds before serving.

Hints & tips

In place of the tahini, stir a little crushed ginger or finely chopped mint through the whipped sauce.

Or for a spicy kick, add a tiny amount of chopped fresh chilli to the carob sauce as the butter melts.

For a delicious party canape, make these tarts smaller by using muffin or even yorkshire pudding trays.

'Carob Mousse'

Ingredients -

For 2 or 4 people -

200 or 400ml	Double cream
30ml or 60ml	Agave nectar
20g or 40g	Carob powder
7.5 or 15ml	Agar flakes
15ml or 30ml	Glucose powder

Method

Pour ½ of the cream into a small saucepan and gently heat until simmering. Remove from the heat and stir in the agave and carob powder.

Allow to cool and infuse. Once the liquid has cooled, sprinkle with agar flakes. Bring to a simmer without stirring - then stir well to combine.

Continue simmering for 4 mins, stirring only occasionally. Once the liquid has simmered, leave to cool for as long as you whip remaining cream.

In a cold bowl, lightly whip the cream and glucose with a whisk. Don't over-whip - it becomes grainy.

Once thickened, lightly fold the cream into the cooled mixture - try to get as much air in as possible to produce a lighter texture. Grease your chosen serving bowls.

Place in individual small serving bowls, cover with film and put in the fridge for an hour to set. For quirky presentation, add the mousse to your favourite espresso, small tea cups or maybe a set of measuring cups. If using a cup and saucer, serve with a biscuit, a tsp and small jug of cream!

Use this super easy mousse to fill your choice of low histamine sponge cake - simply halve the ingredients.

Hints & tips

Try flavouring the mousse with finely chopped fresh ginger or mint. Or for the adventurous chef, add a tiny amount of chopped fresh chilli.

As an alternative to carob, and for fruit lovers, simmer mango or apple pieces with a little glucose to make a fruit puree to add to the mousse. Either stir the puree into the mix or line the base of the serving bowls.

'Carob Cereal Cakes'

Ingredients -

Makes 6 or 12 cakes -

½ or 1 cup	Oats
60g or 120g	Butter
45g or 90g	Glucose powder
10 or 20ml	Carob powder

Optional -
Replace the glucose with 45ml (or 90ml) of agave nectar.
Or -
Try adding crushed seeds or almonds to the crispy mix before it cools.

Method

This is a famously easy recipe that even young children like to get involved with. If so, please be extra careful when melting the butter on the hob. Hot butter and glucose can get very hot and burn little fingers!

Firstly, pulse the oats in a blender until roughly ground. Gently melt the butter in a large saucepan on the hob, pour in the glucose and stir until dissolved. Add the roughly ground oats and stir to coat well in sweetened butter. Cover pan with a lid and allow to cook on a low heat for 2-3 mins until they start to soften.

Add the carob powder and stir well to combine. Cover and cook again for another minute on a low heat.

Meanwhile, prepare your cake cases. Use either tin foil or paper cases and place in muffin tins for stability.

Remove the oat mix from the heat and stir well. If children want to help, allow the mix to cool slightly before dividing between the cases.

Use a spoon to scoop the cereal mix out of the pan and another to spoon it into the cases. To make this much easier to do, dip the spoons in a cup of warm water every so often.

Put the filled cases into the fridge until the mix sets. Eat same day.

Hints & tips

For a more 'grown up' treat, add finely chopped fresh ginger or chilli.

Or serve the slightly cooled 'Carob Butter' (without the oats) as a dip for your favourite low histamine fruits. Try a combination of fresh organic - apples, pear, mango, rhubarb, figs, lychees, watermelon, honeydew or cantaloupe melons.

'Chilli Carob Truffles'

Ingredients -

Makes 6 or 12 -

¼ or ½ small	Fresh chilli
60g or 120g	Butter
35g or 70g	Carob powder
120 or 240ml	Agave nectar
15ml or 30ml	Tahini - light
10g or 20g	Glucose powder

Method

Finely chop the fresh chilli, removing the seeds. Add to a small saucepan.

Gently melt butter in the same pan. Once melted, stir in 30g (or 60g) carob. Remove the pan from the heat, stir in agave and tahini. Place pan in the fridge to allow the mix to set.

Once set, use a tsp to scoop the set truffle mix out of the pan and a second to spoon it onto greaseproof paper. Put in the freezer for 30 mins.

Finely ground the glucose in a pestle and mortar and combine with the remaining carob powder. Lightly dust a plate with the mixture. Gently roll the truffles to cover in the coating.

If truffles become too soft simply return them to the freezer for a few mins. Once rolled, put them back in the fridge for 5 mins before serving.

Hints & tips

Carob truffles are very rich - only 1 or 2 per portion are more than enough! But they do freeze well.

An alternative coating for the truffles, try rolling in 'Almond Frosting', 'Tahini Frosting' or 'Carob Butter' and place in the fridge (see recipes.)

*Or try the carob truffle recipe (without the chilli!) as the filling for **'Pain au Chocolat'** - using homemade or bought puff pastry:*

Simply roll 1 (or 2) pastry blocks to ½ cm thick and cut into 10cm squares. Cool and form the truffle mix into 10cm lengths and place at one end of each pastry square.

Roll into sausages, flatten slightly with your hand, brush with egg yolk or melted homemade jam. Bake at 200°c for 15 mins until golden.

'Carob Fudge Cake'

Ingredients -

Makes 1 small or 1 medium cake -

85g or 170g	Wholegrain Self Raising flour
75g or 150g	Glucose powder
30ml or 60ml	Carob powder
2 or 4	Organic egg yolks
75ml or 150ml	Almond milk
75ml or 150ml	Rapeseed oil
10ml or 20ml	Beetroot juice
85g or 170g	Glucose powder
35g or 70g	Butter
15ml or 30ml	Carob powder
15ml or 30ml	Agave nectar
30ml or 60ml	Almond milk or double cream

Method

Preheat the oven to 180°c and line 2 small (or medium) cake or loaf tins with greaseproof paper. Brush a little rapeseed oil on top of the paper.

Sieve flour into a mixing bowl. Add the glucose to the bowl. Stir in the carob powder until well combined.

Beat egg yolks in a small bowl. Make a well in the centre of the flour and pour in the egg plus the milk and oil. Whisk gently with a balloon whisk (or electric mixer if you have one) until lump-free. Once smooth, carefully stir in the beetroot juice.

Divide the mix between the 2 prepared tins. Bake in the oven for 30 mins until the tops are firm to touch and the edges shrink from the sides.

Turn out once cooked, place on a cold grill rack and allow to cool.

For the buttercream - While the sponge cools, finely grind glucose in a pestle and mortar, add to a bowl.

Cream the butter and glucose together until light and fluffy. Stir in the carob powder then agave until well combined. Mix in milk or cream.

Spread ¼ of the ganache on the top of one of the layers and press them firmly together. Use the remaining ganache to spread on top and sides.

Hints & tips

The small cake should serve 4 people and the medium cake should serve 8.

***To make smaller portions** - grease 1 ramekin per person, add cake mixture but leave a 2 cm gap at the top. Cook for 18 mins or until the tops are firm to the touch and the edges shrink from the sides. Turn out once cooked and allow to cool. Can be wrapped and frozen before frosting.*

'Carob Brownies'

Ingredients -

For 2 or 4 people -

100g or 200g	Glucose powder
100g or 200g	Butter
2 or 4	Organic egg yolks
75g or 150g	Brown flour
30ml or 60ml	Carob powder
Plus -	
80g or 160g	Glucose powder
35g or 70g	Butter
15ml or 30ml	Tahini - light
25ml or 50ml	Almond milk

Optional - Add 60g or 120g crushed almonds or carob frosting chips (see recipe) to the mix before baking.

Method

Finely grind the glucose in a pestle and mortar until the texture of caster sugar - you may find it easier to do this in batches. Preheat the oven to 180°c and lightly grease a small (or medium) cake or loaf tin.

Gently melt butter in a small pan on the hob. Put the egg yolks in a mixing bowl and beat in the ground glucose until well mixed. Stir butter slowly into glucose and eggs. Keep beating until all the butter is added.

Sieve the flour and carob into the bowl. Fold it into the mixture. Try to get as much air into it as possible.

If adding the almonds or carob chips, carefully stir them into the mix now.

Put the brownie mix into the prepared tin and smooth the surface with the back of a warm spoon.

Bake in the oven for 20 mins or until the top feels springy and the edges shrink away from the sides of the tin.

Once the brownies are cooked and cooled, remove from the tin and place on a board. While the brownies cool, grind glucose as before but this time just a little finer.

Once ground add to a small bowl. Cut the butter into cubes and beat together with glucose. Once smooth, whisk in the tahini and milk. Spread the frosting thickly over the top.

Hints & tips

For grown up treats, remember that a little finely chopped chilli works very well with carob. Simply add it once you've mixed in the flour.

In place of the tahini, try almond butter instead - simply stir through the same amount of almond spread. ...And carob frosting works great!

'Mille-Feuille'

Ingredients -
For 2 or 4 people -

100g or 200g	Puff pastry - store bought or (see recipe.)
30ml or 60ml	Glucose powder
100 or 200ml	Double cream
4 or 8	Passion fruit

Method

Firstly, prepare the puff pastry following the recipe in this book. Wrap in cling film and leave to rest in the fridge. Allow 25 minutes. Alternatively, use frozen pastry and defrost at room temperature instead.

Preheat the oven to 200°c.

On a film surface, roll out the pastry to ¼ cm thick. Cut into 3 rectangles per person approx. 5cmx10cm each.

Brush 1 (or 2) baking sheets with water. Put the pastry on the tray(s) and sprinkle with ½ the ground glucose. Put pastry in the oven for 15 mins until golden and risen. Allow to cool.

As the pastry bakes and cools - In a cold bowl, lightly whip the cream and ½ glucose with a whisk. Don't over-whip so that it becomes grainy.

Once cool, cut each pastry layer in half lengthways. Place two layers on each plate and spread each with double cream. Carefully cut the passion fruits in half. Scoop the seeds out of ½ passion fruit on top of each layer of cream. Place another pastry layer on top. Repeat with the remaining cream and the second passion fruit.

Finish with a final layer of pastry. If preferred, drizzle with a little 'Rhupple' coulis (see recipe.)

Hints & tips

Alternatively, replace half of the double cream with a mix of home-made custard (see recipe) stirred into the lightly whipped cream.

Also vary the fruits, including - rhubarb, apple, pear, mango or figs gently roasted in a little apple juice.

Also tasty made with filo pastry.

'Carob Chip Cookies'

Ingredients -

Makes 4 or 8 big cookies -

For the carob 'chips' -

20g or 40g	Butter
20g or 40g	Carob powder
30ml or 60ml	Agave nectar

For the cookie dough -

40g or 80g	Butter
55g or 110g	Glucose powder
1 or 2	Organic egg yolks
5ml or 10ml	Tahini - light
50g or 100g	Wholegrain Self Raising flour

Optional - Try adding small chunks of almonds, seeds, fresh ginger, apple, pear, fig, rhubarb or mango.

Method

Firstly, prepare the carob 'chips' - Melt the butter in a pan. Remove pan from the heat, add the carob powder and agave. Stir well to combine. Spread the mix evenly over a piece of greaseproof paper to around 2-3 mm thick. Put in the fridge to set. If also using the chunks of almonds or seeds, scatter and press into the frosting before refrigerating.

If using the other flavourings, cut and prepare them just before you plan to add them to the dough.

Once set, preheat oven to 190°c. Line 1 (or 2) large baking trays with greaseproof. Lightly brush with oil.

Gently melt the remaining butter in a pan. Put the glucose into a mixing bowl and pour in the melted butter. Stir them together. Add the egg and tahini, stirring into the butter.

Sieve the flour into the bowl, along with a pinch of unrefined sea salt. Stir well. Using clean scissors, cut the set carob frosting into chunks. Fold gently but quickly into the dough.

Drop heaped spoons of the mix onto the prepared baking sheets. Press them down a little with your hand. Allow room for them to spread out. Bake in the oven for 10 mins or until they turn a light golden brown. When baked, remove from the sheet after 3 minutes and put on a cooling rack.

Hints & tips

Alternatively, make the cookie dough without the carob chips and bake them as usual. Instead, as the bars cool, make the carob chip mixture. But don't put it in the fridge just yet; partly dip the cookies into the carob first - THEN refrigerate them!

Use this technique with other low histamine biscuits - (see recipes.)

'Duo Cake'

Ingredients -

Makes 1 or 2 loaf cakes -

110g or 220g	Butter
110g or 220g	Glucose powder
3 or 6	Organic egg yolks
110g or 220g	Wholegrain Self Raising flour
60ml or 120ml	Almond milk
15ml or 30ml	Tahini - light
15ml or 30ml	Carob powder

Optional - Vary this duo cake by adding a little fresh ginger to the tahini mix. Also, try adding beetroot juice to make a pink and cream duo cake.

Method

Take the butter from the fridge a few mins before you want to use it to allow it to soften slightly. Cut into cubes and add to a mixing bowl.

Finely grind the glucose in a pestle and mortar until the texture of caster sugar - you may find it easier to do this in batches. Preheat the oven to 180°c and lightly grease a small (or medium) cake or loaf tin.

Cream the butter and glucose together until well combined. Then mix the egg yolks into the butter and glucose one at a time. Sieve the flour into the bowl, add milk and fold them into the mix - try to get as much air in the mixture as possible.

Pour half of the mix plus the tahini into a clean bowl. In the first bowl, add the carob powder. Stir both bowls well with different spoons.

Use the two spoons to alternate the mixes into the prepared tin. Make sure there is a complete layer at the bottom. Shake the tin a little to remove any air pockets. Use a knife to gently swirl the mixes together. Be careful not to over do this part.

Bake in the oven for 30 mins or until a skewer or cocktail stick comes out clean. After 2-3 mins, turn onto a grill rack and allow to cool. This soft, crumbly cake works really well with a fresh mint afternoon tea.

Hints & tips

To make a similar 'Simple Sponge Cake' - do not use carob flavouring. Instead, divide the mix into two tins and bake until springy on top and the sides shrink away from the sides.

Once cooled, spread one layer with whipped double cream and the other with homemade jam. Press together - sprinkle with finely ground glucose.

'Fruit Salad'

Ingredients -

For 2 or 4 people -

2 or 4	Figs
½ or 1 whole	Mango
6 or 12	Lychees
½ or 1 whole	Cantaloupe melon
2 or 4	Passion fruit

<u>Optional -</u>

15ml or 30ml	Glucose powder
	Filtered water

<u>Other options -</u> Organic under-ripe starfruit, peaches, apple, pear, honeydew, galia or watermelon.

Method

If making a sweet syrup, start by adding the glucose and water to a pan on the hob. Gently heat, stirring until the glucose dissolves. Allow to cool before pouring over the fruit.

To prepare the fruit salad -

When buying and storing fruit - be very careful to buy fruit that is firm and undamaged, always store in a cold refrigerator and eat within a day or two. When cutting fruit for a fruit salad, or even as a snack, make sure to eat it straight away.

Wash the fruits in warm soapy water and rinse well. Cut figs into eighths (you only need to peel them if the skin is rough) and place in a bowl. Lay the mango on its wide edge and cut approx. 1 cm up from the centre to avoid the stone. Peel and cut into small chunks. Add to the bowl.

Peel the lychees, cut around the stone and remove. Cut into quarters. Cut the melon in half and then half again. Remove the seeds, peel and cut into small pieces. Stir into bowl.

Carefully cut the passion fruit in half and scoop the seeds out with a spoon on top of the fruits in the bowl.

If using the cooled syrup, pour over the fruits and stir well to combine. Serve with whipped double cream.

Hints & tips

Fruit salad also works well served with cheese. Try feta, buffalo mozzarella and halloumi (Watermelon is traditionally served with halloumi!)

In place of the sugar syrup try adding the same quantity of organic apple juice. Alternatively, make an apple or pear juice jelly with agar flakes and stir through a selection of fruits before putting in the refrigerator.

'Fritters'

Ingredients -

For 2 or 4 people -

10g or 20g	Glucose powder
65g or 130g	Brown flour
120 or 240ml	Carbonated water
1 or 2 whole	Mango
Approx. 500ml	Rapeseed oil
25g or 50g	Ground almonds
50g or 100g	Brown flour
In place of the mango -	
2 or 4 hard	Pear
2 or 4	Apples

Serve sprinkled with ground glucose and drizzled with carob sauce or a 'Rhupple' coulis (see recipes.)

Method

Finely grind the glucose in a pestle and mortar until the texture of caster sugar If making savoury fritters, replace with quarter quantities of finely ground unrefined sea salt.

Sieve the flour and glucose into a bowl. Slowly add the water, beating with a fork until completely smooth.

When buying fruit - be very careful to buy fruit that is firm and undamaged, always store in a cold refrigerator and eat within a day or two.

Wash the mango in warm soapy water and rinse well. Lay the mango on it's wide edge and cut approx. 1 cm up from the centre to avoid the stone. Repeat for all sides. Peel and cut into slices approx. 1 inch thick.

Heat oil into a small pan. Be very careful when cooking with hot oil. Drip a small amount of batter into the oil - if the batter quickly rises to the top, it's ready to use.

On a plate, mix together the almonds and the flour. Dip a mango slice into the powder to coat each side.

Coat mango in batter and carefully lower into the oil. Fry in small batches for 5-6 mins until light and crispy. Remove with a slotted spoon.

Hints & tips

Add extra 'zing' to the fritters by adding fresh crushed ginger or very finely chopped chilli to the batter.

Or try making 'Fish & Chip Shop Fritters' - finely chop an onion and mix together with either mashed sweet potato, smashed peas or sweetcorn. Season. Form into patties and put in the freezer for 30 mins before dipping into the batter and frying.

'Drizzle Cake'

Ingredients -

Makes 1 or 2 loaf cakes -

<u>For the sponge cake -</u>

110g or 220g	Butter
110g or 220g	Glucose Powder
3 or 6	Organic egg yolks
110g or 220g	Wholegrain Self Raising flour
60ml or 120ml	Almond milk
1 or 2	Apple juice

<u>For the drizzle sauce -</u>

45ml or 90ml	Apple juice
45g or 90g	Glucose powder

Method

Take the butter from the fridge a few mins before you want to use it to allow it to soften slightly. Cut into cubes and add to a mixing bowl.

Finely grind the glucose in a pestle and mortar until the texture of caster sugar - you may find it easier to do this in batches. Preheat the oven to 180°c and line 1 (or 2) small loaf tins with greaseproof paper.

Cream the butter and glucose together until well combined. Then mix the egg yolks into the butter and glucose one at a time. Sieve the flour into the bowl, add the milk and fold them into the mixture. Peel and grate the apple and stir into the mix.

Pour the cake mix into the prepared tin(s.) Shake the tin a little to remove any air pockets. Smooth the top of the cake with a warm spoon.

Bake in the oven for 30 mins or until a skewer or cocktail stick comes out clean. Meanwhile, gently heat the juice and glucose in a small pan, stirring, until the glucose has dissolved.

As the cake cools, prick the cake all over with the skewer and spoon ½ syrup over. After 2-3 mins, repeat.

When cool, tip the cake onto a plate and serve. This soft, crumbly cake works well with a fresh mint tea.

Hints & tips

Turn this into an 'Upside Down Cake' - simply add a layer of roasted apple, pear, rhubarb, figs or mango to the bottom of the tin (with a spoonful of reduced cooking liquor) before topping with the cake batter mix.

Serve the cake freshly made with homemade ice cream, custard or 'Rhupple' coulis (see recipes.)

'Jelly Delights'

Ingredients -

Makes 1 or 2 trays -

100 or 200ml	Apple juice
100 or 200ml	Pear juice
30ml or 60ml	Glucose powder
22.5 or 45ml	Agar flakes
1 or 2 drops	Beetroot juice

For the coating -

3ml or 6ml	Glucose powder
30ml or 60ml	Corn flour

Method

Pour apple and pear juices into two separate saucepans. Divide glucose evenly between the juices and gently heat. Stir the juices over the heat until the glucose dissolves. Cool.

Once cooled, divide the agar flakes between the pans by sprinkling onto the surface of the liquid. Again bring the pans to a gentle simmer without stirring. Then stir well to combine.

Simmer for 4 mins - stirring only occasionally. Once the liquids are clear, stir the beetroot juice into the pear juice. Then carefully spoon all juices into an ice cube tray(s).

Place the ice cube tray(s) into the refrigerator for 45 mins or until fully set. Boil kettle and pour 1 cm of hot water into a baking tray or dish. Place the chilled tray(s) into the water for 3-4 mins to loosen the jellies.

Remove tray(s) from the water and carefully use a sharp knife along the side of each of the cubes - then tip the jellies out onto a board.

Once removed, grind the remaining glucose in a pestle and mortar until the texture of icing sugar. Mix well in a large bowl with the flour. Put each jelly into the bowl then toss in the powder coating. Tap the jellies on the side of the bowl to remove the excess powder. Serve immediately.

Hints & tips

Alternatively, use other pure organic fruit juices such as 'Rhupple' or mango. Try suspending broken almonds into the jelly or spread one side with 'carob frosting'.

If making a softer jelly in a larger mould for a child's party for example, use half the quantity of agar flakes for the same amount of liquid.

Change for (A Better) Life!

Before my major histamine episode (the one I couldn't ignore any longer) I just loved to cook. I'd make meals packed with tomatoes, olives, and cheeses, while enjoying a large glass (okay, perhaps two) of red wine. That's how I unwound after a hectic day.

Food and drink was 'My Thing.' So after I had an anaphylactic reaction to (yep, you guessed it...) red wine, I felt a bit lost. But, do you know what? I've learnt to accept what I couldn't change and moved on: Found a new 'Thing.'

As with any diet, giving favourites up can feel like a daunting sacrifice at first. Don't feel down. If it wasn't doing you any good anyway. Is that brief moment of pleasure from eating a tomato, or chocolate, or strawberry really worth the hours or days of miserable symptoms that follow? I'm not so sure. You might like them, but they don't like you back. Remind yourself; *those foods are not your friends!*

And as you walk past the liquor aisle, remind yourself that not only can alcohol inhibit DAO, but drinking with meals may also reduce your ability to digest foods properly - a double whammy! Change might feel tough sometimes, but you *can* get there. Just remind yourself that your homemade parsnip crisps (or brownies, or ice cream...) can taste so much yummier than the store-bought varieties!

Plus, histamine can also be stimulated by many factors besides food: cosmetics and household cleaning products may trigger reactions. Buying the environmentally friendly brands may help. Try not to stress out, but equally, be careful how you relax: massage and some other beauty treatments can also stimulate the release of histamine. Even sex (or rather, orgasm,) has been known to release histamine!

Histamine influences sleep and you may experience wakefulness and vivid dreams. In fact, some sleeping tablets contain anti-histamines. Even the inflammation caused by tattoos and body piercing (like other wounds,) can produce histamine.

But by reducing the histamine burden from our food these other factors can be less of a risk, so following a modified diet may enable a more 'normal' life elsewhere. Going Low-Histamine *is* an upheaval: It means changing priorities and thinking more carefully about things we once took for granted. But in the end, a more enjoyable and healthy way of life can be our reward!

Drinks

'Juice Bar'

Ingredients

For 2 or 4 people -

50g or 100g	Glucose powder
60ml or 120ml	Filtered water
6 or 12 cms	Fresh ginger
60ml or 120ml	Apple juice
400 or 800ml	Carbonated water
Or -	
3 or 6 cms	Fresh ginger
2 or 4 sprigs	Fresh mint
1 or 2 stalks	Lemongrass
400 or 800ml	Apple or pear fruit juice
Or -	
400 or 800ml	Apple or pear fruit juice
200 or 400ml	Carbonated water

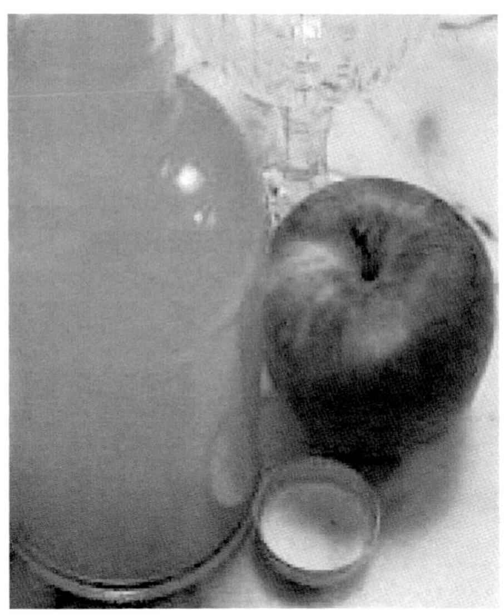

Method

Gingerale - Pour the glucose and water into a pan over a low heat. Stir until the glucose dissolves. Bring to the boil then simmer for 2 minutes.

Prepare ginger by finely dicing. Sprinkle with glucose, and crush with back of a knife. Add to the glucose syrup as it boils. Strain if you prefer.

Mix with apple juice and fizzy water.

Ginger, mint and lemongrass infusion - Prepare ginger by finely dicing. Sprinkle with glucose, and crush with the back of a knife. Finely chop the mint. Remove the outer layers of the lemongrass and hit several times with a rolling pin to bruise it.

Add to a pan and cover with fruit juice and a dash of filtered water. Cover and simmer for 5 mins. Strain and serve warm or cold with ice.

Fizzy 'pop' - Combine juice and carbonated water just before serving.

To make slush puppies - Pour juice into a container. Freeze for 1 ½ hours. Stir every 30 mins with a fork to break down any large ice crystals as they form.

Serve cold drinks with - fruit juice ice cubes, frozen pieces of fruit or a combination of the two. (Try freezing mint leaves inside these ice cubes!)

Hints & tips

You can make these drinks from homemade juices - or from pure organic juices from the store! Walking around the supermarket, it may seem that your juice drink options are somewhat restricted. Do try these recipes to update those (non-fermented!) store-bought juices.

Enjoy juice frozen in ice pop makers!

'Homemade Teas'

Ingredients

For 2 or 4 people -

For digestion -
2 or 4 sprigs Peppermint leaves
2 or 4 sprigs Rosemary leaves

To relieve colds -
2 or 4 sprigs Sage leaves
2 or 4 sprigs Thyme leaves

To relax -
2 or 4 sprigs Lemon balm leaves

For allergies -
2 or 4 sprigs Nettle leaves

Method

There is a more delicate but refreshing taste to fresh herb teas than with store bought dried versions.

To make a hot tea, the trick is to ensure that the water has only recently fully boiled.

Drop your choice of herbs into the base of the cup and pour water over to fill the cup.

Allow the herbs to sit (steep) in the water for 5 minutes, then stir well and remove, if preferred, before drinking.

Served cold, herbs can be added as a garnish to filtered still or sparkling water or juices.

Also try freezing whole herbs in ice cubes for attractive summer drinks.

A maximum of 4 cups per day of **peppermint tea** is usually recommended.

A maximum of 3 cups per day of **rosemary tea** is usually recommended. It is also not suitable if suffering from high blood pressure.

Do not drink **sage tea** if pregnant or breastfeeding.

Hints & tips

***For a spicy winter pick me up**, try adding ginger to hot water. Be careful to crush the ginger with the back of a knife - as whole chunks of ginger can often be too overpowering.*

Sage leaves work particularly well with passion fruit and mango drinks.

'Rhupple Punch'

Ingredients

For 2 or 4 people -

2 or 4 stalks	Rhubarb
1 or 2 firm	Pears
½ or 1 litre	Apple juice
1 or 2 inch	Fresh ginger
1 or 2 sprigs	Fresh mint

Other variations could include -

1 or 2 firm	Apples
1 or 2 firm	Mangos (peeled)
2 or 4 firm	Figs
2 or 4 firm	Peaches

Method

Many of the roast fruit recipes in this book are designed so that the cooking liquor can be retained and used as a fruit punch. Drink diluted to taste (they can be surprisingly strong) and serve hot or if cold - still or sparkling.

Alternatively, pour into an ice cube tray and place in the freezer. Add to summer drinks or defrost to use in sauces over ice cream or fruit salad.

However, you can of course make the punch the other way around and freeze the fruit pulp!

Do not take fruits out of the fridge too early. Work quickly so they remain firm. Do not use bruised or overripe fruit.

Prepare the rhubarb and pears by cutting into chunks 1 cm thick. Leave skins on for maximum colour.

Preheat the oven to 220°c. Place the fruit in a loaf tin. Pour over the apple juice and cover with foil. Roast in the oven for 10-15 minutes, until tender.

When the fruits are soft, remove from the cooking liquor and place in a sealed container in the freezer.

Carefully taste the remaining liquor (it will be hot) and dilute to taste with water or apple juice.

Hints & tips

Experimentation really is the key to creating these punches. Start with a base of apple or pear juice and vary the fruits, fresh spices and herbs to create a variety of 'cocktails'.

Frozen fruit pulp can be used as pie or pastry fillings and added to flavour ice creams or sorbets.

'Smoothies'

Ingredients

For 2 or 4 people -

2 or 4	Apple or pear
120 or 240ml	Apple juice
With -	
1 or 2	Mango
Or -	
500g or 1kg	Cantaloupe
Or -	
500g or 1kg	Watermelon
Or -	
500g or 1kg	Honeydew
Or -	
2 or 4	Kiwi fruit
Or -	
2 or 4	Carrots
2 or 4 sticks	Celery

Method

Use either a juicing machine if you have one, or alternatively a blender. This results in different textures of smoothie. With a juicer the bulk of the fruit is left behind, and produces a much smaller yet clearer drink.

For day-to-day 'smoothies' I tend to use a blender (method below) as I find it easier to clean more often. However, for special occasions I will go to the extra effort of using a juicer. If you do so, be careful to follow the manufacturer's instructions.

Use apples or pears as a base for the smoothie and add variety with other soft fruits, vegetables or herbs.

Firstly, wash all ingredients and peel the soft fruits. If making a vegetable smoothie, peel non-organic carrots . And if you prefer, peel the string from the celery.

Core apples or pears and chop into chunks. Chop the soft fruit into similar sized pieces. If adding ginger or herbs and spices, prepare them now.

Place apples or pears into the blender, add juice, cover and blend for 2-3 minutes. Remove the lid, add the soft fruit or vegetables (and any added herbs or spices.) Stir, cover and blend until it gets to the desired consistency. Serve straight away.

Hints & tips

Fresh ginger adds a 'kick' to any of these drinks. Prepare by finely dicing and crush with the back of a knife. As it's raw, start with a small amount - you can always add more!

See the 'Juice Bar' page for how to make the most of small, clear juices made with a juicer. Such as 'slush puppies' or infusions. Take a peek at the 'Sorbet & Ice Cream' page too!

'Sorbet & Ice Cream'

Ingredients

For 2 or 4 people -
For the sorbet -
90ml or 180ml Filtered water
60g or 120g Glucose powder
2 or 4 Apples or pears
120 or 240ml Apple juice
1 or 2 Mango
For the ice cream -
250 or 500ml Almond milk
70g or 140g Glucose powder
1 or 2 Cantaloupe
60ml or 120ml Apple juice
For both -
Add mint or ginger - even fresh chilli!

Method

For the sorbet - Pour the water and glucose into a pan. Bring to the boil and stir until the glucose has dissolved. Boil gently for 5 mins. Allow to cool as you prepare the fruit.

Wash fruits and peel the mango. Core apples or pears and chop into chunks. Chop the mango into similar sized pieces. If adding ginger or herbs and spices, prepare them now.

Place apples or pears into the blender, add juice, cover and blend for 2-3 minutes. Remove the lid and add the mango. Stir, cover and blend again until soft. Stir the glucose syrup into the fruit puree.

For the ice cream - Pour the almond milk and glucose into a pan. Bring to the boil and stir until the glucose has dissolved. Then turn off heat. Allow to cool as you prepare the fruit.

Wash and peel the melon. Chop into chunks. If adding ginger or herbs and spices, prepare them now. Put in the blender with the juice, cover and blend until soft. Stir the almond milk syrup into the fruit puree.

For both - Pour mix into a container. Freeze for 2 ½ hours. Stir every 30 mins with a fork to break down any large ice crystals as they form. As homemade ices can be quite hard, defrost slightly before serving.

Hints & tips

Other flavour options - watermelon, honeydew, rhubarb, passion fruit, apricot or peach. Serve drizzled with 'rhupple' coulis (see recipe.)

Try carob or crushed almond ice cream. Even savoury pea & mint ice cream (no glucose) - served with burgers, inside lentil loaf or kievs.

'Milkshake'

Ingredients

For 2 or 4 people -

Hot milk version -

400 or 800ml	Almond milk
6 or 12 cms	Fresh ginger
2 or 4 stalks	Rhubarb

Cold milk version -

2 or 4	Peach
10ml or 20ml	Glucose powder
120 or 240ml	Apple juice
300 or 600ml	Almond milk

Ice cream version -

50g or 100g	Almonds
300 or 600ml	Homemade ice cream (see recipe)
100 or 200ml	Almond milk

Method

Below are three basic types of milk drinks - served hot, ice cold or thick and creamy made with homemade ice cream. Always sweeten to taste.

For hot milk drinks - Prepare the ginger by finely dicing. Sprinkle with a little glucose and crush with the back of a knife. Add to a pan.

Cut the rhubarb into 1 cm pieces and add to the pan with the ginger. Pour the almond milk over and simmer gently (but do not boil!) for 5 mins. Remove from the heat and crush the rhubarb and ginger with a fork. Sieve the milk mixture before serving.

For cold milk drinks - Finely chop the fresh fruit and add to a pan. Pour in the glucose and apple juice and bring to the boil. Simmer for 5 minutes or until soft. Allow to cool and puree with a blender.

Either combine the fruit syrup with the milk directly from the pan or sieve first for a smoother drink.

For ice cream milkshakes - Preheat oven to 180°c. Spread almonds out onto a un-greased baking sheet. Bake for 10 mins, shaking from time to time, until golden. Allow to cool.

Place almonds, ice cream and milk into a blender, cover and blitz until you get to your preferred texture.

Hints & tips

Do not worry if the milk curdles at any point - simply blitz with a hand blender and sieve before serving.

Alternatives - hot carob & mint, apricot syrup or mango ice cream milkshakes (add the mango straight to the blender - so no need to roast!) Vary the thickness of the milkshake using less or more almond milk.

'Mocktails'

Ingredients
For 2 or 4 people -

300 or 600ml	Carbonated water
With -	
100 or 200ml	Glucose powder
100 or 200ml	Apple juice
Plus - (I)	
2 or 4 sprigs	Fresh mint
2 or 4 whole	Peach
Or - (II)	
1.5 or 3 cms	Fresh ginger
4 or 8 whole	Lychees
Or - (III)	
¼ or ½ whole	Watermelon
Or - (IV)	
½ or 1 whole	Mango
2 or 4 whole	Passion fruit

Method

To make 'glucose syrup' - Pour 50g (or 100g) glucose and 50ml (or 100ml) filtered water into a pan over low heat. Stir until glucose dissolves. Bring to boil, simmer for 2 mins.

If using fresh mint or ginger - prepare them by chopping very finely and adding to the syrup as it cools.

For the peach Mocktail - wash the peach and remove the stone. Chop very finely and add to a pan containing glucose syrup and apple juice.

For the lychee Mocktail - wash the lychees and remove the seeds. Chop very finely and add to a pan containing glucose syrup and apple juice.

For the melon Mocktail - wash the melon and remove the seeds. Chop very finely and add to a pan containing glucose syrup and apple juice.

For the mango Mocktail - wash the mango and remove the stone. Chop very finely and add to a pan containing glucose syrup and apple juice.

Cut each passion fruit in ½ and scoop the flesh into a blender. Pour in the juice mixture from the pan. Pulse the blender for up to 1 min to separate the passion fruit from the seeds. Do not over-blend and break the seeds.

For all the Mocktails - Crush the fruit into the liquor (unless blended.) Pour into a jug and add fizzy water, ice and apple slices. Strain into glasses.

Hints & tips

Try freezing these Mocktails to make your own slush puppies (see recipes.)

In place of mint, experiment with fresh kaffir lime leaves or basil or sage (these work well with mango.) Also try using a variety of melons - such as cantaloupe or honeydew.

For Friends & Family

Histaminosis doesn't only touch the lives of those people with the condition: Partners, parents, children and friends are also affected. To every friend and relative who's perhaps bought or read this book without being asked to, and who actively support his or her loved-one everyday: "*Thank you for your wisdom, courage and strength.*"

Unfortunately however, all too often I hear about people's friends and relatives who seem to feel more sorry for themselves than for their histamine intolerant loved-one. This page is for them ...

As distressing as it is to watch a loved-one suffer with ill health, you must accept that nothing gets better by doing nothing: That means making changes. When those changes involve giving up popular foods, or finding different ways of socialising that are less dependent on pubs and pizzerias, friends or relatives occasionally resist. Help them by not clinging onto a former life that just doesn't work anymore.

When it comes to well-known illnesses with obvious symptoms, many people will offer all the support and sympathy they can. Yet others will respond with denial - maybe even hostility - about less well-known conditions like Histaminosis.

If that sounds like you: Please Stop. Your loved-one has found the strength to make a life-changing decision to reduce histamine. They should be applauded! Offer your support and encouragement. Remember that you'll benefit too, once your loved-one is healthier, happier and enjoying life so much more.

There may be times when you don't fully understand. Try just that little bit harder: Learning is how problems get solved. Maybe occasionally you won't care if you never hear the word 'Histamine' again. Unfortunately, it isn't going to go away - as testing and treatments become more available, and as more of us experience the benefits.

In the meantime, embrace your loved-one. Support them in the doctor's office, shop with them and compliment their early attempts at home cooking. Heck, cook some of them yourself. They've all been test-driven on real families. Read these recipes: fold over the corners on the ones you'd like to try. Remember and appreciate all the quality, and love, put into these meals.

There may even be times when eating lower-histamine makes you feel better too :-)

My Story

I felt rotten before I started a low-histamine diet. I honestly think I might not even be here today if I hadn't resolved to make these changes to my life.

One of my earliest childhood memories is the 'prickly heat' I first endured one hot summer weekend when I was about 3 years old. This was followed by 20-or-so years of creative, and sometimes downright odd, attempts to alleviate it. But recalling it now, I realise that this (Solar) Urticaria (as it's properly known) was actually an early warning sign for my own Histaminosis.

In common with many high-histamine types, I was a sensitive child and a perfectionist. My teen-years and early twenties were a time of incredible highs and lows. One day I'd be top of the tree; full of energy and enthusiasm: and the next I'd feel bottom of the heap; a reject. And that hurt. It really, really hurt.

I was prescribed several courses of antibiotics for the usual childhood illnesses, and again as a young adult relating to a minor operation on my foot. Little did I realise then that those antibiotics were starting to wreak havoc on the balance of bacteria in my gut - ultimately encouraging my histamine levels to skyrocket!

By my mid-twenties, I was a new mum with an exciting job in Internet marketing in the finance industry; yet dealing with all the stresses that career and early parenthood brought. Suddenly, I was struck with episodes of dizziness and feeling faint.

I dismissed them at first, but I couldn't deny something was wrong after an espresso from a continental deli made me so unwell I was taken to hospital.

My GP spent the next 3 years trying to convince me that I'd suffered from panic attacks, even prescribing Diazepam, until I had another - even stronger - string of reactions. All after the smallest sip of red wine! My blood pressure plummeted, my pulse raced, my skin flushed and I could barely breathe. All this is alarmingly close to anaphylaxis, enough for me to carry adrenaline with me.

I soon realised that I needed to follow a lower histamine diet. The slightest deviation resulted in symptoms.

Then followed another 18 months of misdiagnosis. Unfortunately, many of the 'experts' I consulted were unsupportive. Some offered dubious advice, which only lightened my bank balance and increased my stress. In hindsight, they probably knew less about Histamine Intolerance than I did. The reward I got for following this advice was a very much lighter bank balance, greatly increased stress - and the development of painful, scary, and erratic heartbeats.

Friends and family inevitably struggled to understand. Relationships were strained as the advice I was given differed from my symptoms. It was either fight or give in. But giving up could never be an option - I was a mum and was responsible for my child. Yet I'd become so ill I was almost bed-ridden: Not an easy thing for me to accept.

There had to be another way. Tenaciously, I began piecing together the clues for myself, learning about Histamine Intolerance and Histaminosis and the role that food could play in their management.

So I persevered: I quickly realised that personally, I'd need to follow a low-histamine diet all of the time. Even the slightest lapse made my symptoms return. I put my high-histamine perfectionism and tenacity to good use. I researched ingredients: What foods had high histamine? Which liberated histamine in the body? How did fermentation and decay increase histamine?

And all this while I was developing over 2,000 low-histamine recipes. The Red Wine Headache Cookbook was born!

Spurred on, in March 2009, I finally made the appointment with Dirk Budka that I'd been promising myself. His tests confirmed my low levels of Diamine Oxidase and that I was also positive for SIBO (in my case meaning that my body was already producing much more histamine than I could break down.)

Within weeks I had joined Dirk's enzyme research trial. I had a 6-month check and my DAO levels were on the rise - slowly but surely - and following treatment, my SIBO had gone.

Time and again, people tell me they feel isolated; but trust me you really aren't alone! Through my participation with the enzyme research, my own website (www.lowhistaminerecipes.com) and via my facebook profile, I've been lucky to meet many wonderful people who just happen to be intolerant to histamine.

My Story

My biggest hope in writing this book is that by reading it and enjoying the recipes, you'll feel better supported and informed, and far more optimistic about your future.

As for my own progress, I'm nearly there. When asked, I tell people that I feel about 90% well. The low-histamine diet has made a huge difference to my life. I don't react to food anymore, and my Urticaria's as good as gone. But as I don't have the energy levels I used to I can tire pretty easily, and I'm still troubled by the heart-pains that health professionals have now suggested are 'histamine-induced vaso-spasms.' So I don't yet trust myself to travel alone.

However, our stories don't end here. I'm already researching ways to maximise the nutrition from low-histamine ingredients even further for another book I'm developing called 'Living With HIT'. This book will address many day-to-day histamine challenges like long-distance travel, cosmetics & toiletries, and exercise & relaxation therapies - many based on case studies of other patients.

Excitement about our future is tangible. I'm keen to see the impact these books have on people's perception and under-standing of the condition. I'm also looking forward to the next phase of the enzyme treatment too and as it becomes available in pharmacies. I'd love my histamine friends to get the chance to see if it helps them too!

Last summer as I began to cut down my original, ridiculously long list of recipe ideas to a more sensible 300+, I got the very real sense of a brighter-looking future for us all.

So here's to the start of a Low-Histamine revolution!

Resources

The ingredients used in this book can usually be bought from major supermarkets or high-street health food stores. However, if you are struggling to find any products, search on-line or try the links below for the products that I personally use at home -

* Fortified non-hydrogenated dairy-free spread (a source of B_{12})-
http://www.puredairyfree.co.uk/sunflower.php

Carob powder -
http://www.cotsherb.co.uk

Agave nectar -
http://www.groovyfood.co.uk/index.html

Beetroot juice -
http://www.beet-it.com

Unrefined sea salt -
http://www.thesaltseller.co.uk

A selection of organic products -
http://www.goodnessdirect.co.uk

Glucose powder -
I buy this from my local pharmacy.

There are also many online sources of Histamine Intolerance information and support. A small selection of these are provided below -

The website for this book -
http://www.lowhistaminerecipes.com
Or search for 'Ella Elizabeth' on facebook

To contact Dirk Budka -
http://www.immuneclinic london.com part of the One Life Clinic Group
London, Belgium, Bahrain

I especially offer my thanks to Dirk for his guidance and support over-seeing this book, and for checking that what I have written has been accurate and fair.

A general scientific review of histamine and histamine intolerance -
http://www.ajcn.org/cgi/content/full/85/5/1185

Acknowledgements

Firstly, to Dirk, for his insatiable desire to research Histamine Intolerance and Histaminosis, promoting scientifically-based treatment. Dirk's enthusiasm and sense of humour are compelling - there aren't many of you around! (And a special thank you to Barbara too!)

To my GPs, Dr Justine Reid and Dr Primal Johnson, for being interested in, and supportive of, the needs of my condition.

To Dr Woods, Dr Savic and staff at the Allergy and Immunology department at St James' Hospital, Leeds. Thank you for taking me on, answering my questions and recognising Histamine Intolerance.

To Dr and Mrs McCance, for determining that my heart is 'structually healthy' and for your interest in the histamine connection. Let's see if HIT really will be "the Coeliac of the next decade!"

To my parents, for accepting the diagnosis and for finding an innovative way to help complete this book. One day I shall be driving!

To my grandparents, for always being there and believing in me. Thank you for encouraging me and for sharing beautiful crockery.

To Linda, for looking after Danny when I needed to attend many hospital appointments at short-notice. I miss you everyday, chic!

To Nele, and all my online friends, for sharing with me your own experiences of HIT. Thanks for being cheerleaders for the cause!

To Steve Pendleton at Progressive Printers, for your expertise and assurance that it would be possible to produce this book.

To Julian, for being certain that I had to write it all down. And for always being ready to dash to the supermarket to pick up that last minute ingredient! The best of luck with your new adventures too!

Most of all to Danny, for everything - for understanding when and why you need to reduce histamine foods to relieve your eczema, for believing in and being proud of your mum (especially when I've been too busy to talk about your latest invention!) and for all those well-timed hugs and kisses. What would I ever do without you?

You've defied the odds to understand this unusual condition! x.

Index of Recipes

Index of Recipes

Index of Recipes